Understanding Primary Mathematics

Related titles of interest

Suggate, Davis & Goulding: *Mathematical Knowledge for Primary Teachers*
ISBN: 1-85346-750-2

Hopkins, Gifford & Pepperell: *Mathematics in the Primary School*
ISBN: 1-85346-592-5

Harlyn: *The Teaching of Science in Primary Schools (third edn)*
ISBN: 1-85346-564-X

Hayes: *Foundations of Primary Teaching (second edn)*
ISBN: 1-85346-563-1

Wilson: *Language Knowledge for Primary Teachers: A Guide to Textual, Grammatical and Lexical Study*
ISBN: 1-85346-753-7

Ager: *ICT in Primary Schools: Children or Computers in Control*
ISBN: 1-84312-042-9

Understanding Primary Mathematics

CHRISTINE HOPKINS, SUE POPE AND SANDY PEPPERELL

 **David Fulton** Publishers

David Fulton Publishers Ltd
The Chiswick Centre, 414 Chiswick High Road, London W4 5TF

www.fultonpublishers.co.uk

First published in Great Britain in 2004 by David Fulton Publishers

10 9 8 7 6 5 4 3 2 1

Note: The right of Christine Hopkins, Sue Pope and Sandy Pepperell to be identified as the authors of this work has been asserted by them in accordance with the Copyright, Designs and Patents Act 1988.

David Fulton Publishers is a division of Granada Learning Limited, part of ITV plc.

British Library Cataloguing in Publication Data

A catalogue record for this book is available from the British Library.

ISBN 1 84312 012 7

Typeset by Ann Buchan (Typesetters), Shepperton, Middlesex
Printed and bound in Spain

Contents

Preface

This book attempts to provide the background subject knowledge and insight needed to teach mathematics effectively in the primary school. It draws on the work of the team of mathematics tutors at the University of Surrey, Roehampton. As well as the three named authors, contributions were made to the writing and editing by Julie Alderton, Kay Alldridge, Sue Gifford, Freda Rockliffe, Leo Rogers and Peter Tallant. The book is based on the experiences of teaching and of research, of planning and revising courses and observing students in school. The process involved individual writing followed by group editing to discuss the choice of approach, the emphasis and the relevance to primary education. Individual tutors contributed according to their special interests in mathematics, in history, in pedagogy or social context. We hope that the resulting book will prepare its readers to teach effectively and to draw their children into a deep understanding of and pleasure in mathematics.

Introduction

Primary teachers need to develop their expertise across a wide range of subjects. It is encouraging to note that many students report great pleasure and satisfaction in teaching mathematics to children even when mathematics was not a subject in which they felt very confident at the start of a course. Whether or not your memories of school mathematics are positive we hope that you will find that when, as an adult, you revisit the mathematics you are able to gain an overview of the subject, a sense of what is important and what to emphasise, which will guide your teaching. The book is designed to emphasise general principles and themes which you can draw on when planning your teaching and responding to children's questions. The format of each chapter is described below.

HISTORICAL AND SOCIAL CONTEXT

Each chapter starts with a brief section entitled historical and social context. This is intended to give a sense of when and for what purposes the mathematical knowledge in the chapter was developed. It is hoped that these sections will give a sense of perspective. Many of the ideas which children now learn about in school took centuries to develop. This section also indicates some of the applications, for good or for ill, for which the mathematics has been used.

MATHEMATICAL CONTENT

The main section of the chapter sets out the mathematical knowledge needed to teach mathematics effectively in the primary school in the areas of Number, Algebra, Shape, Space and Measures and Handling Data. An additional chapter emphasises the importance of problem-solving, reasoning and proof in the learning of mathematics.

IMPLICATIONS FOR TEACHING

The mathematical content is appropriate for primary teachers and students. Although focused on the curriculum for young children it draws on more complex and far-reaching ideas so that the teacher has a good understanding of how the small element on which the children are working fits into a larger mathematical pattern. These sections are designed to give just one or two examples of how an awareness of themes and connections can enhance teaching in the nursery and throughout the primary school.

SELF-ASSESSMENT

Most people work through mathematics books a small section at a time. These questions are provided so that readers can develop their understanding of the mathematics presented in the chapter. Full answers and notes are provided at the end of the book.

CD-ROM

The CD-Rom accompanying the book provides additional practice and may be particularly useful if you have not used your mathematical skills for some time. It includes a mental mathematics check and multiple choice questions on the topics covered in the book to help you check out your mathematical understanding.

1 The number system and number operations

'Accurate reckoning. The entrance onto the knowledge of all existing things and all obscure secrets.' (Rhind Mathematical Papyrus, Egypt c. 1800 BC)

ORIGINS OF COUNTING – WORDS AND SUPERSTITIONS

The real origins of mathematics lie deep in the past before any kind of recording, and so any story about the beginnings of counting needs to be situated in the cultural context of the time. Thinking ourselves back into a time before counting, two crucial questions need to be addressed:

'Why do you need to count?'
In many domestic activities today like shopping, cooking, etc., there is still no need to count. You know when you have enough. When hunting, gathering fruits and seeds, or even herding animals, you know if you have enough to feed the family, and you know if a wolf has taken one of the sheep, or if you have lost a spear. Counting does not happen unless there is a need. The idea that the shepherd had to count his sheep to know if one was missing is a myth. Every person who works with animals develops a relationship with them and 'knows' if one is missing.

'What do you need to know in order to be able to count?'
Counting is a powerful activity. So is knowing someone's name. Remember the feeling in your stomach when your name was called out by the class teacher 'Oh dear! What have I done now?' Or when you enter a room full of strangers, and someone calls your name 'Who is that? Somebody knows who I am!'

Because counting people is a very powerful (even magic) thing to do, every culture has many superstitions attached to counting and numbers. In the past, only special people (the king, the priest, the chief) were allowed to do this. Nineteenth-century English administrators in Africa were sometimes killed for trying to take a census because only the witch doctor was allowed to count. In the *Book of The Maccabees* in the Bible, counting the army was done by soldiers each putting a stone on a pile, so the stones were counted and not the men.

There is a theory that suggests that the reason for these superstitions was that

1

the beginnings of counting had nothing to do with arithmetic as we now know it, but was related to early rituals like the rebirth of the land in the spring, or the coming of rains. 'Counting' therefore was originally a chant for calling people in to the ritual area to perform the ceremony, and the words were later transferred to counting objects.

A SEQUENCE OF WORDS

So counting begins with a list of words. The other essential is a series of pointings which associates the words (or symbols) with the objects to be counted. The answer to 'How many?' was the noise you made when you stopped speaking, and you knew 'seven' was more than 'five' because the noise 'seven' came after uttering 'five'.

COMPARING COLLECTIONS OF OBJECTS

Comparing two or more collections of objects in terms of their numerosity can be done in two ways. Direct comparison puts the objects into one-to-one correspondence, like sharing a bag of sweets between people. If there is a remainder, the collections are not equal. A next stage can be where tokens (stones, models, or counters) represent the objects to be shared, so the comparison can be made between the representations of the objects. These actions concern the relative size of collections. A further step is to develop a written symbol system for the objects or for a group of objects. So now we have number symbols and a way of comparing collections of objects indirectly by noting the symbol when we finish 'counting' each collection.

AN INFINITE PROCESS

Once you have a set of names for the numbers, and once you have a system for repeating them, you can always go on. Whatever number you give me I can always add one more! This makes counting a potentially infinite process.

(This property was later called 'the successor property' by Guiseppe Peano in 1889. The statement 'every number has a successor' is a basic principle of counting.)

Think of a list of numbers: 1, 2, 3, 4, 5 . . . For each of these, we can write its square: 1, 4, 9, 16, 25 . . . For every number there is a corresponding square number. So, the list of square numbers is infinite (this was first demonstrated explicitly by Galileo Galilei in 1638), and so is the list of fractions, and cubes and . . .

(Again, this is the power of the principle of one-to-one correspondence.)

NUMBER SIGNS

Written number signs go back to about 4000 BC in Mesopotamia. We first find symbols for objects and then for numbers emerging. Archaeologists now think that this was the very first writing – even before any literature. In the early stages in Mesopotamia about 60 different numerical sign systems were in use.

A wide variety of counting systems evolved, using what we today call different bases. Cows were different from the fish caught from the river and different again from the corn harvested, and so each collection of objects was counted in a different way. In the early twentieth century in England it was still possible to find that the measure for a bushel of corn was different in different market towns.

Still, in certain parts of Polynesia, numbers for a feast are counted in fours, because four people sit round the traditional palm mat where the food is placed. In Japan, five eggs are sold in neatly woven baskets.

Other cultures developed different systems independently: Egypt, Babylonia, China, India, The Mayas, etc. These are the most outstanding, but many other systems appeared according to people's needs at the time. The English Imperial systems for money, weight, volume, and so on contain mixed measures (12 pence in a shilling, 20 shillings in a pound, etc.) and are remnants of these cultural practices.

CALCULATING METHODS

Ancient arithmetic methods were very simple in principle. Tables of products, divisions and fractional parts were used a lot as aids like 'ready-reckoners'. Multiplication and division were achieved by doubling and halving and to multiply by 5 you multiply by 10 and halve the result. Division was achieved by successive subtractions, a method similar to what we teach today as 'chunking'. Many sets of tables developed by ancient people were still in use up to Renaissance times.

The Egyptians did not calculate using the hieroglyphic numbers as this would have been a very cumbersome process. Hieroglyphs are only found on tombs and official monuments; for calculations written on papyrus, hieratic symbols (a kind of shorthand) were used. While notations developed in different ways, calculating methods relied on practical tools like counters, tally sticks, counting boards, the abacus, and so on. For a long time there were only a few people in the culture who knew how to count and calculate (reckon) beyond very simple calculations. This put the Notaries (in Italy and France) or Reckoning Masters (in Germany) in a very powerful position in society.

Another calculating aid developed from mediaeval times was the reckoning board which was marked out in columns and rows according to the goods to be counted. The board was kept in the 'counting house'. This is where many different kinds of goods were counted by moving tokens on the board to represent the different amounts. Counters were moved from one column to another according to the particular table – one table for quantities of grain, another for sacks of wool, etc. To 'go before the board' originally meant going to the counting house to have your goods valued by the experts. (Remember the nursery rhyme – 'The king was in the counting house counting out his money . . .')

The problem with this situation was that it was cumbersome, it could only be done in a few places (although some portable 'boards' made of cloth were used), and it could only be done by specially trained people (hence the power was in the hands of a few). Because only the result was written down, the stages in the calculation were lost in the process and so you could not check if it was right. However, some checking methods like 'casting out nines' were developed specially for this.

DECIMAL NOTATION

Leonardo Fibonacci was the son of a merchant who travelled extensively in the Mediterranean and the Middle East, and wrote 'The Book of the Abacus' (Liber Abaci 1202) which was a summary of the calculating methods that had been known to merchants for ages and in this book he introduced the Hindu-Arabic notation to Europe. The base ten number system and Hindu-Arabic notation eventually greatly accelerated the development of calculating methods. The town of Treviso in northern Italy lay on the direct route from the trading city-states of Genoa and Venice into southern Europe and there the famous Treviso Arithmetic was published in 1478. This book contained all sorts of instructions for merchants to calculate profit and loss, rates of exchange and the shares in investments, and here we find the first appearance of the 'times tables' exactly as they are familiar to us today. (Treviso Arithmetic 1478, see Swetz, F. 1987 *Capitalism and Arithmetic*.)

FRACTIONS

Fractions appeared very early when it became necessary to divide the group of objects or the quantity into smaller parts. 'I only need half that fish today' and we have the development of 'natural' fractions and combinations of these: halves, thirds, quarters, fifths, sixths, and so on. Egyptian fractions (represented by $1/n$ where the numerator is always one) are known as 'unit' fractions and were used mainly for sharing out resources, grain, beer, etc. All fractional representation was in terms of unit fractions, so for example, 3/4 was written as two separate unit fractions 1/2, 1/4. It is possible to obtain many different kinds of unit fractions by judicious use of various 'natural' fractions.

The introduction by the Dutchman Simon Stevin in *The Art of Tenths* 1585 of a 'complete' decimal system where he developed symbols for decimal fractions and showed how to use these for counting and calculating, still did not persuade many people of the advantages of a unified system. Even now, many calculations are still done by goldsmiths, apothecaries and others using the traditional fraction systems; and astronomical measurements still use sexagesimal fractions (sixtieths).

Further reading

Joseph, G. 1991 *The Crest of the Peacock: non-European roots of Mathematics* London: Tauris
Katz, V.J. 1998 *A History of Mathematics: an introduction* Harlow: Addison-Wesley

1.2 DEVELOPING THE NUMBER SYSTEM

NATURAL OR COUNTING NUMBERS

A number system requires an ordered set of number names and a symbol for writing each name. Around the world a rich variety of systems for naming and writing numbers was developed. One way of reducing the number of symbols is shown in the Mayan system where the symbol for 7 is a combination of the symbol for 5 and the symbol for 2.

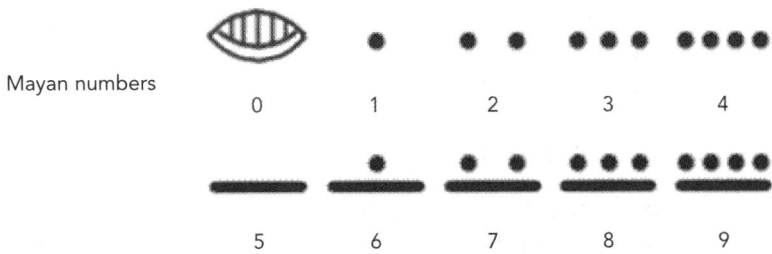

Mayan numbers

In the Aztec system the number of symbols you had to draw was reduced by inventing symbols for large numbers.

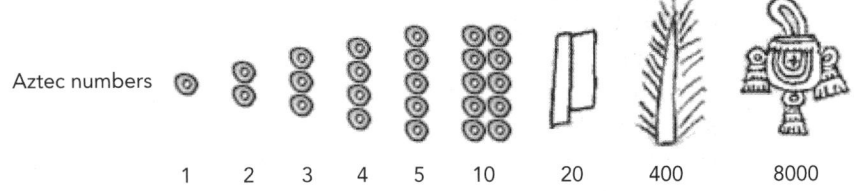

Aztec numbers

CARDINAL AND ORDINAL

To count some objects in any of these systems you recite the number names in order whilst pointing to each object in turn. The number of the final object is the total number of objects.

This is called the *cardinal property* of numbers.

Numbers can also be used to indicate position as in 1st, 2nd, 3rd . . . this is the *ordinal property* of numbers.

PLACE VALUE

The Mayan system substantially reduced the number of symbols needed by giving a different value to a symbol in a changed position. Mayans wrote their numbers vertically. When the symbol for one is moved up, it means 20.

So the number shown in Figure 1a is 25.

The Mayans also had a symbol for zero which tells you that the position is empty. The dot is now in the upper, or second position, as in Figure 1b, and has a value of 20.

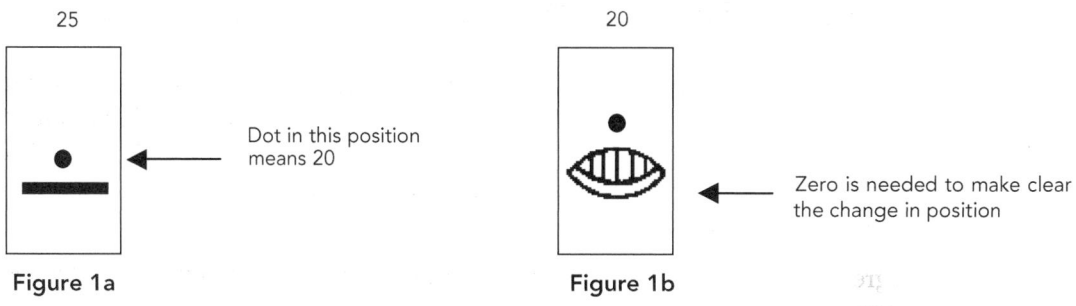

Figure 1a

Figure 1b

The Hindu-Arabic number system was developed in India and adopted and spread by the Arabs. It uses ten symbols. These are 1, 2, 3, 4, 5, 6, 7, 8 and 9, known as digits, which, when written singly, are the first nine natural or counting numbers, and 0, a symbol for zero, which acts as a place holder. The next number is formed by moving the symbol for one along to the left and inserting the symbol for zero. This gives the number 10 meaning one ten and no units.

Two-digit numbers form a regular pattern of numbers 11, 12, 13, . . . , 19, 20, 21, . . . , 98, 99 up to nine tens and nine ones or units. The words for the numbers are not completely regular in some of the European languages, including English, although they are regular in many far Eastern languages, i.e. Chinese, Japanese and Korean. Some of the difficulties our children encounter are:

13	thirteen	Syllables of the word are in opposite order
ten and three	*three and ten*	to the digits for thirteen to nineteen
20	twenty	Right order but two is distorted to twen-
two tens		Three is thir- in 30 and five is fif- in 50
60	sixty	Sixty is clear
six tens		So are seventy, eighty and ninety

It is not unusual to see young children write thirteen as 31, having heard 'thir' and written that first. The error arises in trying to make sense of the system.

After 99, we need a third position or place to create three-digit numbers. The digit one can be used to represent the numbers 1, 10 or 100 simply by virtue of where it is **placed**; this is known as *place value*.

Our place value system has a base of ten with ten ones making ten, ten tens making a hundred and so on.

Million	Hundred Thousand	Ten Thousand	Thousand	Hundred	Ten	One

This base-ten place value system represented a radical breakthrough for arithmetic when it was introduced into Europe. For the first time the way in which numbers were recorded could also be used for computation. Previously numbers had been recorded using one set of symbols e.g. Roman numerals, whilst a counting board or abacus was used for calculating.

A great strength of this number system is that it can be extended to numbers as large as you please.

However many digits are being used, when every place is filled with 9, the next number will have an additional digit. There is a 1 in the additional place and zeros everywhere else.

Nine million, nine hundred and ninety-nine thousand,
nine hundred and ninety-nine **9 999 999**

is followed by ten million **10 000 000**

Starting at zero the numbers go through: tens, hundreds, thousands and on to billions, trillions . . .

With all these numbers it might seem that the task of creating a number system is complete.

NEGATIVE NUMBERS

However, as more complex calculation developed the need to invent new numbers arose.

What can be done with counting numbers? If you choose any two and add them together there is always another counting number which is the answer to your calculation. The natural or counting numbers are all the numbers we need if we restrict ourselves to the operation of addition, as can be shown on the number line:

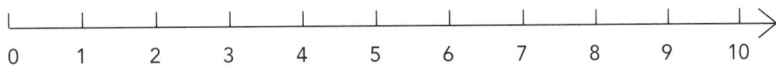

Now consider the operation 5 take away 3. The answer is 2. Just try, however, to work out 3 take away 5 and there is no number representing the answer anywhere on the number line we have established so far. There is a need to name and give a magnitude to the result of 3 minus 5 which indicates that there is a lack of two. The notation which is used to indicate this deficit of 2 is ⁻2 or *negative two*.

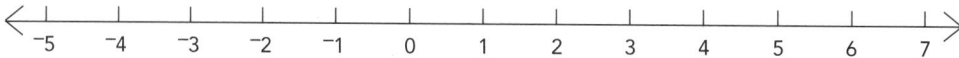

This notation is useful in many different contexts. If you have £50 in the bank, this can be thought of as +£50. Now write a cheque for £60 and your bank balance can simply be represented as ⁻£10.

The zero is the base position from which measurements are made. In trying to indicate and communicate the heights of mountains for example, you need to have a base position from which to measure. The base position is chosen as representative of sea-level around the world. Mount Kenya is 5199 m above sea-level whilst the surface of the Dead Sea is 396 metres below sea-level, that is ⁻396 m.

INTEGERS

The positive numbers, and the negative numbers, together with zero, are called integers.

The root of the word *integer* is the same as that of the word integral meaning *whole*.

Integers are whole numbers.

- If you choose any integer and add or subtract another integer your answer will always be an integer.

  $5 + 3 = 8$

  $4 - 7 = {}^-3$

- If you choose any integer and multiply by another integer your answer will always be another integer.

  $5 \times 7 = 35$

  ${}^-6 \times 2 = {}^-12$

As long as addition, subtraction and multiplication are the only calculations, we have all the numbers we need. However, just as introducing the inverse operation for addition required an extension of the number system from natural numbers to integers, so too does introducing the inverse operation for multiplication require a further extension of the number system.

Consider 5 divided by 2. The answer is not 2 and it is not 3 but somewhere in between. There are still more numbers to be included on the number line.

RATIONAL NUMBERS

The result of 5 divided by 2 can be written as $\frac{5}{2}$ or $2\frac{1}{2}$.

These new numbers, known as the rational numbers are numbers that can be expressed as one integer divided by another.

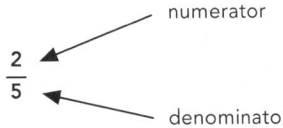

Rational numbers are commonly known as fractions.

Fractions whose numerator exceeds the denominator are often referred to as top-heavy fractions, and can be written as mixed numbers which include both a whole number and a fractional (i.e. less than one) part e.g. $\frac{5}{2} = 2\frac{1}{2}$.

- All the integers are rational numbers as they can be written as one number over another:

$$\frac{1}{1}, \frac{2}{1}, \frac{3}{1}, \frac{4}{1}, \frac{5}{1}, \ldots$$

In between these integers are millions of other rational numbers. If you include not just fiftieths and hundredths but thousandths, millionths, billionths you can imagine how densely packed the numbers are on the number line. It is always possible to write another fraction in between any two you choose.

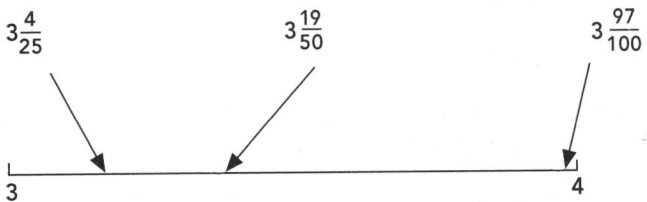

FRACTIONS, DECIMALS AND PERCENTAGES

The Egyptians worked only with fractions with the numerator one.

They would write three-quarters as the sum of a half and a quarter: $\frac{3}{4} = \frac{1}{2} + \frac{1}{4}$.

Writing fractions in particular ways is not unique to the Egyptians. There are two alternative ways of writing fractions that we come across every day, percentages and decimals.

Percentages are just an alternative notation for fractions with a denominator of 100:

$$40\% = \frac{40}{100} \, .$$

The place value system can be extended to very small numbers as well as to very large ones. These are called **decimals** or **decimal fractions**. If one unit is divided into ten equal pieces we obtain tenths. Dividing a tenth into ten equal pieces gives hundredths. This can continue repeatedly.

The decimal point is used to separate the whole number from the fractional part.

Hundred	Ten	One		Tenth	Hundredth	Thousandth
100	10	1		$\frac{1}{10}$	$\frac{1}{100}$	$\frac{1}{1000}$
1	1	1	.	1	1	1

The further the digit is to the right of the decimal point the smaller the fractional part of a whole. If we wrote our numbers so that the area of each digit was proportional to its value it would be obvious how the numbers after the decimal point become smaller and smaller.

$$1.1_1$$

Are decimal numbers rational numbers?

Rational numbers are defined as numbers which can be written as one integer divided by another.

So is 0.42 a rational number?

$$0.42 = \frac{4}{10} + \frac{2}{100} \quad \text{and} \quad \frac{4}{10} = \frac{40}{100}$$

so

$$0.42 = \frac{4}{10} + \frac{2}{100} = \frac{42}{100}$$

Therefore 0.42 can be written as $\frac{42}{100}$, a fraction, which is a rational number.

In this way a decimal with any fixed number of decimal places *can* be written as a fraction.

So all these numbers, because they can be rewritten as one integer divided by another, are rational numbers:

$$\frac{32}{80} \qquad 4\frac{1}{3} \qquad {}^{-}82 \qquad 0.3 \qquad 0.1789 \qquad 30\%$$

REAL NUMBERS

There are some numbers which cannot be expressed exactly as decimals however many decimal places are used, and there is no predictable pattern in their decimal expansion. Examples of numbers like this are π (the ratio of the circumference of a circle to its diameter) and $\sqrt{2}$ (the square root of two).

These numbers are known as irrational numbers and fill up the number line.

The rationals and irrationals together are called the real numbers. The number line is now complete.

1.3 CALCULATING WITH NATURAL NUMBERS

The operations of addition, subtraction, multiplication and division on simple numbers can be carried out in the head. As numbers become more complicated some informal recording helps the memory. Standard methods evolved for business use are often very compact. This may have been important when calculations were recorded in elegant handwriting in ledgers but slightly more extended methods often make the underlying stages much clearer and easier to understand. For each of the operations, mental methods, informal written methods and standard methods will be considered. Standard methods are simply those that have become commonly used in a particular culture. There are other effective methods which have been used at different times and in different cultures. To understand how quick mental methods and formal written methods have evolved it is necessary to consider some basic characteristics of operations and the relationships between them.

CHARACTERISTICS OF THE OPERATIONS

The operations of addition, subtraction, multiplication and division have distinctive properties, also referred to as principles or laws, which are used in devising mental and written methods. Teachers need to be aware of these properties so that they can guide and help children in developing efficient methods and avoiding misconceptions.

COMMUTATIVE PROPERTY

- If you add 2 and 5 then you get the same answer as when you add 5 and 2. When you combine two sets it doesn't matter which set you start with as $2 + 5 = 5 + 2$. This is the commutative property of addition.

  For any numbers a and b:

  $a + b = b + a$

- The answer to $5 - 2$ and $2 - 5$ is not the same so subtraction is **not** commutative.

- Multiplication is commutative as 3 sets of 5 is the same as 5 sets of 3.

  For any numbers a and b:

  $a \times b = b \times a$

- $10 \div 5$ is not the same as $5 \div 10$. Division is **not** commutative.

Making use of the commutative property of addition

This property is useful for children when they realise that you can choose to start with the larger set and count on.

Example: To find $3 + 15$, you can start with 15 and count on 16, 17, 18.

It is not usual to use the word commutative with young children but the idea is an important one for developing addition skills.

Realising that subtraction is not commutative

Children working out problems such as

$$\begin{array}{r} 483 \\ -247 \\ \hline \end{array}$$

sometimes make the error of taking the 3 away from the 7. They need to understand that you start with the 483 and are taking away the 247.

When the children are working on addition, because addition is commutative, this problem doesn't arise. It can be helpful, when working on formal addition calculations, to make the contrast with subtraction by emphasising that it doesn't matter which number you start with in addition.

Making use of the commutative property of multiplication

If a child knows that seven fives are thirty-five then they also know that five sevens are thirty-five.

$7 \times 5 = 35$ $\qquad$ $5 \times 7 = 35$

Realising that division is not commutative

When working out a division problem on a calculator you need to think carefully about which number to put in first. This is not a problem with multiplication as multiplication is commutative.

To summarise

- Addition and multiplication are commutative
- Subtraction and division are **not** commutative

This understanding may give some insight into why there are easy methods for addition and multiplication and why misconceptions can arise with subtraction and division.

ASSOCIATIVE PROPERTY

Addition, subtraction, multiplication and division all work on pairs of numbers.

Addition

When you are asked to add three numbers such as 5 + 7 + 3, does it matter whether you add the 5 and the 7 first or the 7 and the 3?

For addition it does not matter whether you start by adding the first two numbers or the last two numbers. This is described formally by saying that addition is associative. Associativity refers to this pairing without altering the order.

$$(5 + 7) + 3 = 5 + (7 + 3).$$

Subtraction

Is subtraction associative?

Does $(12 - 7) - 3 = 12 - (7 - 3)$?

$(12 - 7) - 3$ gives $5 - 3$ which is 2,

but $12 - (7 - 3)$ gives $12 - 4$ which is 8.

Subtraction is **not** associative.

Multiplication

Is multiplication associative?

Does $3 \times (2 \times 10)$ give the same answer as $(3 \times 2) \times 10$?

Just calculating the answer will show you that it does work for these numbers.

To see that it works for any numbers:

- Imagine multi-link cubes fitted together to make a cuboid with a base of 3×2 cubes and a height of 10 cubes.
  That will be $3 \times 2 = 6$ cubes in the bottom layer. There are 10 layers so that is 60 cubes.

- Knock the cuboid over so that the base is now 2 × 10 and the height is just 3 cubes. The base now has 2 × 10 = 20 cubes and there are 3 layers so that is 60 cubes.

The number of cubes is 60 in each case, it does not change.

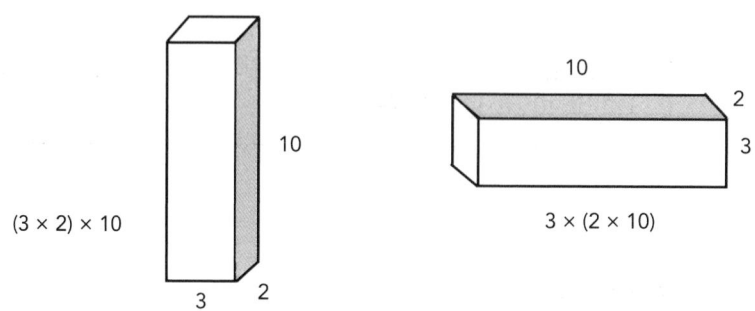

Division

Consider 24 ÷ 6 ÷ 2.

(24 ÷ 6) ÷ 2 gives 4 ÷ 2 which is 2

24 ÷ (6 ÷ 2) gives 8.

So division is not associative.

To summarise

- Addition is associative.
- Subtraction is not associative.
- Multiplication is associative.
- Division is not associative.

Notice that once again addition and multiplication are the easier operations to deal with.

Making use of the associative property

Children use this property when they calculate 5 + 7 + 3 by first working out 7 + 3 and then adding 5.

It can be useful with multiplication too, as when calculating 17 × 5 × 2 by working out 5 × 2 and then multiplying by 17 to get 170.

Because addition and multiplication are both associative and commutative these operations are very flexible. In a list of numbers to be added any pair may be chosen first.

Examples

   $3 + 5 + 7 + 5$

This can be calculated by noticing that the 3 + 7 make 10 and then adding on the 5 + 5.

   $4 \times 12 \times 25 \times 11$

This can be calculated by finding $4 \times 25 = 100$ and $12 \times 11 = 121$ then multiply 121 by 100 to get 12 100.

DISTRIBUTIVE PROPERTY

Many mental and written methods for multiplication depend on the distributive property.

Examples

To find 5×12.

Partition the 12 into 10 and 2, work out 5×10 and 5×2 and add the results.

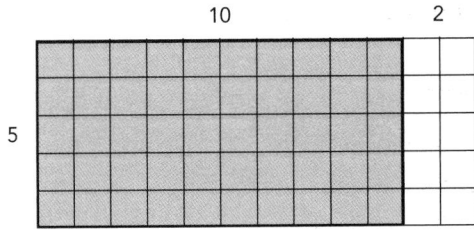

Formally we say that multiplication is distributive over addition:

   $5 \times 12 = 5(10 + 2) = 5 \times 10 + 5 \times 2$

To find 5×18.

Here you can over-calculate by finding 5×20 and then subtracting 5×2.

This works because multiplication is distributive over subtraction:

   $5 \times 18 = 5(20 - 2) = 5 \times 20 - 5 \times 2$

This distributive property underpins almost all the mental and written methods of multiplication.

RELATIONSHIPS BETWEEN THE OPERATIONS: INVERSE

Addition and subtraction are inverse operations.

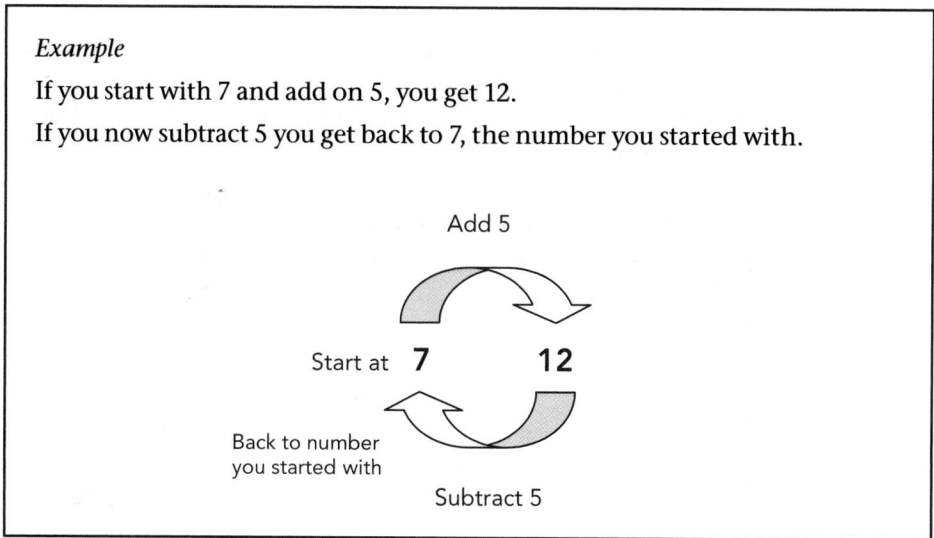

Example

If you start with 7 and add on 5, you get 12.

If you now subtract 5 you get back to 7, the number you started with.

Add 5

Start at **7**   **12**

Back to number
you started with

Subtract 5

As addition and subtraction are inverse operations 12 – 5 can be calculated by adding on from 5 to 12 as well as by subtracting from 12.

Multiplication and division are also inverse operations.

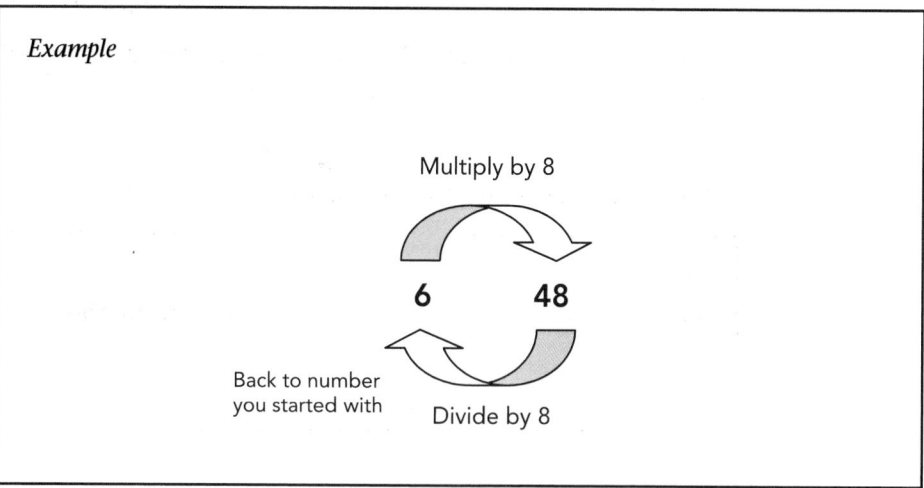

Example

Multiply by 8

6   **48**

Back to number
you started with   Divide by 8

As multiplication and division are inverse operations 48 divided by 6 can be calculated, not only by subtracting sixes from 48, but also by recalling that 6 × 8 = 48 and knowing immediately that 48 divided by 6 must be 8. Almost all quick methods of division rely on this inverse method.

ADDITION

For each of the operations of addition, subtraction, multiplication and division there are useful images and a range of associated language. Although the images used may seem very simple they embody the underlying properties of the operations and of the number system.

1. The image of combining groups of objects

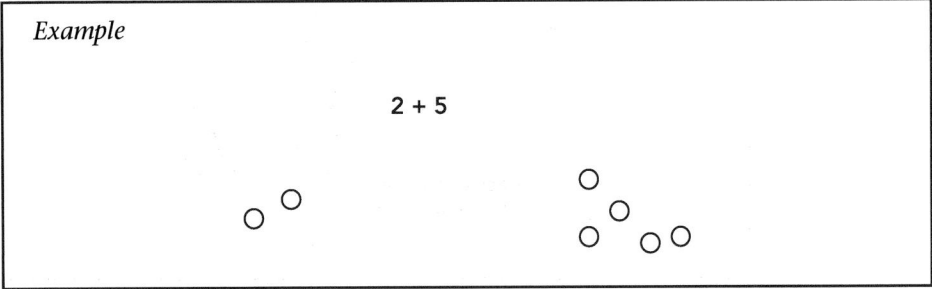

Example

2 + 5

There are three ways of calculating the sum of 2 and 5.

- Count all. Put all the objects together and count 1, 2, 3, 4, 5, 6, 7
- Count on. Start with the 2 objects and count on 3, 4, 5, 6, 7
- Count on from the larger. Start with the larger group and count on 6, 7

As addition is commutative (2 + 5 = 5 + 2) all of these methods will give the correct result though the last one is the most efficient.

2. The image of movement along the number line

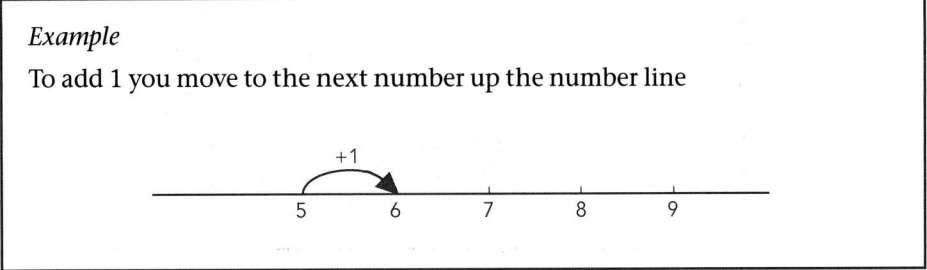

Example

To add 1 you move to the next number up the number line

This image uses the number 5 on a number line rather than 5 objects. The regular spacing of the number line emphasises the relative size of the numbers and the curved arrow represents the operation of addition. This image can be extended to larger numbers by hopping in different sized steps.

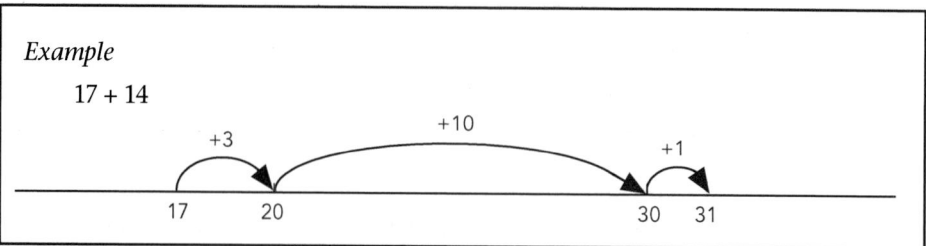

Example

17 + 14

The words most frequently used to indicate the operation of addition are:

add, sum, total, how many altogether?

MENTAL METHODS FOR ADDITION

Counting forward in different sized steps is directly related to addition:

Example

counting in tens: 10, 20, 30, . . .

counting in fives: 5, 10, 15, 20, 25, . . .

counting in twos, firstly from zero and then from any number:

0, 2, 4, 8, . . . and 13, 15, 17, 19, . . .

Counting is a prerequisite to being able to cope with addition, but is not the only valuable process. Other important strategies include the use of:

- **Complements to ten or number bonds**
  Recognising pairs of numbers which sum to ten, known as the complements of ten.
  This knowledge is used to 'bridge through the ten'.

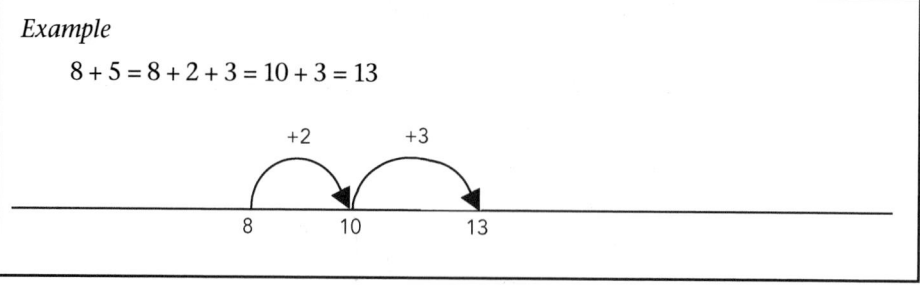

Example

$8 + 5 = 8 + 2 + 3 = 10 + 3 = 13$

- **Doubles**
  Being able to double numbers and recognise doubles or near doubles.

Example

$7 + 8 = 2 \times 7 + 1 = 14 + 1 = 15$

- **Commutative property**
  Using the commutative property, i.e. reversing additions to make them easier.

Example

$1 + 9 = 9 + 1 = 10$

- **Associative property**
  Using the associative property, i.e. bundling up a calculation to make it easier but without altering the order.

Example

$2 + 3 + 7 = 2 + 10 = 12$

- **Partitioning and recombining**
  Partitioning numbers into tens and ones and then recombining.

Examples

$23 + 35 = 20 + 30 + 3 + 5 = 50 + 8 = 58$

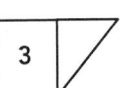
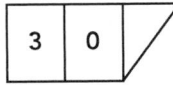

Alternatively start with the 35, add the twenty and add the three.

$23 + 35 = (35 + 20) + 3 = 55 + 3 = 58$

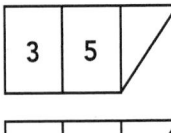
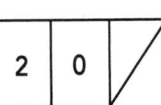
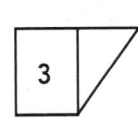

- **Compensating**
  Using an easier number and then compensating for the difference.

> *Example*
>
> $25 + 19 = 25 + 20 - 1 = 45 - 1 = 44$

Familiarity with all these methods, together with an ability to choose which one to use and also to combine several methods, will lead to confident manipulation of numbers.

When you combine the associative and the commutative property of addition you can add a list of numbers in any order you like.

INFORMAL WRITTEN METHODS FOR ADDITION

As more complex additions are attempted some informal method of recording is helpful.

> *Example*
>
> Find $365 + 457$.
>
> | | | |
> |---|---|---|
> | Add hundreds first as in mental methods: | $300 + 400$ | 700 |
> | then the tens | $60 + 50$ | 110 |
> | and the units | $5 + 7$ | 12 |
> | | So $365 + 457$ is | 822 |

FORMAL WRITTEN METHODS FOR ADDITION

The traditional algorithm begins by dealing with ones or units first. So the extended recording becomes:

$$
\begin{array}{r}
3\,6\,5 \\
+\,4\,5\,7 \\
\hline
1\,2 \\
1\,1\,0 \\
7\,0\,0 \\
\hline
8\,2\,2 \\
\end{array}
$$

Add units first
then the tens
and the hundreds

The extended recording helps children to understand what is happening and can be recalled when and if children have difficulty with the compact method of recording, shown below:

$$
\begin{array}{r}
3\,6\,5 \\
+\,4\,5\,7 \\
\hline
8\,2\,2 \\
\hline
{\scriptstyle 1\ 1} \\
\end{array}
$$

SUBTRACTION

1. The image of removing objects from a group of objects

Addition can be modelled by combining groups of objects or adding objects to a group and the inverse operation of subtraction can be modelled by removing objects from a group of objects.

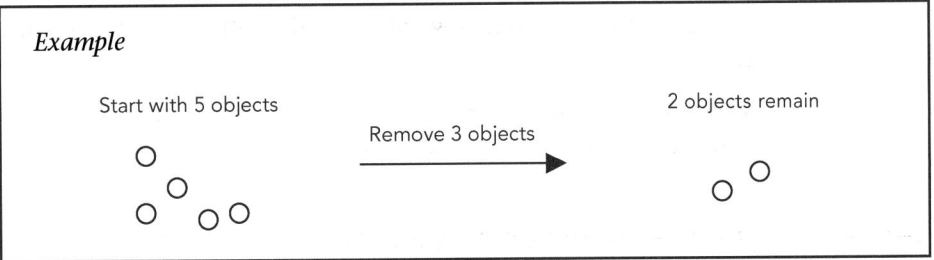

This image is a practical one which emphasises the starting number of 5 and the physical operation of taking away objects whether that is described as 5 take away 3, or as 5 minus 3, or as 5 subtract 3. The image can be extended using Dienes' apparatus so that it is possible to consider larger numbers without continual counting.

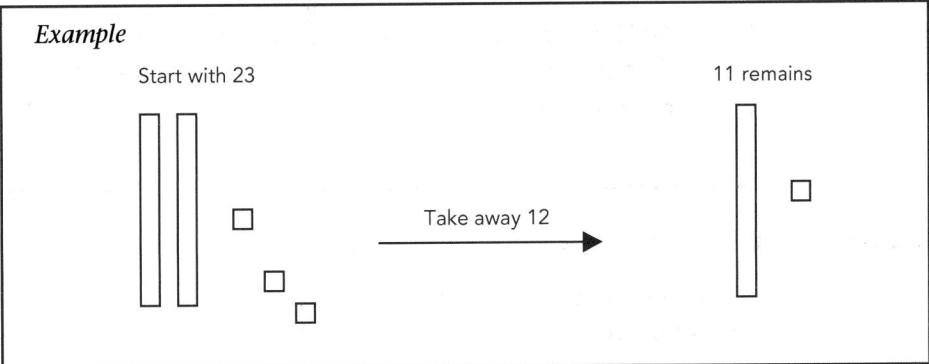

The image can be used to emphasise that addition and subtraction are inverse operations.

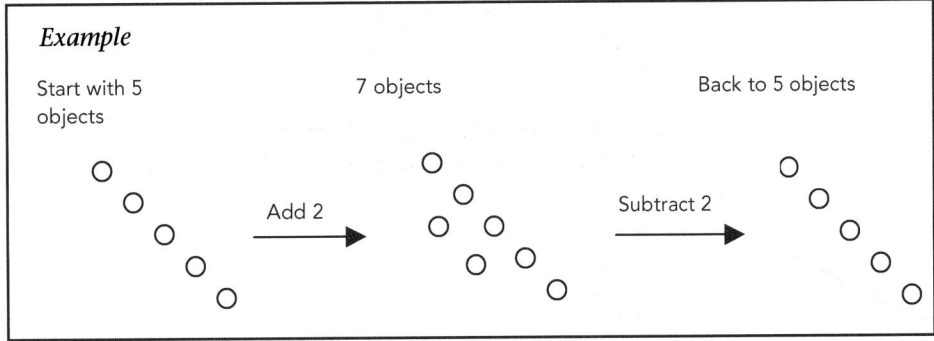

2. The image of comparing two groups

Placing two groups of objects alongside each other to show how many more objects are in the larger group.

Example

I have 6 cubes and you have 2, how many more cubes do I have?

☐
☐
☐
☐
☐ ☐
☐ ☐

Here the image represents the *difference* between 6 and 2.

3. The image of movement along the number line

(a) Counting back from a point on the number line

To add 1 you move on to the next number up the number line; so to take away 1 you move back 1 on the number line.

Once this understanding is established then the problem 5 subtract 3 can be interpreted as:

'If I start on 5 and count back 3 where will I land?'

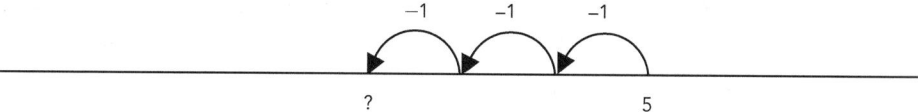

This image can be extended to larger numbers by hopping back in different sized steps.

Example

23 take away 11

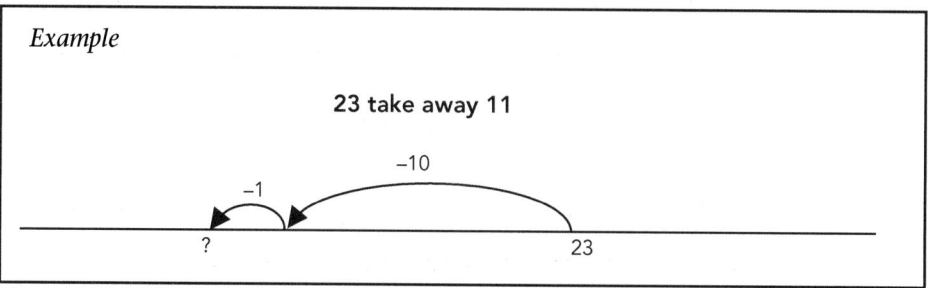

This method extends naturally to standard algorithms for subtraction.

(b) Adding on

It is always possible to solve a subtraction problem by adding on and so change the method of solution from counting back to counting on. This is what many people do when they give change.

Example

To find 23 – 11 you are rewriting the calculation as 11 + ☐ = 23.

The numbers 11 and 23 are fixed on the number line. To solve this problem you start at 11 and see how far you have to hop forward to reach 23

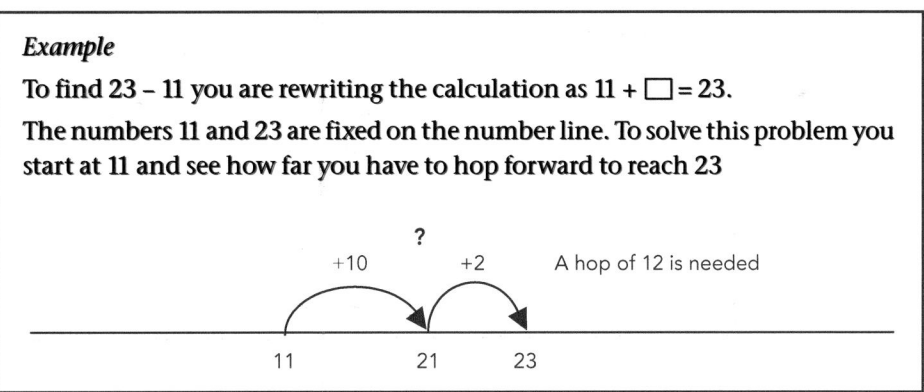

We use a range of different words to pose problems which require the operation of subtraction and to talk about the way the problems can be solved.

I cut 20 cm from an 89 cm length of wood. How long is the remaining plank?

I spend £12.72 from a twenty-pound note. How much change do I get?

Class 1 has collected 237 tokens and Class 2 has collected 483 tokens. How many more tokens has Class 2 collected?

It is possible to identify several categories and sub-categories of word problem but a natural and important distinction is between *reduction* problems and *difference* problems.

A reduction problem gives an initial quantity, states what is taken away and asks for what is left.
The associated image is that of removing objects from a group of objects.
The reduction problem can be restated using the word subtract.

A difference problem gives two starting quantities and asks for the difference between them.
The associated image is of comparing two groups.
The difference problem can be stated as

   'what is the difference between quantity A and quantity B?'

There is then a further step to realise that finding the difference involves subtraction.

Once the word problem has been interpreted as a subtraction problem an appropriate method can be selected for solving it.

MENTAL METHODS FOR SUBTRACTION

Useful strategies for subtracting two- and three-digit numbers include, for example when calculating 93 – 27:

- **Counting up through multiples of ten**
  Either keep count as you hop from 27 to 30 to 90 to 93,
  or from 27 count up in tens to 87 and then add 6.

- **Adjusting to easier numbers and then compensating for the adjustment**
  Round the 27 up to 30 before taking away.
  You have taken away 3 too many so need to add on 3.

- **Shunting the problem along the number line**
  Add 3 to both numbers so the calculation becomes 96 – 30.

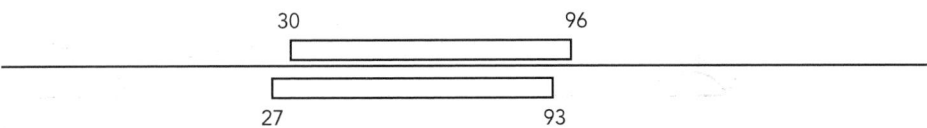

- **Partitioning the number you are taking away into tens and units and sub-tracting it in parts**
  Take away 20 and then 7 more.

 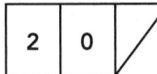 

INFORMAL WRITTEN METHODS FOR SUBTRACTION

When the numbers become difficult to hold in the memory, the approaches used in the mental methods can be developed and recorded, for example when calculating 756 – 78:

- **Compensation method**
  You decide to start by taking away 100 giving 656.
  However you only need to take away 78.
  100 – 78 = 22 so add on 22 because you have taken away 22 too many.
  656 + 22 = 678
  756 – 78 = 678
  The method works reasonably well but can sometimes result in a complex addition.

- **Counting up (complementary addition)**

Go from 78 to 80, the nearest multiple of ten.

After that the steps can get larger to approach the target of 756. You need to keep a tally of the size of the hops and the number reached.

Starting at 78
Add

2	to make 80
20	to make 100
600	to make 700
56	to reach the target of 756
678	So you add 678 altogether

The image on which this method is based is hopping up the number line.

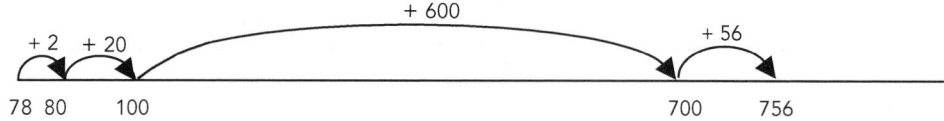

FORMAL WRITTEN METHODS FOR SUBTRACTION

As for addition, formal, standard, written methods were developed which worked for all numbers. An algorithm is rather like a computer program; it is a series of steps which, if carried out in the correct sequence, will lead to the result. The National Numeracy Strategy uses an extended format for formal written methods which is intended to be easier to understand and to explain. Once the extended method is understood the transition can be made to a more concise recording method, as required.

- **Decomposition**

Example

862 – 176

$\dfrac{800 + 60 + 2}{100 + 70 + 6}$	Consider the units: to take away 6 will need to adjust $60 + 2$ to $50 + 12$.
$\dfrac{800 + 50 + 12}{100 + 70 + 6}$	Units are now straightforward. Now to take away 70 you will need to adjust $800 + 50$ to $700 + 150$.
$\begin{array}{r} 700 + 150 + 12 \\ \underline{100 + \ 70 + \ 6} \\ 600 + \ 80 + \ 6 \end{array}$	Subtraction is now straightforward and the answer is 686.

The process is exactly the same as for the concise method but, because the full value of each digit is used, the statements are logical. There is no need to use phrases such as 'carry 1' or, when describing 700 take away 100, '7 take away 1'. Each step of the concise method can be traced and explained by reference to the extended method.

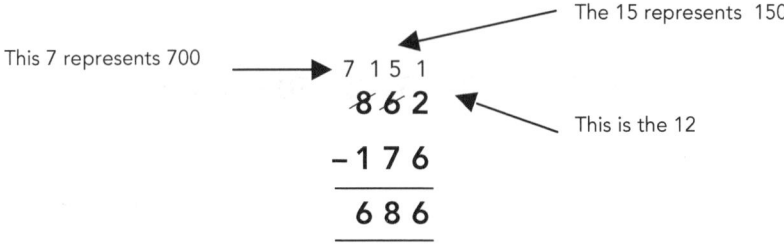

This 7 represents 700

The 15 represents 150

This is the 12

$$\begin{array}{r} 7\ 15\ 1 \\ 8\ 6\ 2 \\ -1\ 7\ 6 \\ \hline 6\ 8\ 6 \end{array}$$

MULTIPLICATION

IMAGES

The natural image for three sets of five objects is of casually grouped objects.

A very useful insight into multiplication is provided by arranging the objects into three rows of five.

From this diagram, called an *array*, it is apparent that $3 \times 5 = 5 \times 3$

This is called the commutative property of multiplication and is very useful for switching between a calculation seen as difficult and a calculation which is familiar.

A child may know that eight fives are forty and use this information to deduce that five eights must be forty as well.

The image can be extended to a grid of squares to represent more complex calculations.

Example

$$5 \times 12 = 5 \times 10 + 5 \times 2 = 50 + 10 = 60$$

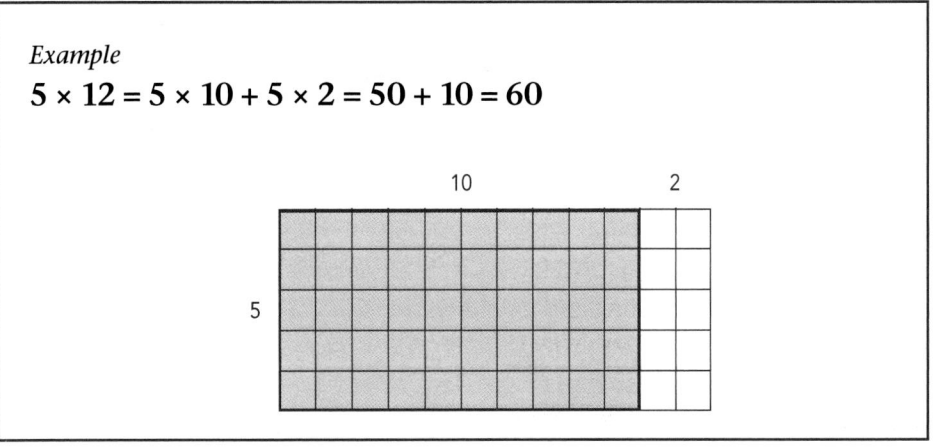

This can be simplified to a rectangle where the numbers represent the lengths of the sides. The numbers multiplied together represent the area.

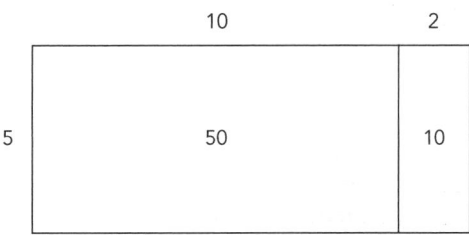

The language associated with multiplication includes:

lots of, multiplied by, times, product of.

Danger of misconception

In everyday language the word multiply is associated with making bigger. Multiplying by a natural number does always make bigger but multiplying by a fraction, e.g 12 × ½ gives 6 which is smaller than the 12 you started with. See the section on multiplying fractions to follow up this idea.

MENTAL METHODS FOR MULTIPLICATION

A variety of methods can be used to make sense of the process of learning basic multiplication facts and using known facts to work out more complex multiplications. The strategies in this list will help to ensure that the learned number facts are supported by a web of interconnections and understandings about the numbers.

- **Repeated addition**
  Finding 5×4 by working out $5 + 5 + 5 + 5$.

- **Deriving facts from the ones you have already memorised**
  Once you have memorised five sevens as 35 then six sevens is 35 plus another seven giving 42.

- **Doubling and halving**
  If doubling and halving numbers is well practised then this can be drawn on to derive further facts.

  If three eights are known to be 24 then six eights must be 48.

  If ten sevens is known to be 70 then five sevens must be half of 70 that is 35.

- **Partitioning and using the distributive law**
  To multiply 43 by 4 the 43 is partitioned into 40 and 3 and the multiplication is done in two stages.

$$43 \times 4 = 40 \times 4 + 3 \times 4$$
$$= 160 + 12$$
$$= 172$$

- **Multiplying by ten**
  Because we have a base-ten number system any integer can be multiplied by ten simply by moving the digits one place to the left and inserting a zero.

$$7 \times 10 = 70 \qquad\qquad 723 \times 10 = 7230$$

- **Rearranging calculations to simplify**
  To work out $25 \times 7 \times 4$, rearrange to $(25 \times 4) \times 7 = 100 \times 7 = 700$.
  There are a limited number of situations in which this is helpful.

- **Breaking multiples of 10 into factors**
$$20 \times 30 = (2 \times 10) \times (3 \times 10) = 2 \times 3 \times 10 \times 10 = 6 \times 100 = 600$$

A **Gattegno chart** is a way of displaying numbers that emphasises the relationship of multiplying and dividing by ten.

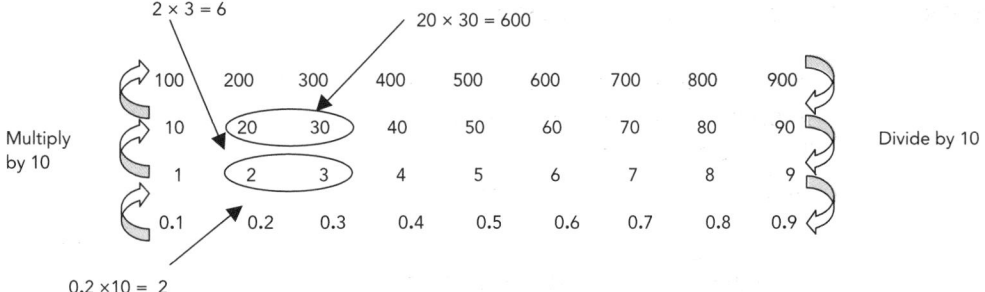

Possible misconception

If children are taught 'to multiply by 10 you add a nought' then this will give the correct solution only when they are multiplying whole numbers.

Now consider 0.2×10. The answer is *not* equal to 0.20.

The correct solution is obtained by moving the 2 one place to the left

$$0.2 \times 10 = 2$$

INFORMAL WRITTEN METHODS FOR MULTIPLICATION

The **grid method** is based on the familiar process of entering the results of a multiplication in a grid.

This is a convenient way of recording the mental method described as: *'partitioning and using the distributive law'.*

Example

32 × 4

×	30	2
4	120	8

$32 \times 4 = 120 + 8 = 128$

The method can be extended to more complex calculations:

Example

32 × 24

×	30	2
20	600	40
4	120	8

$$\begin{array}{r} 640 \\ + \ 128 \\ \hline 32 \times 24 = \ 768 \end{array}$$

FORMAL WRITTEN METHODS FOR MULTIPLICATION

The standard multiplication algorithm is based on partitioning. The extended method shows all the stages of working in a logical way; the compact method uses the same operations but records them in a more compact way.

Extended recording   Compact recording

$$
\begin{array}{r}
243 \\
\times \quad 7 \\
\hline
1400 \\
280 \\
21 \\
\hline
1701
\end{array}
\qquad
\begin{array}{l}
200 \times 7 \\
40 \times 7 \\
3 \times 7
\end{array}
\qquad
\begin{array}{r}
243 \\
\times \quad 7 \\
\hline
1701 \\
\scriptstyle 3 \; 2
\end{array}
$$

DIVISION

IMAGES

As division is the inverse of multiplication the images for division mirror those for multiplication.

Fifteen shared between three is five each.

$$15 \div 3 = 5$$

How many threes in fifteen?

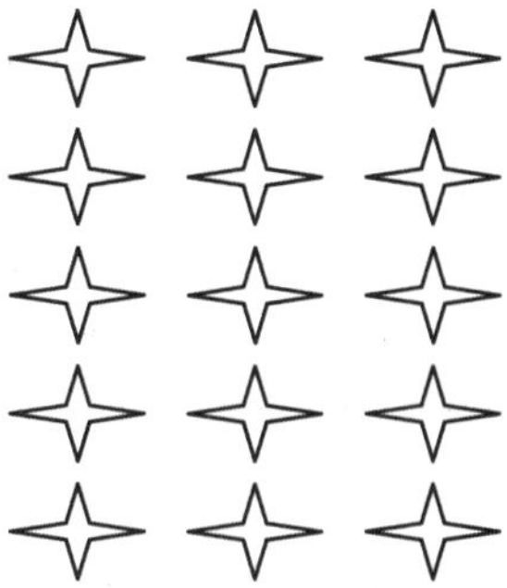

Repeated addition   Repeated subtraction

Repeated addition		Repeated subtraction
3		15
6		12
9		9
12		6
15		3

The language associated with the operation of division includes:

divide, share between, how many . . . in . . . ?

As multiplication and division are inverse operations, the methods for division mirror the methods for multiplication.

- **Repeated subtraction keeping a tally**

> *Example*
>
> 18 ÷ 3 can be solved by repeatedly subtracting 3 from 18.
>
> This gives 15, 12, 9, 6, 3, 0 so 18 ÷ 3 = 6

- **Repeated addition keeping a tally**

> *Example*
>
> 18 ÷ 3 can be solved by repeatedly adding 3 until 18 is reached.
>
> This gives 3, 6, 9, 12, 15, 18 so 18 ÷ 3 = 6

- **Deriving division facts from multiplication facts**

> *Example*
>
> 42 ÷ 7 = 6 because 6 × 7 = 42.

- **Using successive halving to divide by 4 or 8**
  4 = 2 × 2. To divide by 4 you can divide by 2 and then divide by 2 again.

> *Example*
>
> 144 ÷ 4
> First halve 144:   144 ÷ 2 = 72
>   then halve 72:   72 ÷ 2 = 36
>   So 144 ÷ 4 = 36

- **Using division by ten to assist with division by multiples of ten**
  20 = 10 × 2. To divide by 20 you can divide by 10 and then by 2.

> *Example*
>
> 360 ÷ 20
> First divide by 10:   360 ÷ 10 = 36
>   then by 2:   36 ÷ 2 = 18
>   So 360 ÷ 20 = 18

INFORMAL WRITTEN METHODS FOR DIVISION

Chunking

Repeated subtraction can be made more efficient by subtracting multiples of the number you are dividing by. Subtracting multiples of ten is particularly effective.

$143 \div 6$ can be calculated by first subtracting 10 lots of 6:

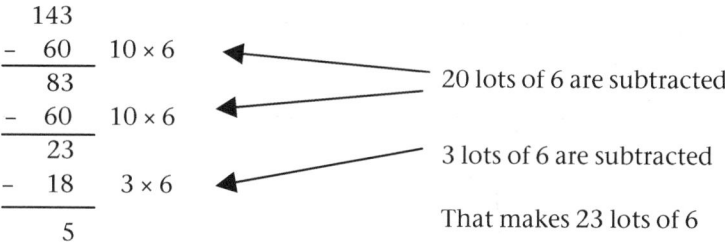

$$143 \div 6 = 23 \text{ remainder } 5$$

FORMAL WRITTEN METHODS FOR DIVISION

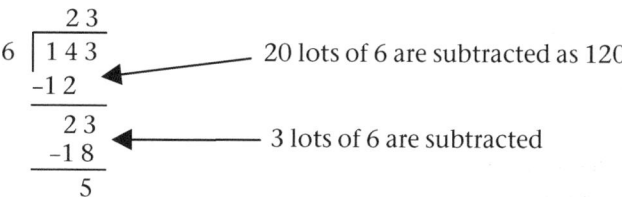

The verbal patter most people use to guide their way through long division ignores place value. Here we say '6 into 14 goes 2'. Compare this with the chunking method above where '20 lots of 6 are subtracted' describes clearly what is happening.

Different ways of dealing with remainders

How remainders are calculated and written depends on the context.

Examples

10 apples divided between 4 children gives 2 and a half apples each.

£10 shared between 4 children gives £2.50 each.

10 pencils divided between 4 children gives 2 each remainder 2.

How many cars are needed for 10 children if each car can take 4 children? 3 cars will be needed.

See the section on fractions and decimals for information on rounding.

1.4 CALCULATING WITH FRACTIONS, DECIMALS AND PERCENTAGES

FRACTIONS

INTERPETING THE NOTATION

It is possible to interpret the same fraction in two different ways:

> *Example*
>
> $\frac{3}{4}$ can be seen as
>
> - a fraction of one whole object
> - a quarter of three objects.

IMAGES

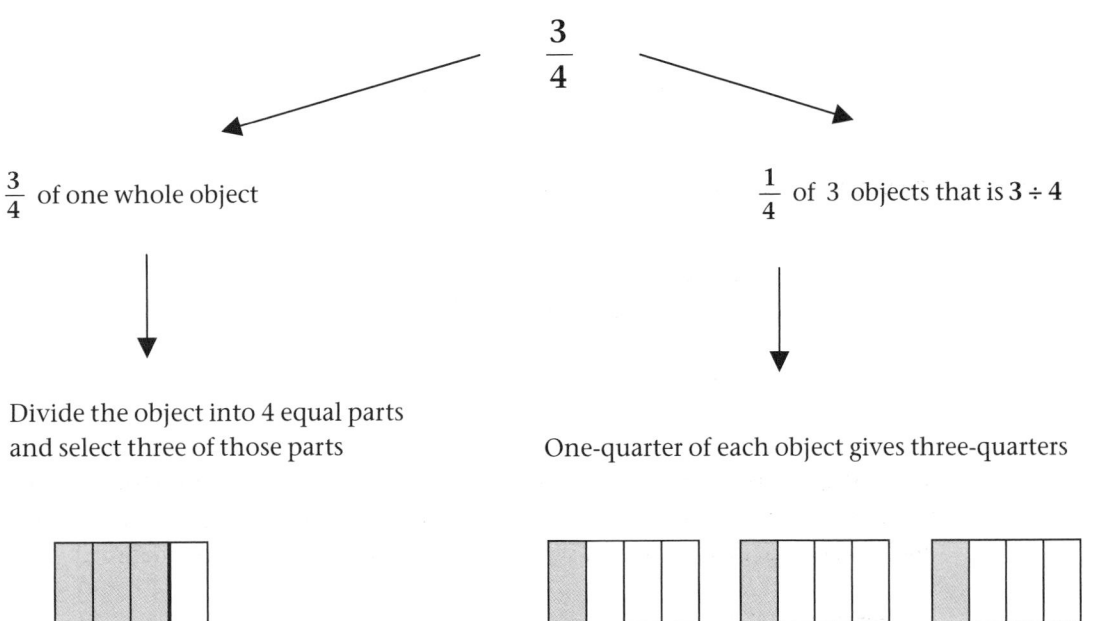

$$\frac{3}{4}$$

$\frac{3}{4}$ of one whole object

Divide the object into 4 equal parts
and select three of those parts

$\frac{1}{4}$ of 3 objects that is $3 \div 4$

One-quarter of each object gives three-quarters

Any fraction can be represented as a number on the number line.

0           $\frac{3}{4}$ 1   2

The insight that three-quarters is the same as 3 divided by 4 is an important one. When using fractions both ideas are needed.

Example

1. interpreting $\frac{3}{4}$ as 3 lots of a quarter is useful

    - when shading a diagram or

    - finding $\frac{3}{4}$ of 12 objects.

2. Interpreting $\frac{3}{4}$ as $3 \div 4$ is useful

    - when changing the fraction to a decimal.

TOP HEAVY FRACTIONS (IMPROPER FRACTIONS)

A top heavy fraction (or improper fraction) is one in which the numerator is larger than the denominator.

Example

$\frac{9}{4}$

Since $\frac{4}{4}$ makes one whole, $\frac{9}{4}$ gives 2 wholes and one extra quarter.

$$\frac{9}{4} = 9 \div 4 = 2\frac{1}{4}$$

EQUIVALENT FRACTIONS AND IMAGES

Take a sheet of paper. Fold it into three equal parts vertically.

Open out the paper and shade as shown.

$\frac{1}{3}$ of the paper is shaded

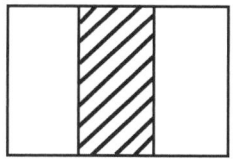

Now fold the paper in half horizontally.

Open out the paper.

Exactly the same amount is shaded but now the paper is folded into twice as many pieces.

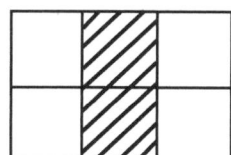

We now have 3 × 2 pieces

       = 6 pieces altogether.

The shaded piece has also been folded into two pieces.

We have 1 × 2 = 2 shaded pieces

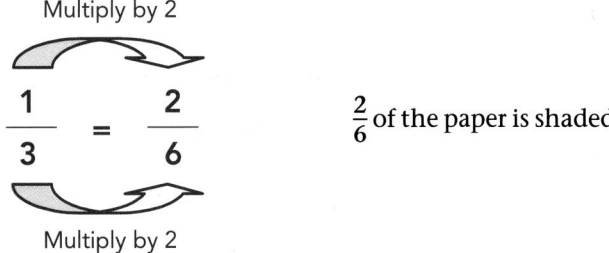

$\frac{2}{6}$ of the paper is shaded

One-third and two-sixths are called equivalent fractions.

Folding the paper into four horizontally would show that

$$\frac{1}{3} = \frac{4}{12}$$

For any fraction it is possible to find an infinite number of equivalent fractions by multiplying the numerator and the denominator by the same number in this way.

$$\frac{2}{3} = \frac{4}{6} = \frac{20}{30} = \frac{2200}{3300} = \cdots$$

CANCELLING DOWN

Fractions are usually cancelled down to their simplest form.

This is the inverse of the procedure above. The numerator and denominator are divided by the same number to give the simplest form of the fraction.

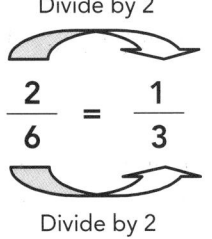

ORDERING FRACTIONS

Which is larger $\frac{3}{4}$ or $\frac{2}{3}$?

This question can be approached in several ways:

1. Intuitive sense of size

When this type of problem arises it can be useful to see how much we need to add to make a whole.

$\frac{3}{4}$ requires an extra $\frac{1}{4}$

$\frac{2}{3}$ requires an extra $\frac{1}{3}$

As $\frac{1}{4}$ is *less than* $\frac{1}{3}$ $\frac{3}{4}$ must be *greater than* $\frac{2}{3}$

2. A visual image of the size of the fraction

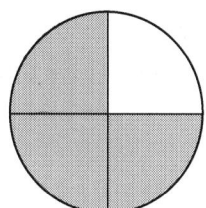 $\frac{3}{4}$ is greater than $\frac{2}{3}$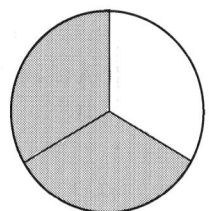

3. Ordering by changing to fractions with the same denominator

Quarters and thirds can both be changed to twelfths as 4 and 3 are both factors of 12.

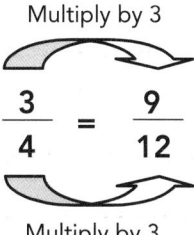

$$\frac{3}{4} = \frac{9}{12} \qquad \frac{2}{3} = \frac{8}{12}$$

Multiply by 3   Multiply by 4

Multiply by 3   Multiply by 4

Nine-twelfths is greater than eight-twelfths so:

$\frac{3}{4}$ is greater than $\frac{2}{3}$

ADDING FRACTIONS WITH THE SAME DENOMINATOR

What is twenty plus seven?	Answer: Twenty-seven
What is one-fifth plus two-fifths?	Answer: Three-fifths

Because of the way in which we name our numbers in bundles of ten, some additions, such as twenty plus seven, hardly seem like calculations at all. They just need an understanding of how numbers are named.

In the same way adding fractions with the same denominator (bottom number) just involves understanding how fractions are named and then adding the numerators (top numbers).

A further step is needed if the answer is greater than one.

Example

Four-fifths plus three-fifths is seven-fifths.

As five-fifths is one whole, seven-fifths is usually simplified to one and two-fifths.

$$\frac{4}{5} + \frac{3}{5} = \frac{7}{5}$$

$$\frac{7}{5} = 1\frac{2}{5}$$

In changing seven-fifths to one and two-fifths, you can either

- use the image of a fraction as a whole divided into parts and think of five-fifths as one whole, or
- consider the fraction as 7 ÷ 5. This gives one remainder two, which is one and two-fifths.

Seeing a fraction as the result of a division in this way is helpful for larger numbers.

Example

$$\frac{27}{4} = 27 \div 4 = 6\frac{3}{4}$$

The wrong method

It may seem perverse to describe a wrong method but so many children will try to add fractions by simply adding the top numbers and adding the bottom numbers that it is worth considering why this method does **not** work.

$$\frac{1}{4} + \frac{1}{4} = \frac{2}{8}$$ **WRONG!**

Two-eighths is just **one**-quarter so it makes no sense for a quarter plus a quarter to make just one-quarter, where the answer is smaller. This is complete nonsense. Try some other additions by this method and convince yourself that it just does not work.

ADDING AND SUBTRACTING FRACTIONS WITH DIFFERENT DENOMINATORS

This is a much more difficult problem as there is no immediate way to compare the size of the two fractions to be added.

Addition

What is $\frac{1}{4} + \frac{2}{3}$?

To solve this problem you need to change both fractions to the same type of fraction (fractions with the same denominator). Once that is done it will be easy to add the fractions using an understanding of how fractions are named.

We know that every fraction has an infinite number of equivalent fractions.

How do you decide which denominator to change to?

- You change to the smallest number that both denominators will divide into because you want the calculation to be as simple as possible. This number is called the lowest common denominator.

To add quarters and thirds you change to twelfths.

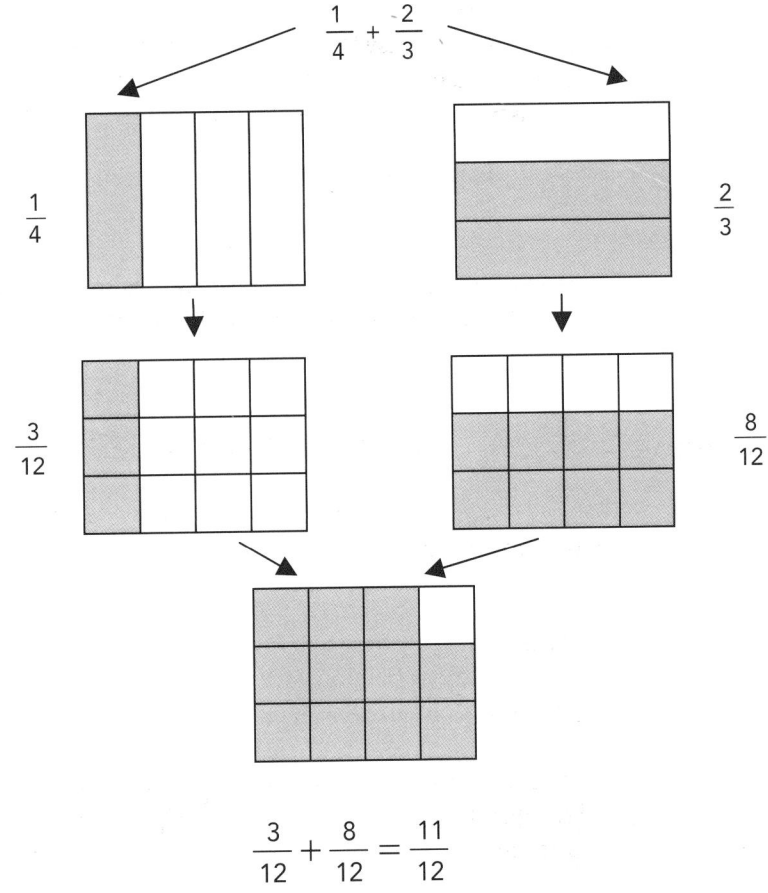

$$\frac{3}{12} + \frac{8}{12} = \frac{11}{12}$$

Using the diagram and looking at the numbers in the fractions:

1. Consider how to change one-quarter into twelfths.

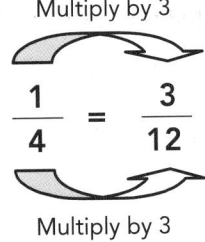

- the denominator 4 is multiplied by 3 to give the 12 parts and
- the numerator 1 is also multiplied by 3

  This shows that 3 of the new smaller parts (now twelfths) are needed to equal a quarter, giving

$\frac{1}{4}$ equal to $\frac{3}{12}$

Notice how you multiply the top and the bottom of the fraction by 3 to find the equivalent fraction with a denominator of 12.

2. To change thirds into twelfths you need four times as many pieces.

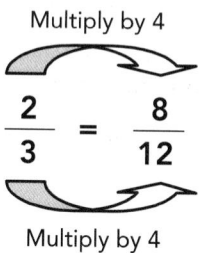

This gives $\frac{2}{3}$ equal to $\frac{8}{12}$

Notice that this time you multiply top and bottom of the fraction by 4 to find the equivalent fraction with a denominator of 12.
Both fractions are now in twelfths and so can be added easily.

To summarise

- Realise that both fractions can be written as twelfths, as the lowest common denominator of 3 and 4 is 12.
- Find the equivalent fractions.
- Add the fractions.

Subtraction
Subtracting fractions works in just the same way as addition.

HOW TO FIND THE LOWEST COMMON DENOMINATOR

Just multiplying the bottom numbers will give you a number that both denominators divide into but will this be the smallest possible denominator?

Denominators with no common factor
Consider fractions with denominator 5 and 7.

5 and 7 have no common factors other than one, so their product, **35** (5 × 7 = 35), is the lowest common denominator.

Example

$$\frac{1}{5} + \frac{2}{7}$$

Find equivalent fractions as described earlier giving:

$$\frac{1}{5} + \frac{2}{7} = \frac{7}{35} + \frac{10}{35} = \frac{17}{35}$$

Denominators with a common factor

Consider fractions with denominator 6 and 9.

Both of these numbers have a factor of 3

$6 = 2 \times 3$ and

$9 = 3 \times 3$

so both numbers will divide into $2 \times 3 \times 3 = 18$

Example

$$\frac{5}{6} + \frac{2}{9}$$

$$\frac{5}{6} + \frac{2}{9} = \frac{15}{18} + \frac{4}{18} = \frac{19}{18} = 1\frac{1}{18}$$

Denominators where one number is a factor of the other

Consider fractions with denominator 12 and 24.

You need to notice that 12 is a factor of 24. Both numbers will divide into 24.

Example

$$\frac{1}{12} + \frac{5}{24}$$

$$\frac{1}{12} + \frac{5}{24} = \frac{2}{24} + \frac{5}{24} = \frac{7}{24}$$

MULTIPLYING FRACTIONS

Surprisingly, multiplying fractions is easier than adding fractions. This is because the intuitive method of multiplying the top numbers and multiplying the bottom numbers does work for the multiplication of fractions (remember it does not work for addition). So multiplying fractions is easy to do but hard to explain.

Example

$$\frac{1}{2} \times \frac{3}{4}$$

$$\frac{1}{2} \times \frac{3}{4} = \frac{3}{8}$$

1 × 3 = 3 and 2 × 4 = 8 so the method is easy but does the answer make sense?

There is a common misconception that multiplying makes things bigger which, of course, it does when you multiply by a whole number.

However in this problem the fraction you end up with is only three-eighths. This is smaller than the half and the three-quarters you are multiplying, so is this answer correct?

To find $4 \times \frac{3}{4}$ you need to find 4 lots of $\frac{3}{4}$.

So to find $\frac{1}{2} \times \frac{3}{4}$ you need to find $\frac{1}{2}$ lots of $\frac{3}{4}$. This is half of three-quarters.

Consider this image:

Half of one-quarter is an eighth   so half of three-quarters would be three-eighths.

The result is correct and it makes sense that it is smaller than three-quarters because multiplying by a half means finding a half of (halving).

Using the same method to find a third of three-quarters

What is $\frac{1}{3} \times \frac{3}{4}$? Or find a third of three-quarters.

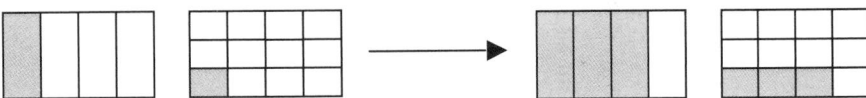

A third of one-quarter is a twelfth

so a third of three-quarters would be three-twelfths; three-twelfths is equivalent to one-quarter.

This gives: $\dfrac{1}{3} \times \dfrac{3}{4} = \dfrac{3}{12} = \dfrac{1}{4}$

Understanding and using the quick method

What is $\dfrac{3}{4}$ of $\dfrac{2}{5}$?

(No diagrams are provided so you will need to visualise what is happening.)

First find $\dfrac{1}{4}$ of $\dfrac{1}{5}$ which is $\dfrac{1}{20}$.

(Each of the fifths is split into 4 giving 4 × 5 = 20 parts.)

Then find $\dfrac{1}{4}$ of $\dfrac{2}{5}$ which is $\dfrac{2}{20}$.

(Two-fifths not one-fifth so multiply previous answer by 2.)

Finally $\dfrac{3}{4}$ of $\dfrac{2}{5}$ which is $\dfrac{6}{20}$.

(Three-quarters not one-quarter so multiply previous answer by 3.)

DIVIDING FRACTIONS

Most people remember the phrase, 'Turn the second fraction upside down and multiply' but can't explain why this works.

Example

$$4 \div \frac{1}{2}$$

This means 'How many halves in four?'

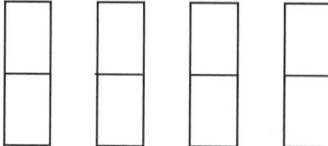

There are 8 halves in four whole ones.

Dividing by a half is the same as multiplying by 2.

Example

$$4 \div \frac{1}{3}$$

This means 'How many thirds in four?' The answer is 12.

$$4 \div \frac{1}{3} = 12.$$

Dividing by a third is the same as multiplying by 3.

So far we have only considered dividing by unit fractions.

Dividing by a non-unit fraction

Example

$$4 \div \frac{2}{3}$$

We are now dividing by something twice as big as last time. The expected answer is twice as small.

The answer is the answer to the previous example divided by 2. This gives 6.

Using the quick method gives

$$4 \div \frac{2}{3} = 4 \times \frac{3}{2} = \frac{12}{2} = 6$$

Using the image shows that you can fit two-thirds into 4 exactly six times.

$$\frac{2}{3} \qquad \frac{2}{3} \qquad \frac{2}{3} \qquad \frac{2}{3} \qquad \frac{2}{3} \qquad \frac{2}{3}$$

Example

$$\frac{3}{2} \div \frac{1}{3}$$

Here you need to find how many thirds there are in $\frac{3}{2}$.

Using the quick method gives

$$\frac{3}{2} \times \frac{3}{1} = \frac{9}{2} = 4\frac{1}{2}$$

Using the image

- divide the whole one into thirds. There are three thirds here.
- divide the half into thirds. This gives one and a half thirds.

Altogether there are four and a half thirds in the whole shape.

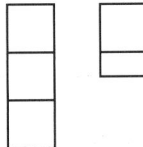

Once you have convinced yourself that the method works, it gives a quick and easy way of calculating fractions. The details of the explanation do not need to be remembered but it is important to realise that all mathematical methods and formulae can be explained logically.

DECIMALS

ADDING AND SUBTRACTING DECIMALS

All the methods for calculating with natural numbers can be extended to working with decimals. In practice just a few of the simpler methods are used for mental calculations and then formal algorithms or a calculator would be appropriate.

Mental methods for addition and subtraction
Counting forwards or backwards in tenths replaces counting in integers

e.g. forward in tenths   2.5,   2.6,   2.7,   2.8,   2.9,   3.0

backward in two-tenths   3.0,   2.8,   2.6,   2.4,   2.2,   2.0

- **Complements to one**

  Recognising pairs of numbers which sum to one. This can be used to add decimals by 'bridging through the integers'.

  Complements: $0.1 + 0.9 = 1$ $0.3 + 0.7 = 1$ $0.2 + 0.8 = 1$

  Bridging: $0.7 + 0.5 = (0.7 + 0.3) + 0.2 = 1 + 0.2 = 1.2$

- **Doubling**

  $0.7 + 0.7 = 0.14$ **WRONG!**

  A common misconception is that double 0.7 is 0.14 This misconception often occurs amongst children who, instead of reading 0.14 correctly as nought point one four, read it as nought point fourteen. The decimal point is seen as a barrier whereas in fact numbers flow across the decimal point as a result of calculations.

  $0.7 + 0.7 = (0.7 + 0.3) + 0.4 = 1.4$

- **Deriving** from known facts about integer calculations

Familiar fact:	$7 + 6 = 13$
Scaling each number up by ten:	$70 + 60 = 130$
Scaling each number down by ten:	$0.7 + 0.6 = 1.3$

Written methods for addition and subtraction

Decimal numbers can be lined up in the correct columns by ensuring that decimal points are underneath each other. If the decimal points are not lined up in a vertical addition the calculation is nonsense as different values are being added together.

$27.03 + 0.0412 + 370$

$$
\begin{array}{r}
27.08 \\
0.0412 \\
+\ 370 \\
\hline
397.1212 \\
\hline
\end{array}
$$

MULTIPLYING DECIMALS

Multiplying by ten

Multiplying decimals depends on a strong sense of how numbers in our base-ten system are multiplied by ten by moving the digits to the left. Moving any digit one place to the left multiplies it by ten, a number with several digits is multiplied by ten by moving each of the digits to the left.

	H T U . tenths	
37×10	3 7	to multiply 7 by ten move the 7 one place left to 70
	3 7 0	to multiply 30 by ten move the 3 one place left to 300
3.7×10	3 . 7	to multiply 3 by ten move the 3 one place left to 30
	3 7	to multiply 0.7 by ten move the 7 one place left to 7 units

Mental methods for multiplication

Mental methods are used for simple calculations and to help develop understanding.

- **Multiplying by multiples of ten and a hundred**
  To multiply by 20 multiply by 2 and then by ten:

  $$2.4 \times 20 = (2.4 \times 2) \times 10 = 4.8 \times 10 = 48$$

  To multiply by 100 multiply by ten and then by ten again, this will move the digits two places to the left.
  So 0.24 multiplied by 100 gives:

  $$0.24 \times 10 = 2.4 \qquad 0.24 \times 100 = 24$$

- **Multiplying by 0.1 and 0.01**
  Multiplying by one-tenth is the same as dividing by ten, multiplying by 0.01 is the same as dividing by one hundred.

  To multiply by 0.1 move the digits one place to the right:

  $$34 \times 0.1 = 3.4$$

  To multiply by 0.01 move the digits two places to the right:

  $$34 \times 0.01 = 0.34$$

  Notice that multiplying by 0.1 or 0.01 gives an answer smaller than the number you started with. A common misconception, based on the experience of multiplying natural numbers, is that multiplication always makes bigger.

  $4 \times 3 = 12$ which is bigger than 4
  $4 \times 2 = 8$ which is bigger than 4
  $4 \times 1 = 1$ which is exactly the same size as 4
  $4 \times \frac{1}{2} = 2$ which is smaller than 4
  $4 \times 0.1 = 0.4$ which is smaller than 4

- **Repeated addition**
  To multiply a decimal by a whole number

  $$5 \times 0.4 = 0.4 + 0.4 + 0.4 + 0.4 + 0.4 = 2$$

- **Partitioning** to simplify a multiplication
  To multiply a decimal by a whole number
  e.g. 3.4×2 partition the 3.4 into 3 and 0.4

  $$3.4 \times 2 = 3 \times 2 + 0.4 \times 2 = 6 + 0.8 = 6.8$$

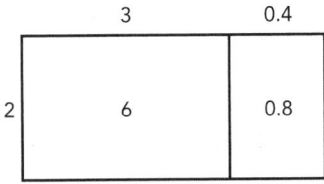

- **Deriving from known facts about integer multiplication**
  To multiply by 0.4 first multiply by 4 and then by 0.1:

  $$0.4 \times 5 = (0.1 \times 4) \times 5 = 0.1 \times (4 \times 5) = 0.1 \times 20 = 2$$

  To multiply 0.4 by 0.5 first multiply 4 by 5 and then multiply the answer by 0.01:

  $$0.4 \times 0.5 = (4 \times 0.1) \times (5 \times 0.1) = 4 \times 5 \times 0.1 \times 0.1 = 20 \times 0.01 = 0.2$$

A well-known rule of thumb for multiplying decimals involves:

ignoring the decimal points and multiplying the numbers

counting up the number of digits after the decimal points

inserting a decimal point to give the same number of decimal places in the answer

The understanding that each decimal place represents a multiplication by 0.1 helps to explain this method which can otherwise seem very strange.

Written methods for multiplication

- **Informal methods**

  The grid method can be extended to decimal calculations. It relies on a good understanding of place value and confidence in mental methods for multiplying decimals.

  Example

  32.5 × 3.4

×	30	2	0.5	
3	90	6	1.5	97.5
0.4	12	0.8	0.2	13
	102	6.8	1.7	110.5

  32.5 × 3.4 = 97.5 + 13 = 110.5

  Check: 32.5 × 3.4 = 102 + 6.8 + 1.7 = 110.5

- **Formal methods**

  WHAT IS 32.5 × 3.4?

  32.5 × 3.4 = 325 × 0.1 × 34 × 0.1 so the answer can be found by multiplying 325 by 34 and then multiplying by 0.01.

  $$
  \begin{array}{r}
  325 \\
  34 \\
  \hline
  \end{array}
  $$

325 × 30	9750
325 × 4	1300
	11050

  325 × 34 = 11 050

  32.5 × 3.4 = 325 × 34 × 0.01 = 110.5

Calculations of this type would normally be carried out with a calculator. For both the calculator and the written method an estimated answer is useful. Simplifying the numbers to just one digit:

32.5 × 3.4 will be in between 30 × 3 = 90 and 30 × 4 = 120.

Notice that the first estimate of 90 is not very close to the precise answer. Children often find estimating harder than calculating. They need to develop a sense of when the answer is completely the wrong size. This is much easier when working on problems in a context and not just on an exercise of calculations.

DIVIDING DECIMALS

Dividing by ten

Division is the inverse of multiplication and this relationship is particularly important in realising that all the methods for multiplying and dividing by ten by moving digits to the left correspond to a method of division by moving digits to the right.

		H	T	U	.	tenths	hundredths	
$37 \div 10$			3	7				to divide 7 by ten move the 7 one place right to 0.7
				3	.	7		to divide 30 by ten move the 3 one place right to 3
$3.7 \div 10$				3	.	7		to divide 3 by ten move the 3 one place right to 0.3
				0	.	3	7	to divide 0.7 by ten move the 7 one place right to 0.07

Relationship between multiplication and division

Dividing by ten is exactly the same as multiplying by 0.1.

This relationship underpins many calculations with decimals.

0.1 is another way of writing the fraction one-tenth $\frac{1}{10}$ which is $1 \div 10$.

So, for example, 4×0.1 is $4 \div 10$ which is $\frac{4}{10}$.

In a similar way dividing by 2 is the same as multiplying by a half.

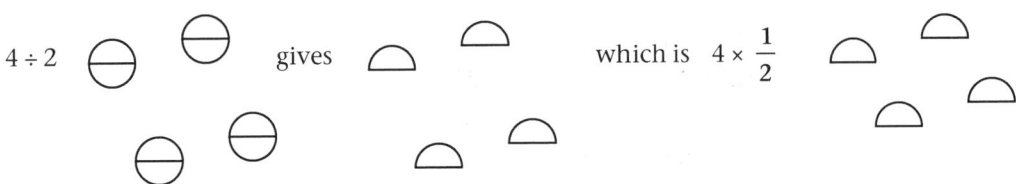

$4 \div 2$ gives   which is $4 \times \frac{1}{2}$

Although the diagram is drawn for just one example you need to see that this would always work.

When a number of objects is divided by 2, each of the objects contributes $\frac{1}{2}$ to the result so this must be the same as the number of objects multiplied by a $\frac{1}{2}$.

Mental Methods for division

These parallel the methods for multiplication but only methods for simple cases are given. These methods are helpful in understanding how division by decimals work but, in practice, more complex calculations would be carried out with a calculator.

- **Repeated subtraction**
  To divide by a decimal count back keeping a tally

  $$2 \div 0.4 \qquad 1.6, 1.2, 0.8, 0.4, 0 \qquad \text{so } 2.4 \div 0.4 = 5$$

- **Dividing by multiples of ten and a hundred**
  To divide by 20 divide by two and then by ten:

  $$2.4 \div 20 = (2.4 \div 2) \div 10 = 1.2 \div 10 = 0.12$$

  To divide by 100 divide by ten and then by ten again, this will move the digits two places to the right.
  So 0.24 divided by 100 gives:

  $$0.24 \div 10 = 0.024 \qquad 0.24 \div 100 = 0.0024$$

- **Dividing by 0.1 and 0.01**
  Dividing by one-tenth is the same as multiplying by ten, dividing by 0.01 is the same as multiplying by one hundred.
  To divide by 0.1 is to multiply by 10 so move the digits one place to the left:

  $$34 \div 0.1 = 340$$

  To divide by 0.01 is to multiply by a hundred so move the digits two places to the left:

  $$34 \div 0.01 = 3400$$

Possible misconception

Notice how counter-intuitive the answer is. Dividing by something very small will give a large answer.

Dividing by a number less than one gives an answer bigger than the number you started with.

Try to visualise how many 0.01s there are in 34.

Well, there are certainly a lot because there are one hundred in each unit and so $34 \times 100 = 3400$ altogether.

When multiplying or dividing mentally by 0.1 or 0.01 it is a good strategy to think first whether the answer will be larger or smaller. Decide whether the result of these calculations will be larger or smaller than the number you start with:

$$25 \times 0.1 \qquad\qquad 25 \div 0.1$$

$$25 \times \frac{1}{10} \qquad\qquad 25 \div \frac{1}{100}$$

Going to extremes – the idea of infinity

Does it make sense to ask the question: What is one divided by zero?

However many zeros you add together you still get zero so how could you stack up enough zeros to make one?

If you start with 1 and divide by 0.1 you get 10

If you start with 1 and divide by 0.01 you get 100

If you start with 1 and divide by 0.001 you get 1000

If you start with 1 and divide by 0.0001 you get 10 000

From this pattern it is clear that as you divide by a number closer and closer to zero your answer becomes larger and larger. If you divide by
0.000 000 000 000 000 000 000 000 000 0001
you get 10 000 000 000 000 000 000 000 000 000 000.

You can never ever get to zero but as you divide by smaller and smaller numbers your answer becomes enormous.

Mathematicians describe this by saying that as the number you are dividing by tends to zero your answer tends to infinity. Infinity is not a number but a way of describing this process of getting larger and larger without end.

Because infinity is such a mind-boggling concept, many puzzles and paradoxes about infinity have been developed. Some of these are described in the section on problem solving, reasoning and proof.

Written methods for division

- **Chunking**, the subtraction of multiples of the number you are dividing by, can be extended to division of a decimal number.

Example

Calculate $106.4 \div 7$

$$
\begin{array}{rl}
106.4 & \\
-70 & \qquad 10 \times 7 \\
\hline
36.4 & \\
-35 & \qquad 5 \times 7 \\
\hline
1.4 & \\
-1.4 & \qquad 0.2 \times 7 \\
\hline
0 & \qquad\qquad \text{So } 106.4 \div 7 = 15.2
\end{array}
$$

- **Changing to an equivalent calculation**
  It is always possible to change a division of decimals to an equivalent form.
  $$2.4 \div 0.3 = \frac{2.4}{0.3}$$

  Multiplying top and bottom by $10 = \frac{24}{3} = 8$

Examples

$$24.4 \div 0.08 = 2440 \div 8 = 305$$

$$0.384 \div 0.04 = 38.4 \div 4 = 9.6$$

ROUNDING

The results of calculations with decimals or percentages can give a long string of digits. How accurately the answer should be given depends on the context. There are two systems for rounding: one fixes the number of decimal places, the other fixes the number of significant figures.

Decimal places

This square measures 1.2 cm to the nearest tenth of a centimetre.

Area of the square = $1.2 \times 1.2 = 1.44$ cm²

How accurate is this answer?

Suppose a slight error had been made in measuring and the length of the side was not 1.2 but 1.3.

Area of a square of side 1.3 cm = $1.3 \times 1.3 = 1.69$ cm²

1.2 cm

1.2 cm

The final area of the square is not known as precisely as the calculated values with two decimal places suggest.

It is usual to round the answer to 1 decimal place.

Area of square of side 1.3 cm = $1.3 \times 1.3 = 1.69 = 1.7$ cm² to one decimal place.

For some calculations with decimals it is even more obvious that rounding is needed to give a sensible answer, e.g.

The area of a rectangle is 5.2 cm²

The length of one side is 3 cm

What is the length of the other side of the rectangle?

Using a calculator   Length of side $= \frac{5.2}{3} = 1.733333333$

Obviously the length of the side of the rectangle is not known to this degree of accuracy.

An appropriate answer is: Length of side = 1.7 cm to one decimal place.

It may be appropriate to give an answer to two or three decimal places. The convention for rounding is the same in each case. Round down if the following digit is less than 5 and round up if it is 5 or more.

To round 5.43621 to two decimal places.

Identify the second decimal place by counting to the right from the decimal point.

The number after the 3 is 6 so round the 3 up to give 5.44 to two decimal places.

To round 0.07234 to three decimal places

Identify the third decimal place by counting to the right from the decimal point.

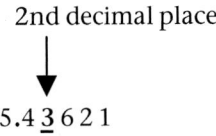

The digit after the 2 is less than 5 so round to 0.072 to three decimal places.

Dividing to find an answer to a given number of decimal places
When a division does not give an exact answer, it is possible with decimals to give an answer to any degree of accuracy required.

So to find £34 ÷ 8

Using the chunking method

```
        34
      − 32          Subtract 4 × 8
      ───────
        2.00        Write the £2 as £2.00
      −  2.00       Subtract 0.25 × 8
      ───────
```

So £34 divided by 8 is £4.25.

Using a standard written method 34 is written as 34.00.

```
        4.25
    ┌────────
  8 │ 34.00
    − 32
    ─────
      20
    − 16
    ─────
      40
      40    So £34 divided by 8 is  £4.25.
    ─────
       0
```

So by adding zeros after the decimal point an answer can be given to any required degree of accuracy. The answer above is given to two decimal places but any other number of places can be used if a particularly accurate answer is required.

Significant figures

From the turnstiles it is known that 15 942 people attended a football match.

A news announcer is more likely to report that nearly 16 000 people attended the match. The thousands are important or significant; the final digit 2 is not significant.

To round 15 942 to two significant figures.

Identify the second significant figure.

The next digit is more than 5 so round up to give 16 000 to two significant figures.

What would 0.000 4725 be to three significant figures?

The most important digit in this number is the 4.

This is the first significant figure.

When counting significant figures you start with the first non zero digit and count to the right.

0.000 4725 to three significant figues is 0.000 473.

2nd significant figure

↓

1 5 9 4 2

3rd significant figure

↓

0.0 0 0 4 7 2 5

Possible misconception

15 942 to 2 significant figures.   Wrong answer: 16

Although only two significant figures are required, it is crucial to add the zeros to show the size of the approximation.   Correct answer: 16 000

RECURRING DECIMALS

Moving from decimals to fractions is straightforward because decimals are fractions with denominator 10, 100, 1000 etc.

0.2   is two-tenths

0.05 is five-hundredths

So what is 0.25 as a fraction?

Each tenth is ten-hundredths so the 0.2 is twenty-hundredths and the 0.5 is five-hundredths so

0.25 can be read directly as 25-hundredths. This is another example of the power of the place value system.

$$0.25 = \frac{2}{10} + \frac{5}{100} = \frac{20}{100} + \frac{5}{100} = \frac{25}{100}$$

Any decimal can be read off as a fraction by finding the place value of the final digit.

0.105 is 105 thousandths or $\frac{105}{1000}$.

Is it possible to start with any fraction and write it as a decimal?

Consider the fraction $\frac{3}{8}$. This means 3 divided by 8. Carrying out the division gives a decimal to any required degree of accuracy.

```
        0.375
    8 | 3.00000
    –   2 4
          60
    –     56
          40
    –     40
```

Some simple fractions give surprising results.

Example

Write $\frac{1}{3}$ as a decimal.

```
        0.3333333333
    3 | 1.000000000
        9
       10
        9
       10
        9
```

This use of the long division algorithm makes it clear that you could go on and on dividing by 3 always getting the same result of 3 remainder 1 so that the decimal equivalent of $\frac{1}{3}$ is

0.33333333333333333333333333333333333333333333333333333333333333333 . . . and so on for ever.

A dot over the three which repeats is used to show this. It looks duller but is short to write: $0.\dot{3}$

This is read as nought point three recurring. This is another situation in which the idea of infinity crops up in what seems to be a very straightforward calculation.

In conclusion it is possible to write any fraction as a decimal by dividing the numerator by the denominator. For some fractions an exact answer is obtained after a finite number of decimal places; these are called terminating decimals. For other fractions a repeating pattern sets in with either one digit or a series of digits being repeated without end. These are called recurring decimals.

The decimal value of $\frac{1}{7}$ repeats after six digits:

0.142857142857142857142857142857142857142857142857142857142857142857 . . .
three dots are traditionally used to indicate that the pattern goes on and on for ever.

The short form of recurring decimals like this is formed by placing a dot over the first number that repeats and over the last number.

So $\frac{1}{7}$ is $0.\dot{1}4285\dot{7}$

Some fractions which give terminating decimals:

$$\frac{1}{5} = 0.2 \qquad \frac{1}{2} = 0.5 \qquad \frac{1}{4} = 0.25 \qquad \frac{1}{8} = 0.125$$

Some fractions which give recurring decimals:

$$\frac{1}{3} = 0.\dot{3} \qquad \frac{2}{3} = 0.\dot{6} \qquad \frac{1}{11} = 0.\dot{0}\dot{9} \qquad \frac{3}{7} = 0.\dot{4}2857\dot{1}$$

It is possible to explore recurring decimals using a combination of a calculator (to speed up calculations) and long division (to make sure the calculator has not introduced rounding errors). Can you predict which fractions will give terminating decimals and which will give recurring decimals? (The answer, you may not be surprised to find, is linked to the base-ten place value system.)

PERCENTAGES

Percentages are a special type of fraction with denominator one hundred. They are useful for comparisons because it is easy to compare fractions with the same denominator.

Example

The machine operators got a rise from £180 a week to £189 a week.

This is a rise of $\frac{9}{180}$.

The supervisors got a rise from £300 a week to £315 a week

This is a rise of $\frac{15}{300}$.

Because the fractions have different denominators it is not easy to compare to see if $\frac{9}{180}$ or $\frac{15}{300}$ is larger.

Changing the fractions to percentages, that is fractions with the same denominator, makes comparison easier:

$$\frac{9}{180} = \frac{1}{20} = \frac{5}{100} = 5\%$$

$$\frac{15}{300} = \frac{1}{20} = \frac{5}{100} = 5\%$$

So the machine operators and the supervisors got the same percentage rise.

Notice that the increase in take-home pay was different. As the supervisors earned more to start with, 5% of £300 meant an extra £15 a week for them. The machine operators' starting wage was £180 so 5% of £180 gave them an extra £9 a week.

The negotiators can argue whether percentage rises are fair. The important mathematical point is that you need to know what the percentage is a percentage of to make sense of a practical situation.

What operations are done with percentages?

The most usual operations are;

Finding a percentage of an amount
Expressing one number as a percentage of another
Increasing or decreasing a number by a given percentage

FINDING A PERCENTAGE OF AN AMOUNT

Remembering that percentages are just fractions, this is the same as finding a fraction of an amount.

- **Informal methods**
  A few percentages such as 50% and 10% are easy to find. From these many other percentages can be calculated.

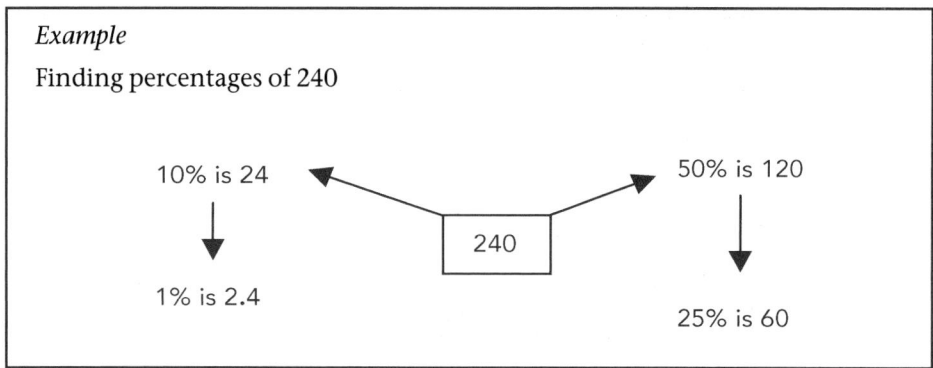

Example

Finding percentages of 240

10% is 24

1% is 2.4

240

50% is 120

25% is 60

1 By building up from simple percentages

10% of 240 is 24,

so 5% of 240 is 12.

So 35% of 240 is 3 × 24 + 12 = 84.

2 By finding 1%

1% of 240 is 240 ÷ 100 = 2.4

Any other percentages can be found from this: e.g 12% of 240 is 2.4 × 12 = 28.8.

- **Formal method**

  12% of 240 can be found by writing the percentage as a fraction and multiplying

  $$\frac{12}{100} \times 240 = \frac{12 \times 240}{100} = 28.8$$

  Alternatively the 12% can be written as a decimal, that is 0.12 and then multiplied.

  12% of 240 = 0.12 × 240 = 28.8

EXPRESSING ONE NUMBER AS A PERCENTAGE OF ANOTHER

In a class of 33 children there are 12 girls. What percentage of the class are girls?

A percentage is just a fraction with numerator 100, so the problem is to find a number such that

$$\frac{?}{100} = \frac{12}{33}$$

This can be solved by finding $\frac{12}{33}$ as a decimal and multiplying by 100.

A calculator gives $\frac{12}{33} = 0.36363636\ldots$

To multiply by 100 the digits are moved two places to the right.

So the percentage is $36.36363636\ldots$

A sensible degree of accuracy is one decimal place, that is 36.4 (36.4 is chosen rather than 36.3 because the next digit is 6).

So the percentage of girls in the class is 36.4 to one decimal place.

Notice that this immediately gives an answer for the percentage of boys in the class as 100 – 36.4, that is 63.6% to one decimal place.

INCREASING OR DECREASING A NUMBER BY A GIVEN PERCENTAGE

Example

£80 is invested in an account earning 5%. At the end of the year the interest is added to the account.

How much money will be in the account after one year?

1 The problem can be solved by working out 5% of £80 and adding it on.

Using the method above: 10% of £80 is £8 so 5% is £4.

After one year there will be £80 + £4 = £84 in the account.

2 Calculating the final amount in one stage.

At the end of the year the account will contain all the money first invested that is 100% plus the 5% of the money invested which is added as interest. So at the end of the year there will be 105% of £80 in the account

$$105\% \text{ of } 80 = 1.05 \times 80 = 84$$

This last method is particularly useful when finding the result of several increases.

After year 2, the amount in the account will be 105% of 84 = 1.05 × 84 = 88.2. So there will be £88.20 in the account.

As long as you don't ever spend any money just multiplying the amount in the account by 1.05 each year will show how the investment grows.

POSSIBLE MISCONCEPTION

On Tuesday a shop puts up the price of a television costing £800 by 15%.

The following day they have a sale and all prices are put down by 15%.

When is the best time to buy the television?

It might seem that it wouldn't matter if you bought the television on Monday before prices were changed or on Wednesday when the prices had gone up and then down again. But try the calculations . . .

On Tuesday the price of the TV is put up by 15%:

15% of £800 = £120, so price is now £920.

On Wednesday the price is reduced by 15%:

15% of £920 = £138, so price is now £782.

It is cheaper to buy the TV after prices have been put up and down.

What is happening? If the price had just been put up by £100 and down by £100 it would have ended up at exactly the same price as it started.

This is because a percentage is a fraction of the price.

To find out how much to increase the price you work out 15% of £800.

To find out how much to decrease the price you work out 15% of the new higher price of £920.

CHANGING BETWEEN FRACTIONS, DECIMALS AND PERCENTAGES

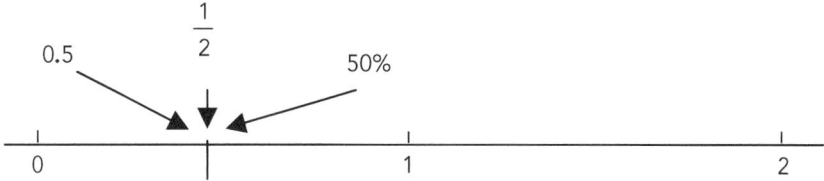

The same point on the number line can be represented in many different ways: as a decimal, a percentage or as a fraction with an infinite number of equivalent forms.

It is useful to be able to move between the different representations so that the most appropriate representation for the context can be chosen.

This diagram shows conversions. The underlying ideas needed to make sense of the conversions are that:

- A percentage is a fraction out of 100.

- 0.3 can be written as $\frac{3}{10}$ or as $\frac{30}{100}$ or as $\frac{300}{1000}$.

- A fraction such as $\frac{3}{4}$ can be thought of as either 3 lots of a quarter or as 3 ÷ 4.

To change	Fractions	Decimals	Percentages
Fractions		$\frac{3}{4} = 3 \div 4 = 0.75$	$\frac{3}{4} = \frac{?}{100}$
Decimals	$0.28 = \frac{28}{100}$		$0.28 = \frac{28}{100} = 28\%$
Percentages	$32\% = \frac{32}{100}$	$32\% = 0.32$	

In the diagram the operation of changing a fraction to a percentage has been left unfinished.

In the example given an equivalent fraction with denominator 100 can be found by multiplying by 25.

$$\frac{3}{4} = \frac{3 \times 25}{4 \times 25} = \frac{75}{100} = 75\%$$

If the denominator of the fraction does not divide exactly into 100 another method is needed.

$$\frac{x}{100} = \frac{2}{3}$$ The problem is to find the unknown number over the 100.

Multiplying both sides by 100 gives

$$x = \frac{2}{3} \times 100 = \frac{200}{3} = 66\frac{2}{3}\%$$

1.5 CALCULATING WITH NEGATIVE NUMBERS

NOTATION

Negative 5 is written $^-5$. The number 5 could be written as $^+5$ to emphasise the distinction but, normally, it is just written as 5. Some calculators have different keys for the sign meaning to subtract and the sign placed in front of a number to show that it is negative.

Example

To enter the calculation $^-5 - 3$ in such a calculator you would need to press

| negative | | 5 | | subtract | | 3 |

Pressing subtract 5 at the start would give an error message.

The distinction between the signs is sometimes made in print by having the sign for negative slightly higher than the minus sign.

ADDITION

Once negative numbers have been defined there will be situations in which calculations with negative numbers are needed. Negative numbers are less tangible than natural numbers but it is still possible to develop images to help with an understanding of the operations of addition and subtraction.

HOPPING ALONG THE NUMBER LINE

To add 1 you move to the next number up the number line.

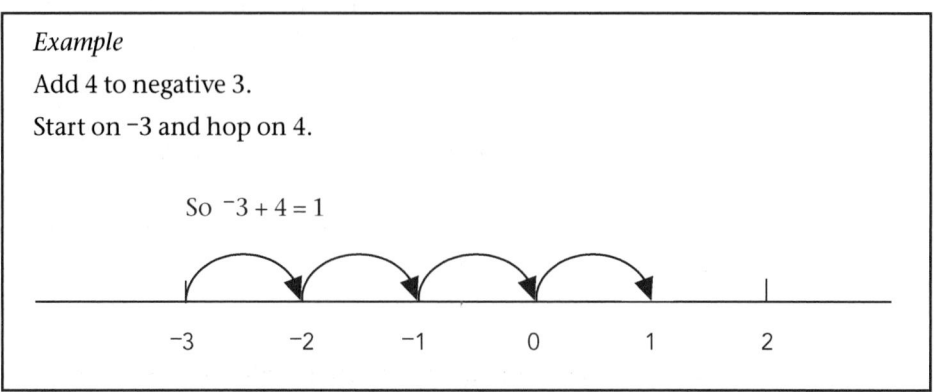

Example

Add 4 to negative 3.

Start on ⁻3 and hop on 4.

So ⁻3 + 4 = 1

But what happens when you add ⁻1? In this case you move back down the number line. If negative one is thought of as a debt of 1 then if you start with 3 and add a debt of 1 then you end up with 2.

+ ⁻1 is the same as –1

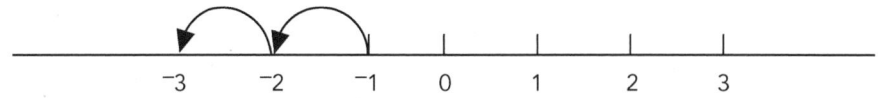

So to work out ⁻1 + ⁻2 you start on ⁻1 and move two steps back down the number line to ⁻3.

Addition is commutative for negative numbers as well as positive ones:

⁻1 + ⁻2 = ⁻2 + ⁻1 = ⁻3

If you start at ⁻2 on the number line and hop back one you get to ⁻3.

> Two of these statements are true. Which one is false?
>
> 4 + ⁻10 = ⁻14
>
> ⁻23 + 12 = ⁻11
>
> ⁻17 + 4 = ⁻13

IMAGES FOR NEGATIVE AND POSITIVE NUMBERS

A variety of images and contexts are used to assist in the understanding of negative numbers. The number line is a strong image emphasising the ordering of the numbers. The idea of height above and below sea level emphasises the base or zero position from which measurements are made. The image of owing money gives a situation where owing money corresponds to a negative amount of money. A similar image, illustrated below, emphasises the essential property of a negative number that $^-1 + 1 = 0$.

Different people will find different images helpful in developing an understanding of the properties of negative numbers.

Positive one is represented by the upper half of the zero sign.

Negative one can then be visualised as the lower part of the zero.

Together they make zero.

$$^-1 \;+\; 1 \;=\; 0$$

Example

To calculate $3 + {}^-1$, you have three upper parts and one lower part.

The lower part and one of the the upper parts make zero; this leaves two upper parts.

| 1 | 1 | 1 | $^-1$ | | 1 | 1 | $^-1$ | | 1 | 1 |

Example

To work out $^-2 + 1$.

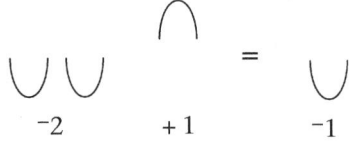

SUBTRACTION

FINDING THE DIFFERENCE

What is the difference between a temperature of ⁻10°C and a temperature of 40°C?

⁻10 to zero is ten degrees , zero to 40°C is 40° so the difference is 50°C.

Formally 40 – ⁻10 = 50.

```
40
30
20
10
 0
⁻10
⁻20
⁻30
```

HOPPING ALONG THE NUMBER LINE

If adding negative one is to add a debt and go one back down the number line, then what does it mean to subtract negative one?

This is the inverse operation, a debt is being removed, to subtract negative one is to move one place up the number line.

Example

2 – ⁻1 = 2 + 1 = 3

−⁻1 is the same as + 1

```
     ⁻3    ⁻2    ⁻1    0    1    2    3
```

IMAGE BASED ON 1 + ⁻1 = 0

Is it possible to use this image to subtract a negative number?

Example

Calculate 2 – ⁻1

Starting with two ones, it is not obvious how a negative one can be removed. However, two is the same as two plus zero.

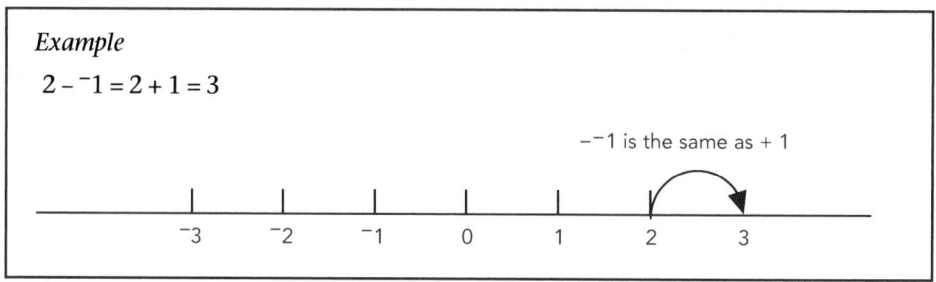

It is now possible to take away the negative one leaving 3.

Symbolically this is the same as saying

2 – ⁻1 = 2 + 0 – ⁻1 = 2 + (1+ ⁻1) – ⁻1 = 2 + 1 = 3

To summarise

The key property of negative numbers is that $^-1 + 1 = 0$ or $1 + ^-1 = 0$.

Adding a negative number sends you back down the number line.

$$5 + {}^-2 = 5 - 2 = 3$$

Subtracting a negative number sends you up the number line.

$$5 - {}^-2 = 5 + 2 = 7$$

MULTIPLICATION AND DIVISION OF NEGATIVE NUMBERS

What is three lots of negative two?

From the work on addition: $^-2 + {}^-2 + {}^-2 = {}^-6$ so $3 \times {}^-2 = {}^-6$

What is negative three multiplied by two?

From the work on addition: $^-3 + {}^-3 = {}^-6$ so $^-3 \times 2 = {}^-6$

What does it mean to multiply negative two by negative three? This is such an abstract idea that the answer has to be found in following the patterns in the mathematics. Formally mathematicians defined the answer to negative two multiplied by negative three to preserve the properties of distributivity and commutativity found in positive numbers. Looking at the patterns in this table may help you to see how the decision was made.

	2	$^-2$
3	6	$^-6$
$^-3$	$^-6$	**?**

Do you think negative three multiplied by negative two should be six or negative six?

If it were negative six then negative three multiplied by two would be negative six and negative three multiplied by something quite different would also be negative six. That is not possible so negative two multiplied by negative three must be positive six.

Following patterns in multiplication can also help to convince us that the only reasonable answer to $^-3 \times {}^-2$ is positive 6.

$^-3 \times 2 = ^-6$

$^-3 \times 1 = ^-3$ Multiply $^-3$ by one less than before and the answer is three MORE.

$^-3 \times 0 = 0$ Three more again.

$^-3 \times ^-1 = ?$ It must be three more which is positive three.

$^-3 \times ^-2 = ?$ Three more again would make positive six.

The next section shows this formally. You could either work through this slowly trying to follow the logic of each step or, if you prefer to focus on patterns, move on to the next table and try to fill in the missing numbers by following the patterns in the rows and columns.

$^-3(2 + ^-2)$ $= ^-3 \times 0 = 0$ Any number multiplied by zero is zero.

$^-3 \times 2 + ^-3 \times ^-2 = 0$ Work out the bracket.

$^-6 + ^-3 \times ^-2$ $= 0$ Add 6 to both sides.

$^-3 \times ^-2$ $= 6$

Follow the patterns in the rows and columns to insert numbers here.

×	$^-3$	$^-2$	$^-1$	0	1	2	3
3	$^-9$	$^-6$	$^-3$	0	3	6	9
2	$^-6$	$^-4$	$^-2$	0	2	4	6
1	$^-3$	$^-2$	$^-1$	0	1	2	3
0	0	0	0	0	0	0	0
$^-1$				0	$^-1$	$^-2$	$^-3$
$^-2$				0	$^-2$	$^-4$	$^-6$
$^-3$				0	$^-3$	$^-6$	$^-9$

SUMMARY

A negative number multiplied by a positive number gives a negative number

e.g. $^-2 \times 7 = ^-14$

A negative number multiplied by a negative number gives a positive number

e.g. $^-2 \times ^-7 = 14$

The same patterns apply to division.

A negative number divided by a positive number gives a negative number

e.g. $^-12 \div 6 = ^-2$

A negative number divided by a negative number gives a positive number

e.g. $^-12 \div ^-6 = 2$

When adding and subtracting, to add a negative number is the same as subtracting the number.

To subtract a negative number is the same as to add the number.

Danger of misconception

In order to remember the result for multiplying a negative number by a negative number it may seem natural to shorten the statement to a negative multiplied by a negative is a positive. This still makes sense, but if the shortening is carried even further to the statement that 'two negatives make a positive' there is a danger that it will be forgotten that this applies to two numbers multiplied together and will be applied in inappropriate situations.

$$^-3 + {}^-1 = 4 \textbf{ WRONG}$$

There may be two negative signs around but the answer is not positive. To solve this problem you have to start on $^-3$ on the number line. Adding a negative will send you back down the number line to $^-4$.

So there are two facts to be remembered. They are a bit lengthy but remembering them in this way will help to avoid a lot of errors.

Subtracting a negative number is the same as adding the number.

$$5 - {}^-2 = 5 + 2 = 7$$

Multiplying a negative number by a negative number gives a positive number.

$$^-2 \times {}^-7 = 14$$

1.6 RATIO AND PROPORTION

The words ratio and proportion are used in everyday language and the distinction between them is not always made clear. This table compares the use of the words in mathematics.

PROPORTION

- The word *proportion* is used to compare part to whole.
- The notation used is that of fractions, decimals or percentages.
  e.g. What proportion of these counters is black?

  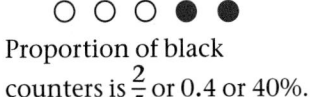

  Proportion of black counters is $\frac{2}{5}$ or 0.4 or 40%.

RATIO

- The word *ratio* is used to compare part to part.
- The notation used is two dots.
  e.g What is the ratio of black to white counters?

  The ratio of black to white counters is 2 : 3.

- Units

  It is necessary to make sure that both part and whole are in the same units before working out the proportion.

  e.g. If the total journey is 1 km and I have walked 200 m, what proportion have I walked?

  $\dfrac{200}{1000} = \dfrac{1}{5}$ of the journey.

- Units

  A pure ratio has no units. If units are still included in a ratio then both numbers need to be changed to the same units before the ratio can be simplified or used in a calculation.

  5 mm : 2 cm is 5 : 20.

DIRECT PROPORTION

As well as the use of proportion described above, which is close to the use of the word in everyday language, the word is used in the phrase, 'direct proportion'. This phrase describes the relationship between two variables and is useful in science and mathematics.

The most important stage is deciding if direct proportion is appropriate.

Consider these questions:

(a) If four bars of chocolate cost £6, how much do two bars of chocolate cost?

(b) If 5 kilometres is approximately the same as 8 miles, how many kilometres is twelve miles?

(c) If Henry VIII had six wives, how many wives did Henry VI have?

In case (a), the cost of the chocolate is directly proportional to the number of bars.

Two bars would cost half as much as four bars; that is £3.

In case (b), the number of kilometres is directly proportional to the number of miles.

Four miles is the same as $2\dfrac{1}{2}$ kilometres, so twelve miles is $7\dfrac{1}{2}$ kilometres.

In case (c), there is no relationship between the number of wives Henry VIII had and the number of wives Henry VI had. The question cannot be answered using direct proportion.

Possible misconception

Although the Henry VIII question is nonsense it draws attention to the need to ensure that the variables are really in direct proportion before starting to calculate. There are many situations in which variables appear to increase steadily with each other but are not in direct proportion.

> *Example*
>
> An electricity bill has a standing charge of £20 and then electricity is charged at 10p per unit.
>
> 500 units of electricity will cost £20 + 500 × 10p = £20 + £50 = £70
>
> 1000 units of electricity will not cost twice as much. It will cost £20 + 1000 × 10p = £120

Graphs to show how variables are related

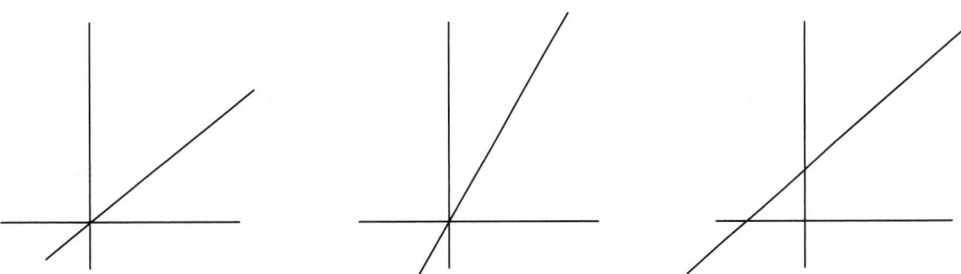

If two variables are directly proportional then their graph will be a straight line graph through the origin.

The third graph does NOT show direct proportion; it could represent a situation like that for electricity where there is a standing charge and so the graph does not pass through (0,0).

RATIO

The most usual operations with ratio are:

- To reduce a complicated ratio to its simplest form
- To divide an amount in a given ratio
- To use a ratio to find an unknown quantity.

To reduce a complicated ratio to its simplest form

> *Example*
>
> If there are 12 boys in a class and 16 girls the ratio of boys to girls is 12 : 16.
>
> Ratios can be simplified in the same way as fractions.
>
> Dividing both sides of the ratio by 4 it is clear that for every four girls there are three boys; that is a ratio of 3 : 4.

Dividing an amount in a given ratio

Ratios are a useful way of working out fair shares. Consider the following problem:

Example

Three people club together to buy a lottery ticket with their spare change. They win £10 000.

How should the winnings be divided if they contributed 50p, 20p and 30p respectively?

The ratio of their contributions was 50 : 20 : 30.

Dividing by ten this simplifies to 5 : 2 : 3. So the first person should get 5 shares, the second 2 shares and the third 3 shares. So the winnings need to be divided into 5 + 2 + 3 = 10 shares.

£10 000

£10 000 divided into ten equal shares makes each share £1000.

So the first person will get £5000, the second will get £2000 and the third will get £3000.

To use a ratio to find an unknown quantity

Example

The scale of the floor plan of a flat is 1 : 40.

If the length of the kitchen on the plan is 8 cm, what is the length of the kitchen?

	1 : 40	(This can be read as: 1 cm represents 40 cm)
	8 : ?	(so 8 cm represents?)

Multiply by 8 $\left\{ \begin{array}{l} 1 : 40 \\ 8 : 320 \end{array} \right\}$ Multiply by 8

So the length of the kitchen is 8 × 40 = 320 cm or 3.2 m.

Unitary ratios

The scale of a map is always written as a ratio in the form 1 to some number. Ratios in the form 1 : number or number : 1 are called **unitary** ratios.

It is sometimes useful to convert a ratio to a unitary ratio to make a problem clearer.

Example

A paint mix contains red and blue paint in the ratio 2 : 7.

If you use 5 cans of red paint , how many cans of blue paint will you need?

2 : 7   (2 cans of red mix with 7 cans of blue)

1 : ?   (so 1 can of red mixes with?)

Dividing by two, the ratio 2 : 7 can be written as 1 : 3.5.

Divide by 2   2 : 7   1 : 3.5   Divide by 2

Final stage is to have 5 cans of red paint.

Multiply by 5   1 : 3.5   5 : 17.5   Multiply by 5

So 18 cans of blue paint will be needed.

IMPORTANCE OF RATIO IN MATHEMATICS

The topic of ratio can seem an abstract one. The formal notation of two dots is, with the exception of scales on maps, seldom seen outside mathematics textbooks. The use of ratio to find an unknown number by multiplying by a scale factor is however present in a very large number of mathematical situations. Studies of misconceptions identified a group of children described as 'adders' who tended to add rather than multiply in situations involving a scale factor. A few examples of the use of ratio may help to show its importance.

- To compare costs, supermarkets provide the unit cost e.g. price of 100 g of biscuits.

- To increase an amount by 5% you multiply by 1.05.

- If this square is enlarged with scale factor two, the lengths of the sides will be doubled. What will happen to the area?

- The cosine of an angle is a ratio. Draw any right-angled triangle with an angle of 60° and the lengths of the sides around the 60° angle will be in the ratio 1 : 2.

 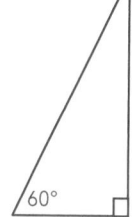

- The gradient of a straight-line graph is found by measuring the ratio

$$\frac{\text{Vertical increase}}{\text{Horizontal increase}}$$

It doesn't matter where on the graph the gradient is measured because the ratio of *vertical* to *horizontal increase* will always be the same. The idea of ratio is needed to understand this although the notation of ratio is not used.

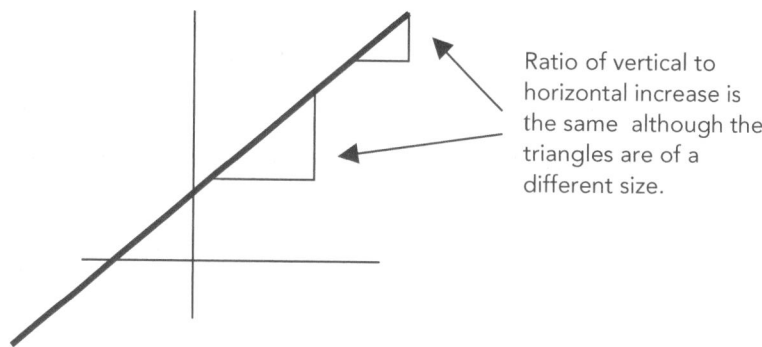

Ratio of vertical to horizontal increase is the same although the triangles are of a different size.

- In solving equations: If $4x = 72$ then the value of one x will be found by dividing 72 by 4 to get 18.

1.7 INDICES

IMAGES OF SQUARE NUMBERS

Sixteen is a square number because 16 objects can be arranged in four rows of four.

That is $16 = 4 \times 4$

The number four multiplied by itself can be written as 4^2.

This is read as 'four squared'.

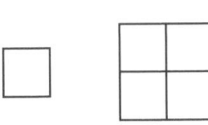 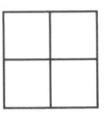 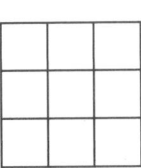 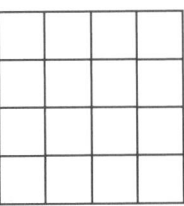

$1 = 1^2$ $4 = 2^2$ $9 = 3 \times 3 = 3^2$ $16 = 4 \times 4 = 4^2$

IMAGES OF CUBE NUMBERS

8 is a cube number because 8 small cubes can be arranged to form a larger cube.

$2 \times 2 \times 2 = 8.$ This is written as 2^3 and read as 'two cubed'.

 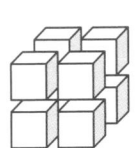 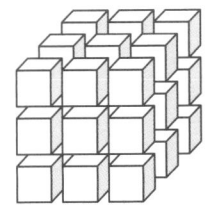

$1^3 = 1$ $2^3 = 8$ $3^3 = 27$

POWERS

The number 3^2 can be read as 'three to the power two' but it is more usual to read it as 'three squared'. The 2 is called the index. 3 is called the base number.

Higher powers do not have special names.

$2 \times 2 \times 2 \times 2$ is written 2^4 and read as two to the power four.

Powers of ten are important because of the links to the base-ten number system.

$$10^1 = 10$$

$$10^2 = 10 \times 10 = 100$$

$$10^3 = 10 \times 10 \times 10 = 1\,000$$

$$10^4 = 10 \times 10 \times 10 = 10\,000$$

This notation allows very large numbers to be written concisely.

The distance from the earth to the sun is approximately 1.5×10^8 kilometres.

To multiply by 10^8 you need to move the digits 8 places to the left so

$$1.5 \times 10^8 = 150\,000\,000 \text{ kilometres that is 150 million kilometres.}$$

It would be useful to have a concise way of writing very small numbers. This can be achieved by considering one divided by a power of ten.

$$\frac{1}{10 \times 10} = \frac{1}{100} = 0.01$$

How can 1 divided by 10^2 be written in index notation?

Looking at the patterns in the powers suggests a way of answering this question.

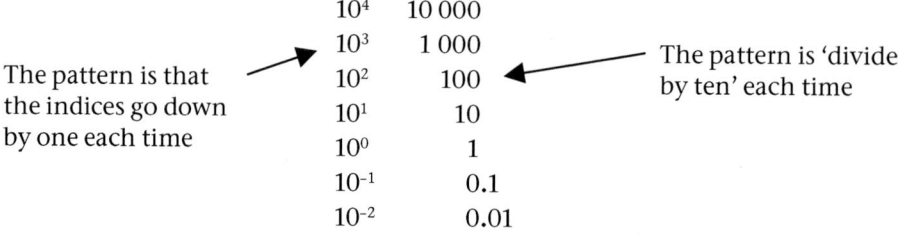

The pattern is that the indices go down by one each time

10^4	$10\,000$
10^3	$1\,000$
10^2	100
10^1	10
10^0	1
10^{-1}	0.1
10^{-2}	0.01

The pattern is 'divide by ten' each time

So following these patterns

$$\frac{1}{10 \times 10} \text{ is written as } 10^{-2}.$$

The negative sign shows that it is not 10^2 but one divided by 10^2. The number 0.01 is small but it is not negative so this is an unusual use of the negative sign which only applies to indices.

Using negative indices very small numbers can be written concisely.

CALCULATING WITH INDICES

MULTIPLICATION

> *Example*
>
> What is $10^2 \times 10^3$?
>
> Writing the calculation out in full gives $(10 \times 10) \times (10 \times 10 \times 10) = 10^5$
>
> As the 10^2 contributes two tens and the 10^3 contributes three tens the answer can be found directly by adding the indices 2 and 3.

Although this is just one example it is clear that the process would work for any powers of ten. The general statement for powers of ten is:

$$10^a \times 10^b = 10^{a+b}$$

Similarly for a different base number, $2^3 \times 2^4 = 2^7$ and so the general law of indices is that:

$$x^a \times x^b = x^{a+b}$$

Possible misconception

This method of multiplication works for powers of any number but notice that the law does not help to multiply powers of different numbers. There is no simple way of calculating $3^4 \times 2^3$.

DIVISION

> *Example*
>
> What is $2^5 \div 2^2$?
>
> $$2^5 \div 2^2 = \frac{2 \times 2 \times 2 \times \cancel{2} \times \cancel{2}}{\cancel{2} \times \cancel{2}} = 2 \times 2 \times 2$$
>
> The pattern in this case shows that to divide the numbers you need to subtract the indices.
>
> The general case is:
>
> $$x^a \div x^b = x^{a-b}$$

Possible misconception

Notice that there are quick ways to multiply and divide numbers written as powers of the same base number but there are no quick ways to add or subtract.

For example $3^4 - 3^3$ would have to be calculated as $81 - 27 = 54$.

RAISING TO A POWER

> *Example*
>
> What is 3^2 cubed?
>
> There is an easy way of squaring or cubing numbers written in index notation.
>
> $$(3^2)^3 = 3^2 \times 3^2 \times 3^2 = (3 \times 3) \times (3 \times 3) \times (3 \times 3) = 3^6$$
>
> The groups of two threes are written three times to find the cube, so the answer is three to the power 2×3.

For any power of three: $(3^a)^b = 3^{a \times b}$

The general case for any base number is: $(x^a)^b = x^{a \times b}$

SQUARE ROOTS

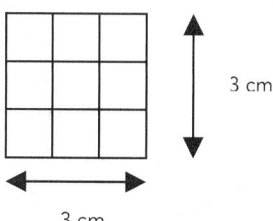

9 cm²

A square with area 9 cm²
must have sides of length
3 cm.

3 cm

3 cm

$9 = 3 \times 3 = 3^2$

The same information can be written as $\sqrt{9} = 3$. This is read as the square root of 9 equals 3.

The square root symbol means find the number which multiplied by itself gives 9.

$$\sqrt{16} = 4 \qquad \sqrt{100} = 10 \qquad \sqrt{64} = ?$$

Square roots can be written as indices. The possibility of indices which are not whole numbers is at first surprising since indices were introduced as a way of recording how many times the base number should be multiplied together. It follows however from a familiar mathematical approach of extending a useful idea to a wider situation.

$$\sqrt{9} \times \sqrt{9} = 9$$

Applying the idea that to multiply numbers you add the indices, this fits with:

$$9^{\frac{1}{2}} \times 9^{\frac{1}{2}} = 9^{\frac{1}{2}+\frac{1}{2}} = 9^1 = 9$$

$$\text{So } 9^{\frac{1}{2}} = \sqrt{9}$$

STANDARD FORM

It is possible to use index notation to write very large numbers in a compact way. To make it easier to compare numbers a standard form of index notation is used.

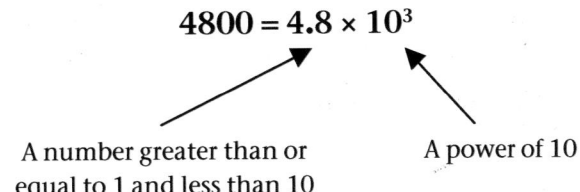

$$4800 = 4.8 \times 10^3$$

A number greater than or equal to 1 and less than 10

A power of 10

As our number system is based on powers of ten it is possible to move easily between standard form and the usual representation of numbers by extending the idea of the column headings for HTU.

Each column heading is written as a power of ten so Thousands is 10^3 etc.

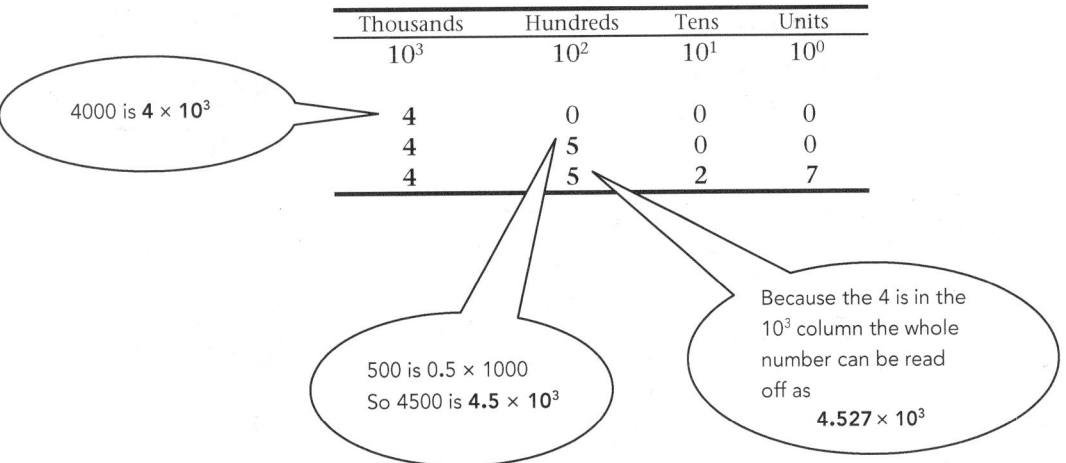

Thousands 10^3	Hundreds 10^2	Tens 10^1	Units 10^0
4	0	0	0
4	5	0	0
4	5	2	7

4000 is **4 × 10³**

500 is 0.5 × 1000
So 4500 is **4.5 × 10³**

Because the 4 is in the 10^3 column the whole number can be read off as
4.527 × 10³

So to change any number to standard form, e.g. 43 260, identify the value of the most important digit: $40\,000 = 4 \times 10^4$

Digits following the 4 are decimal fractions of 10 000.

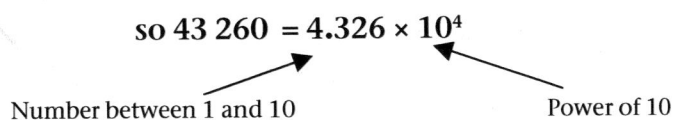

$$\text{so } 43\,260 = 4.326 \times 10^4$$

Number between 1 and 10

Power of 10

The average distance of the moon from the earth is 384 467 km.

The most important digit is the 3 which is in the 10^5 column.

So in standard form this is 3.84467×10^5 km.

When Jupiter is at its furthest distance from the earth it is 968 100 000 km away.

That is 9.681×10^8 km.

Standard form is also useful for very small numbers.

Hundreds	Tens	Units	•	Tenths	Hundredths	Thousandths
10^2	10^1	10^0		10^{-1}	10^{-2}	10^{-3}
		0	•	0	3	
		0	•	0	3	5
			•			

The 3 is in the hundredths column. So that is 3×10^{-2}

The most important digit in this number is the 3 which gives 3×10^{-2}
And the 5 gives 0.5×10^{-2}
So this is 3.5×10^{-2}

Example

Change 0.0027 to standard form.

The most important digit is the 2 which has a value of 2×10^{-3}.

So in standard form the number is 2.7×10^{-3}.

1.8 IMPLICATIONS FOR TEACHING NUMBER SYSTEMS

By deepening your level of mathematical knowledge you can teach for understanding and respond confidently to children's questions. Some issues considered in this section which could be helpful when you are planning your teaching are the importance of the number ten, language, and powerful visual images.

An understanding of place value underpins the later use of standard form and index notation. A real understanding of place value involves an appreciation of the multiplicative structure of the base-ten number system e.g. the relationship between one million and one millionth. If you understand that the position of each digit in a number is worth ten times the one on the right and is a tenth of the one on the left then you have a feeling for what happens when you multiply or divide by ten or 100. Children who use procedures like 'to multiply by ten you add a zero' need help to see that the digits move one position to the left because the digit in that position is worth ten times more. Even with very young children who are learning to recite numbers to 50 you can appreciate that they are gaining insights into the tens structure of the number system through the pattern in the words.

The number ten is an important theme in primary mathematics. Younger children can use a ten-sided die with faces showing multiples of ten and a similar unit die and record the two-digit numbers they have produced using arrow (sometimes called place value) cards and represent the numbers using Dienes' equipment or sticks of multilink in tens. Variations include using money or anything that is packed in tens. They could also represent the numbers on the computer with clipart pictures grouped in tens.

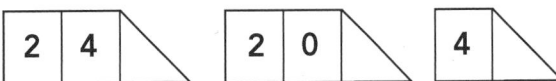

For older children a memorable activity is to explore what happens when two-digit numbers are multiplied or divided by ten. You need some large cards for digits one to nine and several zeros. Set out chairs labelled hundreds, tens, ones and tenths, separated by a chair with a decimal point label. If two children hold up large digit cards with 2 and 4 the class can discuss where they should sit to show 24 and what would happen when the number is multiplied by ten. This clearly shows that the digits move one place to the left when multiplying by ten and that zero is needed as a place holder. When dividing by ten the children can see that the digits move to the right and they can begin to appreciate the value of the position after the decimal point as tenths. Similarly they can investigate multiplying and dividing by hundreds and thousands.

NUMBER OPERATIONS

It is important that teachers know the characteristics of the operations so that they can give children experience of different kinds of problems involving the same operation and familiarise them with a range of associated language. This helps children to realise that a problem like:

How much more do you need to save if you want £5.25 and you have £3.68 so far?

can be checked on the calculator by using the minus sign. Children who have only been taught to read the minus sign as take away and connect counting up only with addition, will not readily realise this. Later on, children trying to calculate $8 \div \frac{1}{2}$ need to interpret this as a grouping problem. How many halves in 8 makes sense, whereas 8 shared between a half does not.

Similarly teachers need to be aware of the effect of using different kinds of numbers in examples and how this affects the choice of method for solution. For the example above children might solve it by complementary addition or counting up. Altering the numbers to £5.25 – £4.26 would give children the opportunity to use a rounding and adjusting method. Whereas for £5.25 – £4.30 children could choose to count back.

For younger children telling them a different kind of subtraction story each day will give them experience in associating the minus sign with a range of language. For example the following problems can all be represented by 12 – 8:

1. Sue has £12 and spends £8. How much does she have left?
2. Sue has saved £8 and wants £12 to buy a football. How much more money does she need?
3. Sue is given £8 and her sister gets £12. How much less than her sister has Sue got?

Children could be asked to use a calculator to check the problems.

Older children could be set the task of how to use a grid to multiply 5 by 18 in lots of different ways. The teacher will be aware that this is a demonstration of the distributive law.

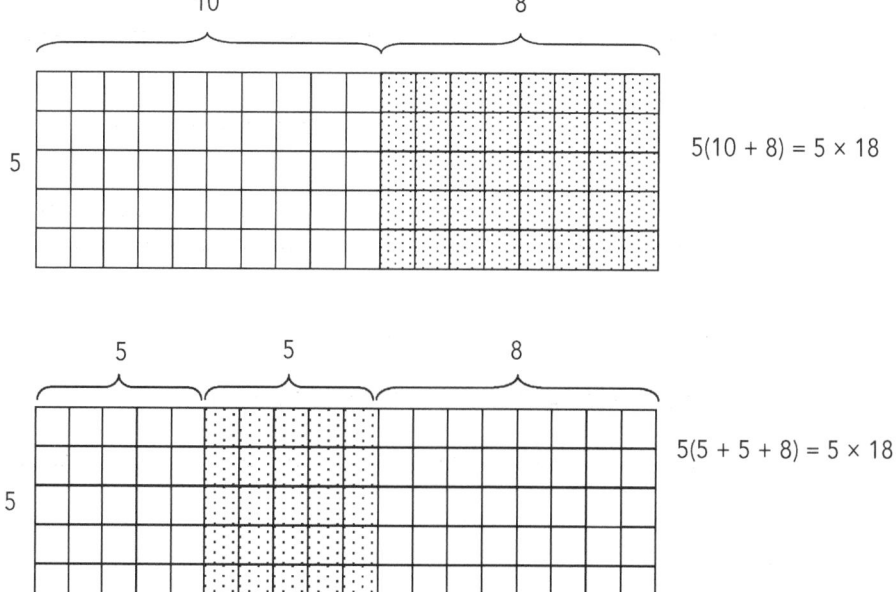

$5(10 + 8) = 5 \times 18$

$5(5 + 5 + 8) = 5 \times 18$

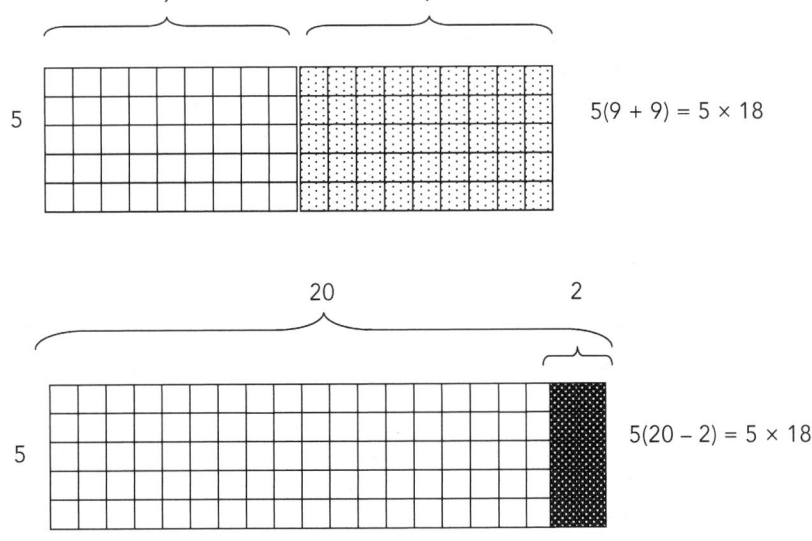

Children could investigate other ways of partitioning both numbers using addition and subtraction.

1.9 SELF-ASSESSMENT QUESTIONS · The number system and number operations

Use these questions to check your understanding of number operations

SUBTRACTION AND DIVISION OF NATURAL NUMBERS

1a. Work out 534 −147 using the formal written algorithm most natural to you.

1b. Compare your method with those described in the text.

1c. Repeat the calculation using the formal algorithm described in the National Numeracy Strategy if this is not your usual method.

1d. Repeat the process for 489 divided by 17.

ADDITION AND MULTIPLICATION OF FRACTIONS

First estimate the approximate size of the answer and then calculate:

2a. $\frac{2}{3} + \frac{4}{5}$

2b. $\frac{2}{3} \times \frac{4}{5}$

Repeat for other fractions to develop your understanding.

2c. Explain the difference in the procedures for adding and for multiplying fractions.

MULTIPLICATION AND DIVISION OF FRACTIONS

3a. Estimate $\frac{2}{3} \times \frac{3}{4}$. Will the answer be larger or smaller than $\frac{3}{4}$?

Now calculate the answer.

3b. Estimate $\frac{3}{4} \div \frac{2}{3}$. Will the answer be larger or smaller than $\frac{3}{4}$?

Now calculate the answer.

3c. Explain clearly, with diagrams if helpful, how to calculate $4 \div \frac{1}{3}$.

Will the answer to $4 \div \frac{2}{3}$ be larger or smaller than $4 \div \frac{1}{3}$?

DECIMALS

4a. Arrange in order of size, smallest first:

0.71   0.17   0.07   0.65   0.625

4b. Starting with $5 \times 6 = 30$, use multiplication and division by any multiple of 10 to derive other multiplication facts.

e.g. $0.5 \times 6 = 3$ $5 \times 0.06 = 0.3$

Use your usual method for multiplying decimals to check the accuracy of your statements.

4c. Work out 2.4×5.3 using at least two different methods.

Explain any difficult stages in the working.

4d. Use two different methods to calculate 7 divided by 1.25.

SIGNIFICANT FIGURES AND DECIMAL PLACES

5. For each of these statements decide if you would:

- leave the numbers in the form given
- state the numbers to a certain number of significant figures
- round the numbers to a certain number of decimal places.

Write each statement in a sensible form and justify your answers.

5a. It is easy to see which match was more popular as for the match with Fulham 24 042 tickets were sold but for the match with West Ham only 16 971 tickets were sold.

5b. The length of the piece of wood to be cut up is 17 cm. We have to cut it into three pieces each of length 6.333333 cm.

5c. Using measurements of 750 m from the base of the cliff and an angle of 15°, I calculated the height of the cliff to be 201 m.

PERCENTAGES

6a. Find as many different percentages of 320 as you can, making a spider diagram similar to the one in the text.

6b. Select out from the diagram the percentages you need to calculate to find 17.5% of 320.

FRACTIONS, DECIMALS AND PERCENTAGES

7a. Explain how to change:
- percentages to fractions and then to decimals
- fractions to decimals
- decimals to fractions.

7b. Change all these numbers to decimals and arrange in order of size:

65% $\frac{3}{5}$ 0.425 $\frac{5}{8}$ 42%

NEGATIVE NUMBERS

8. $2(5 - 1) = 8$ $^-2 \times {}^-2 + 4 = 8$ $4 - {}^-2 + 2 = 8$

Write down expressions with a value of 8.

Each expression must contain a subtraction sign and/or a negative number.

Enter the expressions into a calculator. Score 1 for each expression which gives eight, −1 for an error.

Stop when your score reaches 10.

RATIO

9. On squared paper draw axes and join the origin (0, 0) to the point (10, 15).
   Choose any two points on the line.
   Starting from the lower point move horizontally and then vertically to the higher point – this will give a right-angled triangle.
   Find the ratio

$$\frac{\text{Vertical distance}}{\text{Horizontal distance}}$$

Repeat for several triangles and compare the ratios.

INDICES AND POWERS

10. Which of these numbers have exactly the same value

   0.25 $\frac{1}{100}$ 1000 10^{-2} 10^{3} 0.01 2^{-2}

STANDARD FORM

11a. Here are some measurements in centimetres. Which of these numbers are not in standard form? Explain your answer.

   5.26×10^{0} 358 9.26×10^{-3} 9.26^{2} 20.1×10^{4}

11b. Put all the numbers into standard form and arrange them in order of size, smallest first.

11c. Which of the measurements could be:
   The height of a child
   The length of a pencil
   The height of a room
   The thickness of a finger nail
   The length of a cross-country run?

SQUARE ROOTS

12.

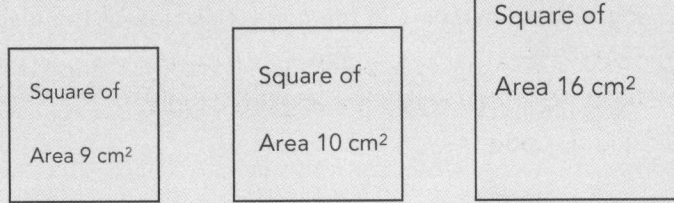

The length of the side of the first square is $\sqrt{9}$ = 3 cm

12a. The side of the second square is $\sqrt{10}$ cm. Estimate this to one decimal place and then find it using a calculator.

12b. Find the length of the side of the third square.

INTEGERS, RATIONALS, IRRATIONALS AND REALS

13.

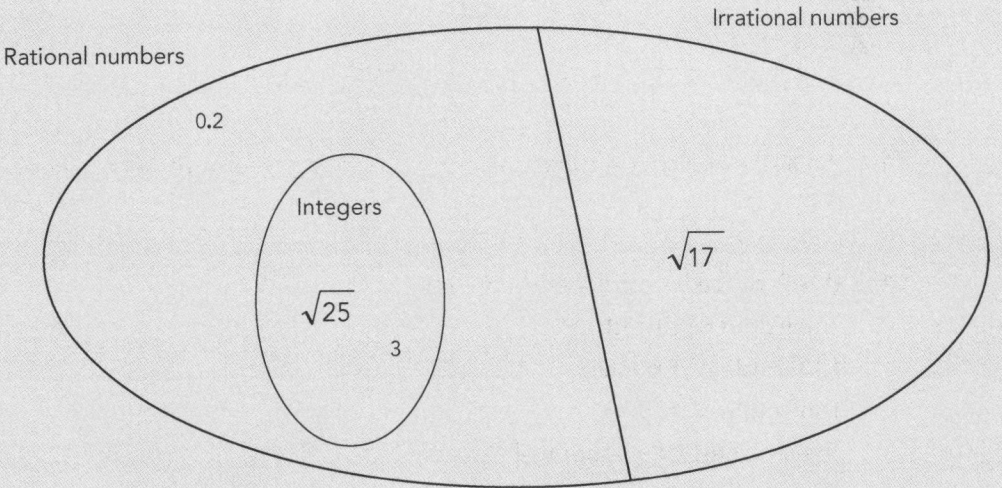

The outer shape represents the **real numbers**.

0.2 can be written as $\frac{2}{10}$ so is a rational number.

$\sqrt{25}$ is 5 so $\sqrt{25}$ is an integer.

$\sqrt{17}$ cannot be written as a fraction and so $\sqrt{17}$ is irrational.

Place these numbers in the correct section of the diagram and explain your reasoning.

$\frac{12}{9}$ 87   87.0001 $\sqrt{87}$ $\frac{8}{4}$

2 Properties of numbers, number sequences, algebra

IN THE BEGINNING

As soon as people began to represent objects by using pebbles or other small tokens, they became aware that they could count them more easily by arranging the stones in patterns. The easiest shapes are rectangles or squares, and this leads to the discovery of some elementary properties of numbers. By arranging two rows of stones we can quickly see whether they are equal or if there is 'one more', and so the basic ideas of even and odd numbers are apparent. Even numbers can always be arranged in a rectangle. Some odd numbers can also make a rectangle, and particular even and odd numbers can make squares. This game with the stones leads to some of the basic properties of numbers: the sum of even numbers is always even, the sum of two odd numbers is always even, and the sum of an odd number and an even number is always odd. The numbers, 4, 9, 25, 36, and so on are called square numbers because the stones can be arranged as such. These properties were certainly well known to ancient peoples by 3500 BC when the first mathematical writing was being developed, and by about 1600 BC in Babylonia we find lists of number triples like 3^2, 4^2, 5^2 and 5^2, 12^2, 13^2 which are squares on the sides of right-angled triangles.

THE PYTHAGOREANS

In about 570 BC, a mystic sect, called the Pythagoreans, was founded in Crotona in southern Italy. Their fundamental belief was that everything was made up of discrete numbers of elementary parts called *monads*. All objects, natural or man-made, people, animals or plants, consisted of a characteristic number of monads. Therefore the relationships between numbers were important to them, and using the knowledge already established, they discovered many more properties which we now think of as elementary number theory.

Arranging elements to make squares gives the following sequence: $1 + 3 = 4$, $4 + 5 = 9$, $9 + 7 = 16$. So, adding an odd number to a square gives you the next square number. The Triangular Numbers 1, 3, 6, 10, 15, . . . are found by adding consecutive numbers: $1 + 2 = 3$, $1 + 2 + 3 = 6$, $1 + 2 + 3 + 4 = 10$, and so on. Dots could be arranged in other plane and solid shapes (pentagons, hexagons, cubes, tetrahedral, etc.), so that many more properties could be discovered. The Pythagoreans also investigated musical harmonies and showed they relied on ratios, for example: 2 : 1 gives the octave; 3 : 2 give a fifth and 4 : 3 a fourth. The Pythagorean sect died out in about 430 BC, and there are no existing texts written by them; we rely on the writings of much later people. However, all this knowledge appears in geometric form in Books 7, 8 and 9 of Euclid's 'Elements', a compendium written in about 300 BC in the library in Alexandria, from where he collected most of the then known mathematical knowledge.

RENAISSANCE ALGEBRA – 'THE COSSICK ART'

In the fifteenth century Johannes Gutenberg, a German printer, invented a printing press with moveable type. The famous 'Gutenberg Bible' was printed in 1455. The next two hundred years saw a radical change in the way that information was transmitted; books could be printed more quickly, and consequently much more mathematics became available. This period was particularly significant for the development of algebra, and after about two hundred years, algebra was being written in a form that is very similar to today's.

The rapid development was motivated by the need to provide the mathematics to support the workings of commerce that had developed principally through the city states of Venice and Genoa, and many 'abacus schools' were set up to teach ways of solving commercial problems.

In 1494 a book by the Franciscan monk, Luca Pacioli, was printed. It was a review of the whole of known mathematics covering arithmetic, trigonometry, algebra, tables of moneys, weights and measures, a large number of 'merchants' problems', games of chance, and a summary of Euclid's geometry. This included the work of Leonardo Fibonacci and the traditional methods of the Abacists, and the techniques developed by the Arabs from earlier Babylonian mathematics. In this book also Pacioli introduced the technique of Double Entry Book Keeping, which included the use of negative numbers. This was a very important step because it introduced a meaning for negative numbers to represent debts.

By the middle of the sixteenth century, practice in the methods developed into a series of problem-solving challenges between mathematicians competing for posts at the Italian universities. These problems were posed in words, usually in verse, challenging other mathematicians to find a solution. The problems were extensions of the old Babylonian theme. Namely, given the sum of two numbers and their product, find the numbers. If the challenger was successful, the incumbent could lose their job. Since the solution of the problem was a closely guarded secret, there are many stories of lies and deceptions in order to discover the solution.

The common language was at first Latin, but then Italian began to be used. The conceptual basis was geometry – we are investigating lengths and areas – so products were thought of as squares, rectangles, cubes or square prisms. This is where the names 'quadratic' and 'cubic' originate. As the problems became more difficult, the solutions became more complicated, and mathematicians got used to handling fractions and irrational numbers.

Perhaps the most famous mathematician in this period is the Italian, Girolamo Cardano. He was originally a doctor, and highly educated, but gained a colourful reputation for being a gambler (he wrote a book on the chances of winning various games – see the Data Handling chapter), a dueller, drunkard, liar and cheat. He was also an outstanding mathematician. His book, 'The Great Art', was published in 1545, and was a collection of all the then known methods for solving quadratic and cubic equations. Because these problems were thought of in terms of areas and volumes, earlier mathematicians had rejected negative answers as not 'real'. Cardano accepted negative answers as logical (but mysterious) results, and went further in solving the problem: 'The sum of two numbers is 10 and their product is 40 – find the numbers'.

By applying the old Babylonian algorithm to this problem, he followed the steps logically to a point where he says, '. . . putting mental tortures behind us, let us proceed. . .'

In the end, he was amazed to find that the sum and the product of the two 'numbers' he found, was exactly that posed in the original problem. Both 'numbers' involved the square root of negative fifteen!

Whilst the square root of positive numbers was understood and negative numbers had a reality in profit and loss, the idea of the square root of a negative number was beyond anyone's imagination. Such numbers became called the 'imaginary' numbers.

This often happens in mathematics where, by following the logical consequences of a process, you can discover new and strange things which challenge the imagination and our powers of explanation. By 1572, another Italian, Rafael Bombelli, had written his 'Algebra' where all the rules for correctly manipulating these imaginary numbers were explained. Right through to the late eighteenth century, mathematicians used these numbers in developing new mathematics without having any clear idea what physical situation they could refer to.

By the late seventeenth century all the basic rules for manipulating algebraic quantities had been well established. Algebra had developed into a sophisticated kind of 'literal arithmetic' where it was generally accepted that letters could be substituted for all kinds of numbers and that the operations of arithmetic 'worked' for any algebraic quantities as well. Mathematicians were manipulating rational numbers, decimal fractions, positive and negative quantities, algebraic numbers, positive and negative square roots, trigonometric and imaginary quantities with ease, but without any logical justification. In the early nineteenth century mathematicians began to look at the logical basis of algebra and searched for some fundamental properties. Because we are so used to using arithmetic, we take for granted the fact that operations like addition and multiplication work the 'other way round'; $3 + 2 = 2 + 3$, and that $5(3 + 2) = 5 \times 3 + 5 \times 2$, are 'obvious', but when we replace these easy numbers by something more complex, it is not so obvious. By comparing different systems, nineteenth-century mathematicians identified the commutative, associative and distributive properties, which are some of the fundamental properties by which we understand algebra today.

Nowadays, 'Algebra' refers not only to the basic school subject, but to a concept which involves looking for, recognising and building logical patterns in almost every area of mathematics.

SYMBOLS AND NOTATION

In different cultures over our history, many notation systems for numbers have been developed, but the notation for algebra that we use today came from the Renaissance and early Modern period (1450–1650). By this time, the base-ten system for numbers had been accepted, and the Hindu-Arabic notation was beginning to be used. It was the spread of ideas by the printed word that was the biggest influence on the development of algebraic notation. In the early part of this period, different mathematicians used abbreviations of words (like p for plus and m for minus) and many different symbols to represent operations and results of operations. However, asking the printer to carve the wooden blocks for new, strange and often bizarre symbols became time consuming and very expensive. Better to use what was already available, and so this was how the convention arose where the letters at the end of the alphabet, x, y and z became used for the unknown quantities, and a, b and c at the beginning were used for known parameters. The symbols for the basic arithmetic operations became quickly standardised to those we use today, and the '=' sign appeared in the work of the English mathematician Robert Recorde (1510–88), where he wrote '. . . I will set to as I doe often in woorke use a pair of parallels or gemowe lines of one lengthe, . . . bicause noe two thynges can be moare equalle . . .'

2.2 ALGEBRAIC NOTATION

But what does x mean?
I don't get it.
What do you mean? How can I choose a value for x?

The introduction of algebraic notation introduces a level of abstraction in mathematics which is both powerful and potentially confusing. We will consider two very different situations in which algebraic notation is used and try to unravel some of the complexities.

SOLVING EQUATIONS: THE AS-YET-UNKNOWN

Example

I think of a number, double it, add 10 and the answer is 16.
What was the number I first thought of?

To solve the problem you need to reverse all the calculations.
Taking away 10 from 16 gives 6. Half of 6 is 3. The unknown number must have been 3.

In this situation enough information is given to pin the number down exactly. Taking x to stand for the unknown number, the information given can be written as:

$$2x + 10 = 16$$

Finding the unknown value is referred to as solving the equation and there is only one possible solution; the unknown number must be 3.

WORKING WITH FUNCTIONS: THE VARIABLE

The diagram shows a function machine with an input and an output. The function machine works by carrying out exactly the same operation on each number that is input.

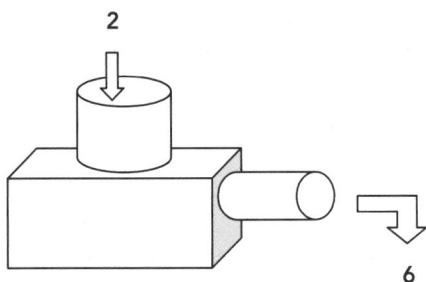

When 2 is entered into this machine the output is 6.

Trying further inputs makes clear what the machine is doing.

INPUT	OUTPUT
2	6
5	15
10	30
6	18

The machine takes the number entered in the machine and multiplies it by 3.

If the number entered in the machine is represented by n, then the output is $3n$.

In this case n can take any value The algebraic expression (called a function) describes what happens to the number n.

If n is 102 then the output will be 306. n can be anything you like.

These very different uses of algebraic notation help to explain how confusions can arise. Using x for the unknown in an equation and n as the variable in a function can help a little to distinguish the situations. It is, however, the convention, especially when plotting graphs, to describe the input to a function as x and the output as y. With this notation the function 'multiply by three' is written $y = 3x$.

Both $2x + 10 = 16$ and $y = 3x$ have equals signs but there are important differences in meaning.

$2x + 10 = 16$ is an equation with an **as-yet-unknown** value x. The value x can be calculated from the information in the equation.

$y = 3x$ is a function containing the **variable** x. x can take any value you like. The expression gives the value of a second variable y corresponding to your chosen value of x. This is why, when plotting the graph of

$y = 3x$

the person plotting can choose any values of x they like.

Choosing the simple values of 0, 1, 2, 3, 4 for x and making a table to show the values of y gives:

Graph of $y = 3x$

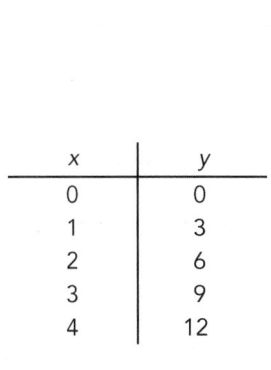

x	y
0	0
1	3
2	6
3	9
4	12

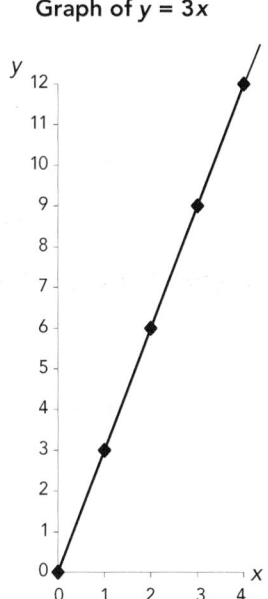

The graph of $y = 3x$ is a straight line.

Functions of the form $ax + b$ are called linear functions.

Functions of the form $ax^2 + bx + c$ are called quadratic functions.

See the section on *Functions and graphs* for more information.

CONVENTIONS IN ALGEBRAIC NOTATION

Whether working with equations or functions there are some conventions about how algebraic notation is used.

$3x$ This means 3 multiplied by x. The multiplication sign is omitted. $1x$ is written just as x.

x^2 This means x multiplied by x or x squared.

$3x^2$ Raising to a power takes priority over multiplication. This means x is squared and the result is multiplied by 3.

$(3x)^2$ Here brackets are used to indicate first multiply the x by 3 and then square the result.

πr^2 There are no brackets in this formula for the area of a circle so this means first square r and then multiply by π.

$2(x + 5)$ When substituting a value for x, the convention is that brackets must be worked out first so this means add 5 to x and multiply the result by 2.

So if $x = 3$, $2(x + 5) = 2 \times 8 = 16$

If you don't know the value of x, your only option is to leave the expression as it is or to expand the brackets (see below).

So algebraic expressions are not just read from left to right, they need to be interpreted using the conventions about the order of operations. The order is:

Brackets   Powers/Indices   Division/Multiplication   Addition/Subtraction

EXPANDING OR MULTIPLYING OUT BRACKETS

Having introduced the notation of brackets it can sometimes be helpful to rewrite an expression without the brackets. This section will deal with some techniques for working with algebraic expressions which are useful in problem-solving situations. What is required is an expression with exactly the same value but written without brackets.

Numbers often provide an indication of how to deal with algebra so consider the expression:

$3(10 + 2)$ since $10 + 2$ is 12, the expression is 3×12 which is 36.

Alternatively, this can be calculated using a grid with width 3 and length $(10 + 2)$.

The calculation is then 3×10 add 3×2, giving 36.

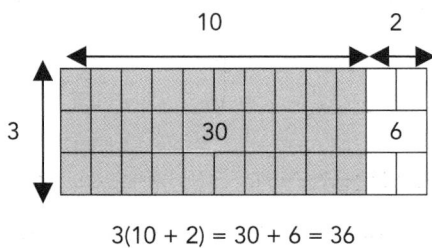

$3(10 + 2) = 30 + 6 = 36$

The grid method can be extended to algebraic expressions such as $3(x + 2)$.

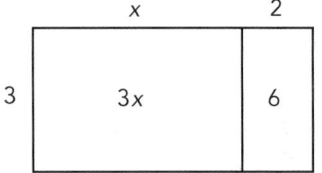

From the grid $3(x + 2) = 3x + 6$

Now consider the numerical expression $(10 + 4)(10 + 2)$ and the algebraic expression $(x + 4)(x + 2)$.

The numerical expression can be worked out by multiplying all the numbers in the grid and adding the values to give $100 + 20 + 40 + 8 = 168$

The expression can also be worked out as follows without drawing a grid

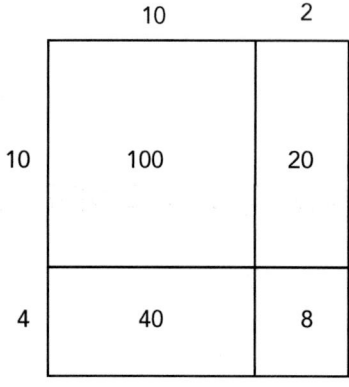

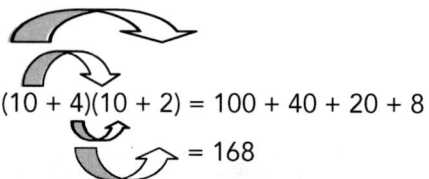

$(10 + 4)(10 + 2) = 100 + 40 + 20 + 8$

$= 168$

The expression $(x + 4)(x + 2)$ is expanded, as shown, using a grid to give four terms:

$$x^2 + 4x + 2x + 8$$

The expression can also be worked out as shown below without drawing a grid.

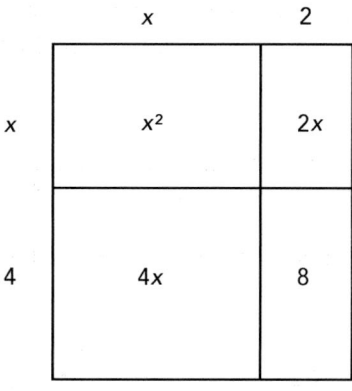

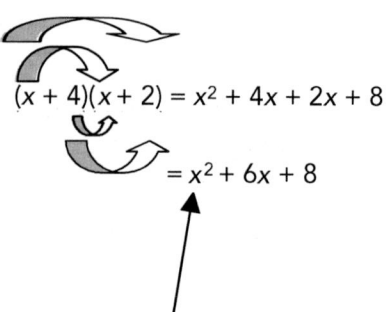

$(x + 4)(x + 2) = x^2 + 4x + 2x + 8$

$= x^2 + 6x + 8$

An expression like this in which the highest power of x is x^2 is called a quadratic expression.

FACTORISING OR INSERTING BRACKETS

Looking at the expression $3x + 6$, it is apparent that both terms are divisible by 3. So a factor of 3 can be taken outside the bracket and the terms inside the bracket adjusted to give the required value.

$$3x + 6 = 3(x + 2)$$

The process is the inverse of multiplying out (expanding) the bracket.

$3(x + 2)$ means 3 multiplied by $(x + 2)$ and so inserting the bracket makes it clear that 3 is a factor of $3(x + 2)$.

$$10 - 5x = 5(2 - x) \quad \text{as 5 is a factor of 10 and a factor of } 5x$$

$$x^2 - 21x = x(x - 21) \quad \text{as } x \text{ is a factor of } x^2 \text{ and a factor of } 21x$$

2.3 NUMBERS AND NUMBER SEQUENCES

PROPERTIES AND TYPES OF NUMBER

ORDINAL AND CARDINAL

 To count the number of objects in this set you need to repeat in order the number sequence 1, 2, 3, 4. The total number of objects is indicated by the final number 4. This is the cardinal aspect of number.

Repeating the sequence 1, 2, 3, 4 in order can also be used to find the 4th object in the set. This is the ordinal aspect of number.

Arranging numbers in order of size
One important property of numbers is their size. Arranging numbers on a number line emphasises the size of a number. The numbers are arranged in order of size from left to right.

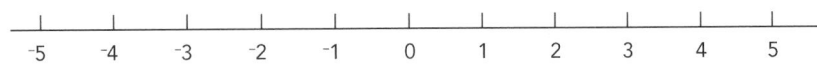

From the number line it is possible to read off the largest and the smallest number in any pair, for example:

$3 < 5$	$^{-}1 < 0$	$^{-}2 > {}^{-}3$
three is less than five	negative one is less than zero	negative two is greater than negative three

It can seem counter intuitive that negative 2 is greater than negative 3 but the image of the number line helps to clarify this.

NUMBER PROPERTIES CONNECTED WITH SHAPE

If the numbers are represented by shapes then the geometric patterns into which the shapes can be arranged provides another means of classification.

Square and cube numbers were considered in section 1.7.

Triangular numbers are formed by adding consecutive counting numbers starting with 1; this can be illustrated by arranging counters in triangles and putting one more counter in each new row:

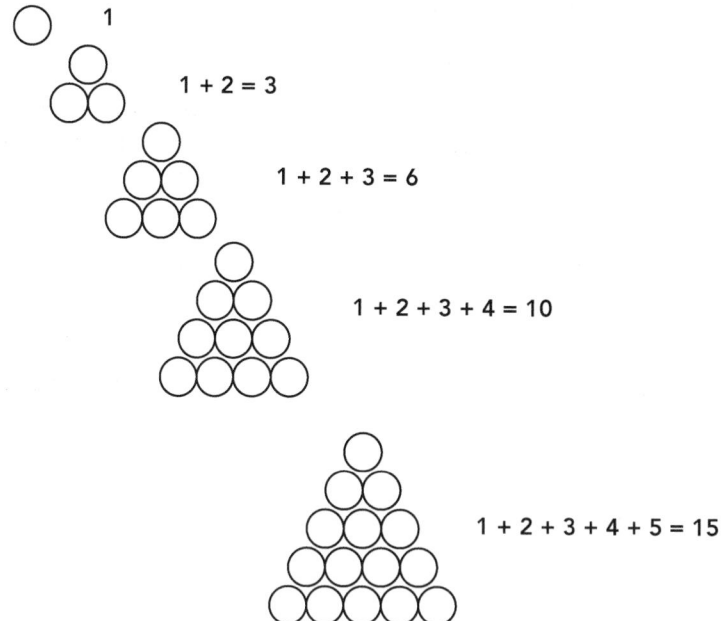

ODD AND EVEN NUMBERS

If you take any number and divide it by two, there are only two possible outcomes: either the number is divisible exactly by two or there is a remainder of one. Numbers which divide exactly by two are called even numbers; numbers which have a remainder of one are called odd numbers. A useful visual image is that even numbers can be arranged in pairs, odd numbers arranged in pairs have one additional unit.

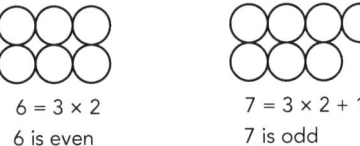

6 = 3 × 2   7 = 3 × 2 + 1
6 is even   7 is odd

Once odd and even numbers are defined in this way, it is apparent that odd and even numbers alternate on the number line.

0 1 **2** 3 **4** 5 **6** 7 **8** 9 . . .

Counting in twos starting from zero gives the even numbers: 0, 2, 4, 6, 8 . . .

Views vary as to whether the terms odd and even apply to negative numbers. In this section only positive numbers are considered.

Reasoning from a definition

Even numbers have two important properties:

They are exactly divisible by 2.

They are alternate numbers on the number line.

Mathematicians work by defining the properties of a group of objects (e.g shapes, numbers) and then deducing further properties from that definition. There is sometimes a choice as to which property is taken as the defining property. As a teacher you will have to decide which idea you introduce to your children first.

1. If you define even numbers as numbers which are exactly divisible by two then it makes sense to ask the question:
   What do you notice about the position of even numbers on the number line?

2. If, however, children learn to count omitting alternate numbers, so 0, 2, 4, 6, 8 . . . and are told these numbers are called the even numbers, then sensible questions are:
   If you arrange counters in pairs to represent even numbers, what do you notice?
   What number divides exactly into all even numbers?

A logical way of introducing even and odd numbers would be to:

- Say 12, 4, 16, 8 . . . are even numbers because 2 goes into them exactly.
  Even numbers are doubles, multiples of 2.

- Make patterns with counters arranged in twos and notice that this can be done exactly.

- Ring the even numbers on the number line and notice that alternate numbers are ringed.

- Say 15, 3, 5, 17. . . are odd numbers because they leave a remainder of 1 when divided by 2.

Combining odd and even numbers

If you add two even numbers will the answer be odd or even?

Thinking visually

The two even numbers can be represented by dots arranged in pairs. There will be no odd dot left over as the numbers are even.

Thinking algebraically

An even number is a multiple of two, that is double a number or twice a number, so it can be written as $2a$ for some number a (a represents the number of dots in each row of the pattern for the even number).

The second even number is also a multiple of two so it can be written as $2b$ for some number b.

$$2a + 2b = 2(a + b)$$

Inserting the bracket shows that the sum of $2a$ and $2b$ is double $(a + b)$ and so is an even number.

This algebraic statement proves that if you add two even numbers you will always get an even number.

The diagram of dots above is very close to a proof because although the diagrams are drawn for the particular values of eight plus ten, it is clear that the argument would work, in general, for any even number.

If you add an even number and an odd number then, thinking visually, there will be one odd dot left over from the pairs and the answer will be odd.

Algebraically, the even number can be represented by $2a$. To represent an odd number you need pairs of numbers and one odd one over, so $2b + 1$ is sure to be an odd number.

$$2a + (2b + 1) = 2(a + b) + 1$$

This is double the number $(a + b)$ plus 1 which is an odd number.

Using this approach it is possible to find the outcomes when adding or multiplying odd and even numbers. Can you fill in the remaining two results in this addition table?

+	Odd	Even
Odd		
Even	Odd	Even

Checking whether large numbers are odd or even

Example

Is 32 504 odd or even?

It is not necessary to divide by two to find out the answer. As 100 is even and 1000 is even and 10 000 is even it is only necessary to check the final digit. 4 is even so any number ending in 4 is even.

Similarly numbers ending in 1, 3, 5, 7 or 9 must be odd. This is a powerful example of defining a set of numbers with a particular property, and then deducing further properties of all the numbers in the set.

In this case the set contains an infinite number of numbers but it is still possible to make confident statements about all the numbers in the set. This ability to deal with the infinite is one of the pervading qualities of mathematics.

MULTIPLES

Even numbers are multiples of 2. It is possible to consider the multiples of any number:

A number is a multiple of 6 if it divides exactly by 6.

6, 12, 18, 24, 30 are some of the multiples of 6.

There are millions and millions of multiples of any number. The list of multiples of 6 never ends; it is always possible to add 6 and form yet another multiple so the number of multiples of 6 is infinite.

FACTORS

A factor of a number divides exactly into the given number.

So are there a large number of factors of 6?

There are very few. The factors of 6 are 1, 2, 3 and 6.

To find all the factors of a number you could try dividing the number by all the numbers less than the number – but there are more efficient methods.

Example

Consider searching for all the factors of 28.

Start with 1	$1 \times 28 = 28$	so 1 and 28 are factors
Then 2	$2 \times 14 = 28$	so 2 and 14 are factors
3 is not a factor		
Try 4	$4 \times 7 = 28$	so 4 and 7 are factors
5 is not a factor		
6 is not a factor		

7 we already know is a factor $4 \times 7 = 7 \times 4 = 28$

There is no need to check further. If a number larger than 7 was a factor we would already have found it paired with a number smaller than 4.

So there are six factors of 28: 1, 2, 4, 7, 14, 28

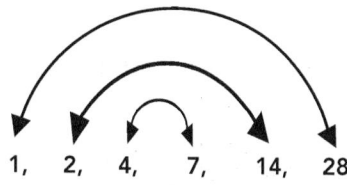

1, 2, 4, 7, 14, 28

Notice that the factors occur in pairs, this is a useful check that none has been omitted.

There are numbers which have an odd number of factors:

Consider the number 16.

$$1 \times 16 = 16, \quad 2 \times 8 = 16, \quad 4 \times 4 = 16$$

The factors of 16 are 1, 2, 4, 8, 16. The factor 4 is paired with itself as $4 \times 4 = 16$.

So all square numbers have an odd number of factors. Notice that this sentence demonstrates another power of mathematics. Square numbers, odd numbers and factors have all been defined and these definitions are now combined to make a powerful general statement. The statement is very concise which makes it powerful but also abstract. Most people need to check out a few examples with particular numbers to make sense of such abstract statements.

15 has factors 1, 3, 5, 15. This is an even number of factors and 15 is not a square number.

100 has factors, 1, 2, 4, 5, **10**, 20, 25, 50, 100. This is an odd number of factors, 10 is paired with itself and 100 is a square number.

Hopefully, it is now obvious to you that, 'All square numbers have an odd number of factors'.

PRIME NUMBERS

The number 7 has factors 1 and 7 but no other factors.

A number which has just two factors, itself and one, is called a **prime** number.

Examples of prime numbers are 7, 13 and 19.

> 2 is a prime number because it has two factors, 1 and 2.
>
> 1 is not a prime number because it has just one factor, the number one.

How do you decide if a number is prime?

An elegant way of finding prime numbers was devised by Eratosthenes.

If you want to find all the primes between 1 and 100 say, you follow the following procedure.

Write down the numbers from 1 to 100, arranged in a square grid.

Circle the first prime number, so circle 2. Now strike out all the multiples of 2, these numbers cannot be prime as they have a factor of 2 as well as 1 and themselves.

Now circle the first number which is not struck out, that will be 3 which is the next prime. Continue in this way until all numbers are deleted because they have a factor other than themselves and 1 or are circled because they are prime. The numbers circled are all the primes less than 100.

A systematic method like this which considers all possibilities is called a proof by exhaustion.

It is useful when considering a finite set of numbers but other styles of proof are more powerful as they can establish truths about infinite sets.

Sieve of Eratosthenes

Factor trees

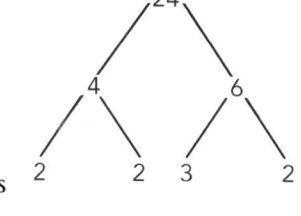

Example

Start with the number 24.

Break it up into two factors that multiply to give 24.

Break up each of the new numbers into factors.

Stop when all the end numbers are prime.

Multiplying all the numbers at the end of the tree builds back up to the starting number so:

$$2 \times 2 \times 3 \times 2 = 4 \times 6 = 24$$

The 24 tree could have been broken up in a different way.

Start with the number 24.

Break it up into two factors that multiply to give 24.

Break up each of the new numbers into factors until each of the end numbers is prime.

Again the end numbers are 2, 2, 3 and 2.

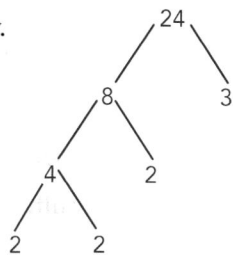

Any number can be split into prime factors which multiply to give the original number. However you break the number down you will always get the same set of prime factors.

Possible confusion

There is an important difference between finding all factors of a number and factorising a number into PRIME factors as in (1) and (2) below.

(1) Find all the factors of 24
The factors of 24 are:
1, 2, 3, 4, 6, 8, 12, 24

(2) Factorise 24 into prime factors
$$24 = 2 \times 2 \times 2 \times 3$$

There are also links between the two ideas. If you choose any of the factors of 24 (with the exception of 1) it can be made by multiplying together some of the prime factors.

e.g $12 = 2 \times 2 \times 3 \qquad 8 = 2 \times 2 \times 2$

Looked at in the other way, multiplying the prime factors of 24 together in all possible ways will give all the possible factors of 24 except 1. The prime factors are the building blocks from which the number is made.

A factor tree can be cumbersome for large numbers. An alternative method of finding prime factors of 24 is to systematically divide 24 by all the possible prime numbers starting with the smallest prime number, which is 2.

2 | 24   There are 12 lots of 2 in 24

2 | 12   Now divide the 12 by 2

2 | 6   Divide by 2 again

3 | 3   Then divide by 3 which is the next prime number after 2

1

So $24 = 2 \times 2 \times 2 \times 3$

TESTS OF DIVISIBILITY

By considering the properties of multiples it is possible to find easy ways of testing if large numbers are multiples of a given number.

Multiples of two are 2, 4, 6, 8, 10, 12, 14, 16, 18, 20 . . . This pattern will include all numbers ending in 0, 2, 4, 6, 8.

> A number is divisible by 2 if its last digit is 0, 2, 4, 6, 8.
>
> Why is this true?
>
> 10 is a multiple of 2.
>
> So any multiple of 10 such as 100, 1000 or a million is a multiple of 2. So to find if a number such as 3044 is a multiple of 2, since we know that 3 × 1000 and 4 × 10 are divisible by 2, we need only consider the last digit.
>
> If the last digit is divisible by 2, that is if the last digit is 0, 2, 4, 6 or 8 then the whole number will be divisible by 2.

For multiples of 4 the situation is not so obvious.

Multiples of 4 are 4, 8, 12, 16, 20, 24, 28, 32, 36, 40, 44, 48, 52 . . .

There is a pattern in the final digits which cycle 4, 8, 2, 6, 0, 4, 8, 2, 6, 0 but not every number which ends in 8 is a multiple of 4, e.g. 18, 38, 58, 2138.

To see that 2138 is not a multiple of 4, decompose it into 2100 + 38.

4 × 25 = 100 so 4 divides exactly into 100.

So 4 will divide into any multiple of 100 such as 21 × 100 = 2100.

All that is needed is to check if 4 divides into the last two digits 38.

4 does not divide into 38 and so 4 is not a factor of 2138 or 52 038 or 216 538 or any other number ending in 38.

> A number is divisible by 4 if its last two digits are divisible by 4.

Similarly, for multiples of 8 you need to consider the last three digits.

The multiples of 9 are 9, 18, 27, 36, 45, 54, 63, 72, 81, 90, 99, 108. . .

The sum of the digits of these multiples is 9 in every case.

For larger numbers such as 999 which is clearly a multiple of 9 the digits do not sum to 9 but to 27 which is a multiple of 9 and if the digits 2 and 7 are added they come to 9.

It seems likely that if the digits of a number sum to a multiple of 9 then that number is divisible by 9.

To prove this for any three-digit number we need to make clear the connection between the digits and the size of the number. Consider the number 753.

$$753 = 100 \times 7 + 10 \times 5 + 3$$

So if the digits of the number are represented by the letters a and b and c:

The number is $100 \times a + 10 \times b + c$. This number can now be rearranged to show which parts of it are divisible by 9.

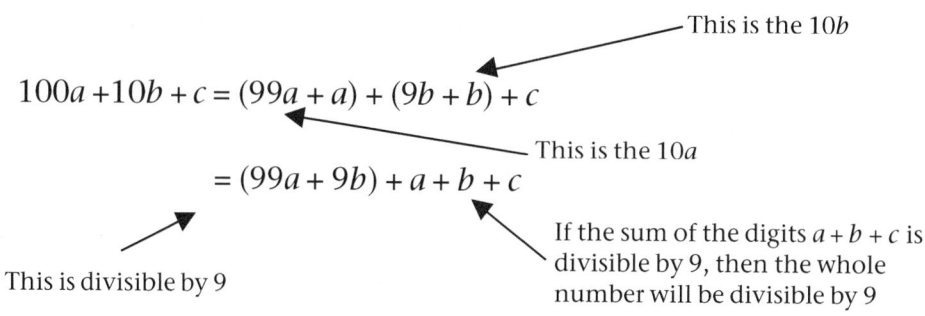

This is the $10b$

$$100a + 10b + c = (99a + a) + (9b + b) + c$$

This is the $10a$

$$= (99a + 9b) + a + b + c$$

This is divisible by 9

If the sum of the digits $a + b + c$ is divisible by 9, then the whole number will be divisible by 9

A number is divisible by 9 if the sum of its digits is divisible by 9.

The multiples of 3 are: 3, 6, 9, 12, 15, 18, 21, 24, 27, 30, 33, 36 . . .

Using the method above but considering dividing the number by 3, it can be shown that a number is divisible by 3 if the sum of its digits is divisible by 3.

A number is divisible by 3 if the sum of its digits is divisible by 3.

A number is divisible by 6 if it is divisible by 2 and 3.

No simple test of divisibility by 7 is known.

NUMBER SEQUENCES

GROWTH PATTERNS

Number sequences can be derived from growth patterns. A growth pattern is a series of shapes where it is quite clear how the next pattern in the sequence is formed.

	1st			2nd			3rd	

(growth pattern of circles forming a cross: 1st pattern with 5 circles, 2nd pattern with 9 circles, 3rd pattern with 13 circles)

How would the tenth pattern in this sequence be made? There are several ways of visualising this.

One is of a circle at the centre with 10 circles on each arm of the cross.

So the tenth pattern in the sequence contains 41 circles.

With this picture in mind, the twentieth pattern would have 20 circles on each arm making $4 \times 20 + 1 = 81$ circles altogether.

How many circles would there be in the nth pattern?

The nth pattern would have one circle in the centre and n circles on each of the four arms making $4n + 1$ circles altogether.

The formula for the nth term of the sequence is: number of circles = $4n + 1$.

Notice that this formula was found by looking at the structure of the shape and breaking it down into a central shape surrounded by four arms. This approach looking at the structure of the problem is often helpful in finding a formula for the nth term.

Another way of defining the sequence is to show how each term is derived from the one before.

In this sequence the next shape is made by adding one extra circle at the end of each arm, that is adding four circles. The first term in the sequence is 5.

The number sequence goes 5, 9, 13, 17, 21 . . .

Taking the last term and adding four will give the next term in the sequence.

This is called a term-to-term or an inductive definition.

DIFFERENCE METHOD

If you have a sequence which goes up by a constant amount each time it is possible to work out the formula for the nth term.

So for the sequence   7   10   13   16   19 . . .

Differences are: 3   3   3   3

The sequence goes up in 3s just like the multiples of 3.

     7   10   13   16   19 . . .   sequence

     3   6   9   12   15 . . .   multiples of 3

Comparing the sequence with the multiples of 3, each value in the sequence is 4 more than the corresponding multiple of 3.

As the formula for the multiples of 3 is $3n$, the formula for the sequence is $3n + 4$.

Similarly for the sequence 3 , 8, 13, 18, 23 . . .

So for the sequence   3   8   13   18   23 . . .

Differences are: 5   5   5   5

The sequence goes up in 5s just like the multiples of 5.

     3   8   13   18   23 . . .   sequence

     5   10   15   20   25 . . .   multiples of 5

Each value in the sequence is 2 less than the corresponding value in the multiples of 5.

The formula for the nth term of the multiples of 5 is $5n$.

So formula for the sequence is $5n - 2$.

Sequences with a constant difference are called linear sequences.

Consider the sequence of square numbers

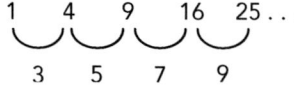

The differences are not constant, they go up by 2 each time.

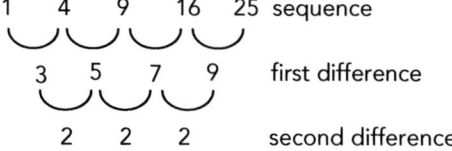

A sequence like this has a quadratic formula; in this case the formula for the *n*th term is n^2.

USING A SPREADSHEET TO GENERATE SEQUENCES

Sequences can be generated using a spreadsheet in two different ways, either by using the inductive definition or the formula for the *n*th term.

Generating a sequence using inductive definition

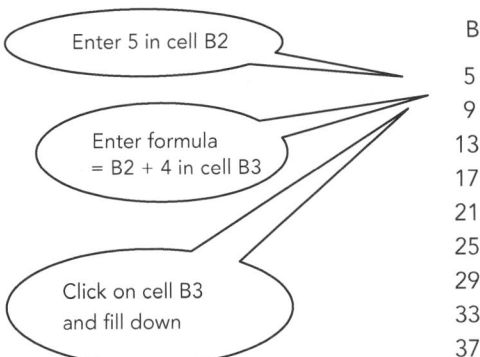

Generating a sequence using formula for the *n*th term

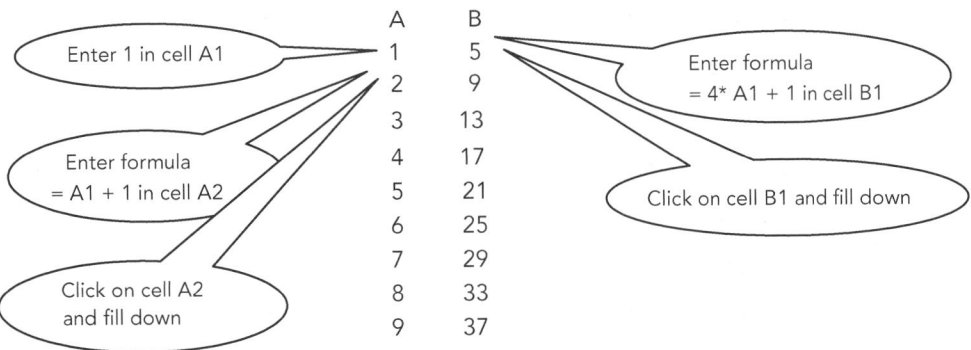

2.4 FUNCTIONS AND GRAPHS

STRAIGHT LINE GRAPHS

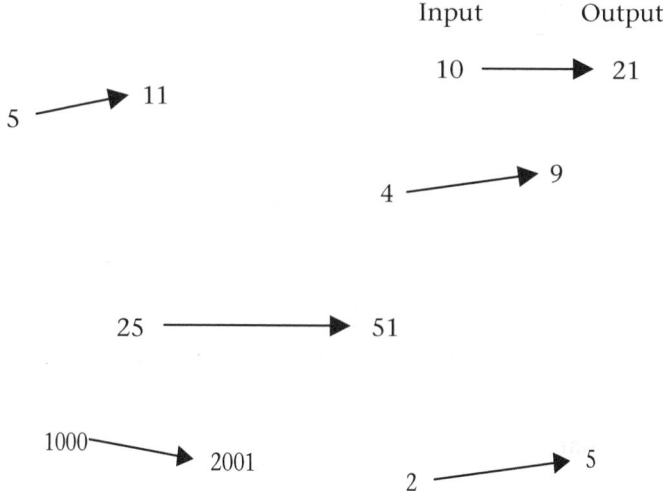

Can you guess the connection between the input number and the output number? More examples can help to check out your ideas.

In this case the input number is multiplied by 2 and then 1 is added.

If n is the starting number that gives: $n \longrightarrow 2n + 1$ (the arrow means 'goes to' or 'is mapped onto').

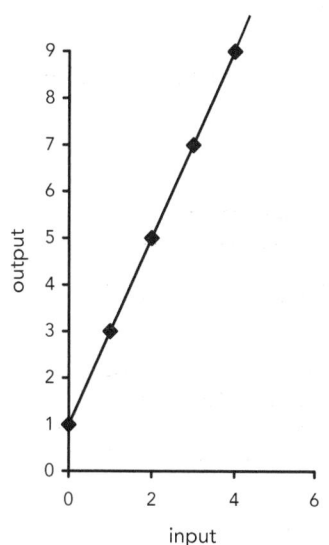

Double and add one

To get an increased understanding of the function, the input and output numbers can be taken as the co-ordinates of points on a graph:

$$(5, 11) \qquad (4, 9) \qquad (2, 5) \text{ etc.}$$

What will the graph look like if these points are plotted?

The function points all lie on a straight line. So do all the other points that fit the pattern, 'output number equals double the input number plus one'.

If the graph is extended the point (1000, 2001) would lie on this line.

If fractional values are used then points such as (2.5, 6) and (3.5, 8) would lie on this line.

Because all the intermediate points have a meaning in this way it is appropriate to join the dots with a straight line. When plotting graphs it is customary to describe the input number as x and the output number as y. With this notation the formula which describes the function is $y = 2x + 1$.

Any function of the form $y = ax + b$, where a and b are constants, will give a straight line graph of this kind, and such functions are described as linear (see Working with functions in Section 2.2).

It is possible to identify specific features of the straight line graph from the equation $y = 2x + 1$.

Consider the equation $y = 2x + 1$

The constant term in this equation is 1.

What connection does that have with the graph?

Well, when $x = 0$, y will be equal to 1, so the graph goes through the point (0, 1).

This co-ordinate gives the point at which the graph crosses the y-axis which is called the intercept.

What information does the other constant, the number in front of the x, give about the graph?

x	0	1	2	3	4
y	1	3	5	7	9

Notice, in the table, that every time the x-value increases by 1, the y-value increases by 2.

Graph of $y = 2x + 1$

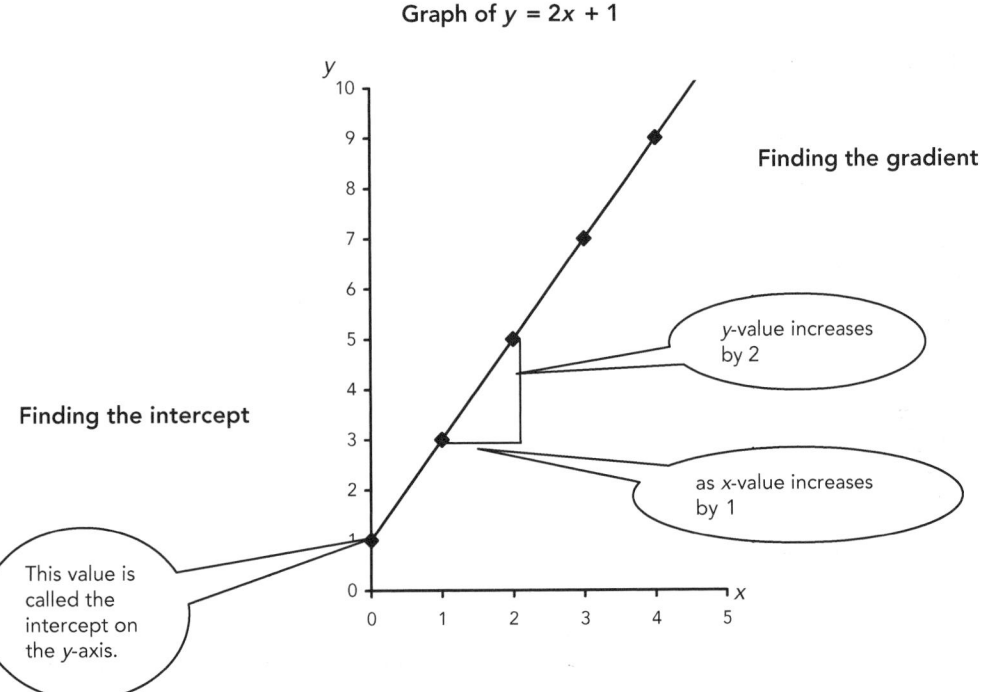

Finding the gradient

y-value increases by 2

as x-value increases by 1

Finding the intercept

This value is called the intercept on the y-axis.

The ratio $\dfrac{\text{increase in } y}{\text{increase in } x}$ is called the gradient. For this graph the gradient is $\dfrac{2}{1} = 2$.

The gradient is measured by choosing any two points on the graph and measuring the increase in y divided by the increase in x.

So for the graph $y = 2x + 1$

This number is the intercept on the y-axis.

This number is the gradient.

Graph of $y = {}^-x - 4$

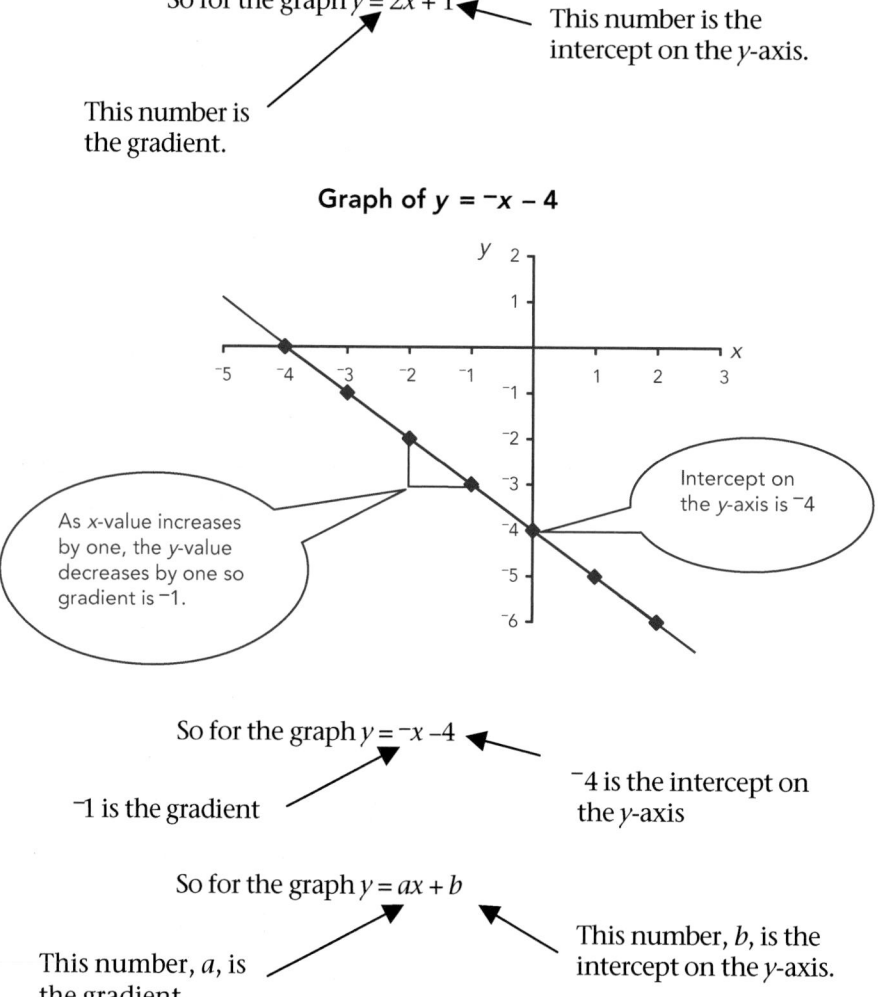

As x-value increases by one, the y-value decreases by one so gradient is $^-1$.

Intercept on the y-axis is $^-4$

So for the graph $y = {}^-x - 4$

$^-1$ is the gradient

$^-4$ is the intercept on the y-axis

So for the graph $y = ax + b$

This number, a, is the gradient.

This number, b, is the intercept on the y-axis.

QUADRATIC GRAPHS

A graphic calculator is useful for exploring more complicated functions. Consider the function which squares the input number.

$(0, 0)$ $(1, 1)$ $(2, 4)$ $(3, 9)$ $(4, 16)$ etc.

When you enter $y = x^2$ into a calculator you might expect to get this:

The calculator, however, plots the function with negative values of x as well. As a

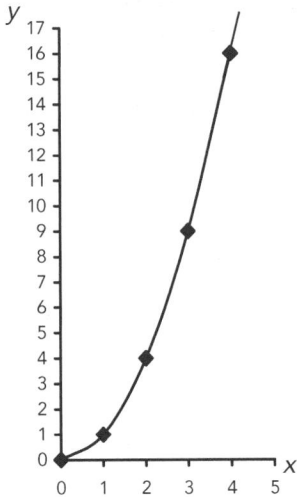

negative number multiplied by a negative number gives a positive number $^-3 \times {}^-3 = 9$, $^-2 \times {}^-2 = 4$. The graph is symmetrical about the y-axis.

Graph of a quadratic function

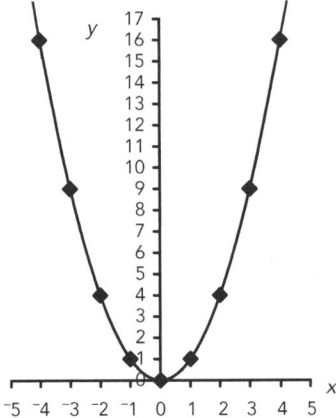

Any graph of the form $y = ax^2 + bx + c$ is a quadratic function; the highest power of x in a quadratic function is x^2.

CUBIC GRAPHS

If the highest power of x is 3, the graph is a cubic, e.g. $y = x^3$.

To get an idea of the general shape of the graph, choose any negative number for x, e.g. $x = {}^-2$

If $x = {}^-2$ then $y = {}^-2 \times {}^-2 \times {}^-2 = 4 \times {}^-2 = {}^-8$

. . . or like this?

Will the graph of the cubic be u-shaped like this?

Graph B

Graph A

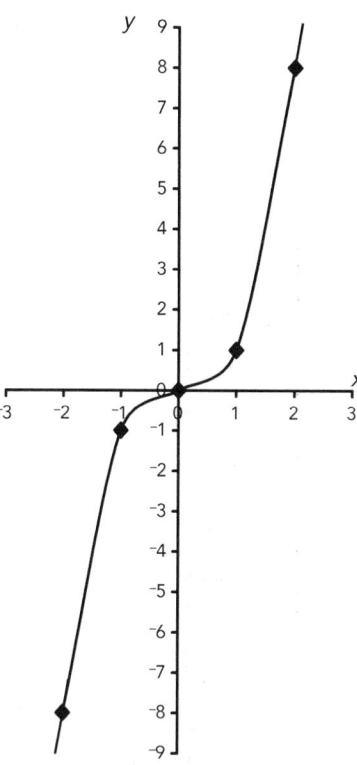

The point ($^-2$, $^-8$) must lie on the graph so the cubic is graph B which has negative values when x is negative.

EXPONENTIAL GRAPHS

The expression 'increasing exponentially' is sometimes used colloquially to describe something which is increasing very fast. Mathematically exponential functions are of the form $y = ka^x$, where k is a constant and a is called the growth factor.

Example

Consider the graph of $y = 3^x$

When $x = 1$, $y = 3^1 = 3$

When $x = 2$, $y = 3^2 = 9$

When $x = 10$, $y = 3^{10} = 50\ 049$. That is a lot bigger than $10^3 = 1000$.

This exponential graph increases far faster than a quadratic or cubic graph when x is positive.

As x increases by 1, the y-value is multiplied by 3.

x	1	2	3	4	5	6
y	3	9	27	81	243	729

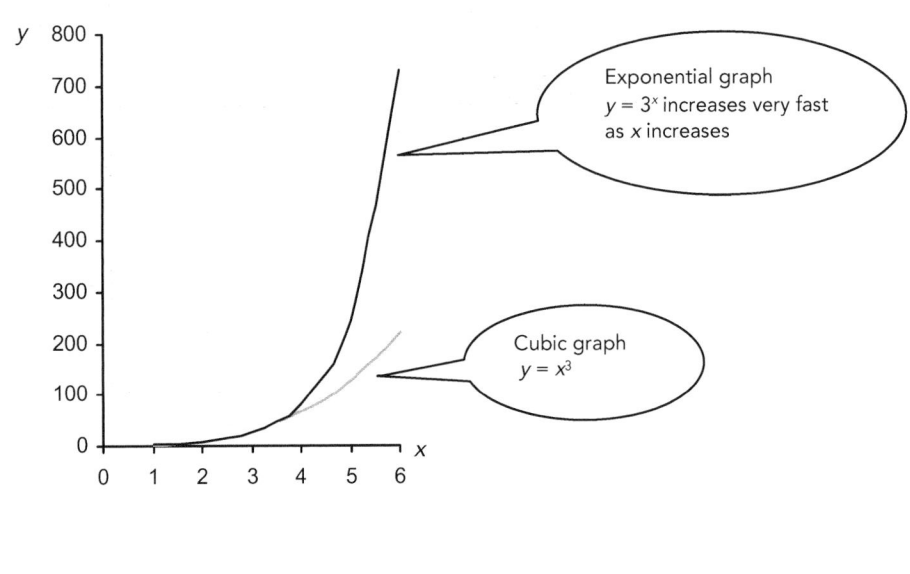

2.5 EQUATIONS

SOLVING EQUATIONS ALGEBRAICALLY

Example

I think of a number, multiply it by 3 and add 4.

The answer is 10. What was the number I first thought of?

This type of problem gives enough information to identify the as-yet-unknown number.

It can be solved by reversing all the processes described.

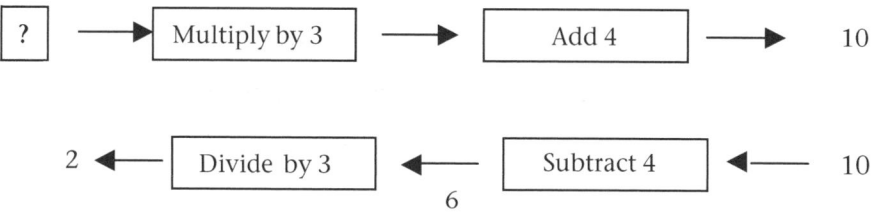

The answer is 10. Before the 4 was added that would have been 6.

The number trebled to make 6 must have been 2.

If x is taken as the unknown number, the problem can be written as an equation. Solving the equation gives the answer to the problem. So we need to solve the equation:

$$3x + 4 = 10$$

The principle which is used to solve equations is that if exactly the same operation is carried out on both sides of the equation then the two sides of the new equation must also be equal. The equation can be thought of as a balance: if the two sides balance initially then adding or subtracting the same weight on both sides means the scales will still balance.

The principle can be illustrated with a numerical example.

Start with the statement	$3 = 2 + 1$	
Add 5 to both sides	$8 = 2 + 1 + 5$	This new statement is clearly true
Subtract 2 from both sides	$6 = 1 + 5$	Again this is a true statement

So to solve an equation we need to:

- Carry out the same operation on both sides.
- Choose operations that will make the equation simpler and simpler until the final line starts '$x =$'.

$$3x + 4 = 10 \quad \text{Subtract 4 from both sides of the equation}$$

$$3x = 6 \quad \text{Divide both sides by 3}$$

$$x = 2$$

With more complicated equations more stages are required to reach the final solution but the principles are exactly the same.

$$3x - 5 = x + 7 \quad \text{Add 5 to both sides}$$

$$3x = x + 12 \quad \text{Subtract } x \text{ from both sides}$$

$$2x = 12 \quad \text{Divide both sides by 2}$$

$$x = 6$$

$$2(5x - 7) = 13 \quad \text{Multiply out the brackets}$$

$$10x - 14 = 13 \quad \text{Add 14 to both sides}$$

$$10x = 27 \quad \text{Divide both sides by 10}$$

$$x = 2.7$$

SOLVING EQUATIONS GRAPHICALLY

Example

To solve $3x + 4 = 10$ graphically, you need to plot the graph of $y = 3x + 4$.

The point on the graph we are interested in is the point where $y = 10$. Drawing a line across from y-axis from the point (0, 10) locates the point on the graph where $y = 10$. The value of x at this point can be read from the x-axis. It is usual to draw a line down to the x-axis to ensure an accurate reading.

Graph of $y = 3x + 4$

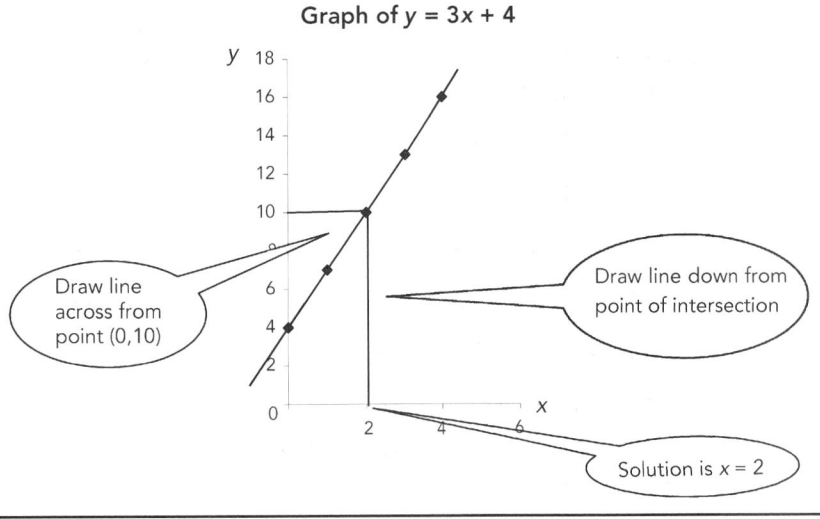

The method above wouldn't work for equations which have x on both sides.

> *Example*
>
> $3x - 5 = x + 7$
>
> To solve this equation graphically you need to draw two straight lines representing the two sides of the equation: $y = 3x - 5$ and $y = x + 7$.
>
> The x-value at the point where the two lines cross gives the solution of the equation. The graphs can be plotted on paper or using a graphic calculator. The trace function on the calculator enables you to move a flashing cursor along the graph to the point of intersection. The co-ordinates of the cursor are displayed on the screen so you can easily read off the x-value at the point of intersection.

USING A GRAPHIC CALCULATOR TO SOLVE EQUATIONS

The graphical method of solution can be extended to more complicated equations using a graphic calculator to plot the graph.

> *Example*
>
> In trying to solve the quadratic equation: $2x^2 - 2x - 3 = 0$
>
> First plot the graph of $y = 2x^2 - 2x - 3$.
>
> The graph crosses the x-axis in two places. There are two values of x which make $2x^2 - 2x - 3 = 0$.
>
> Using the trace button, the value of x at the points where the graph cuts the x-axis can be read off.
>
>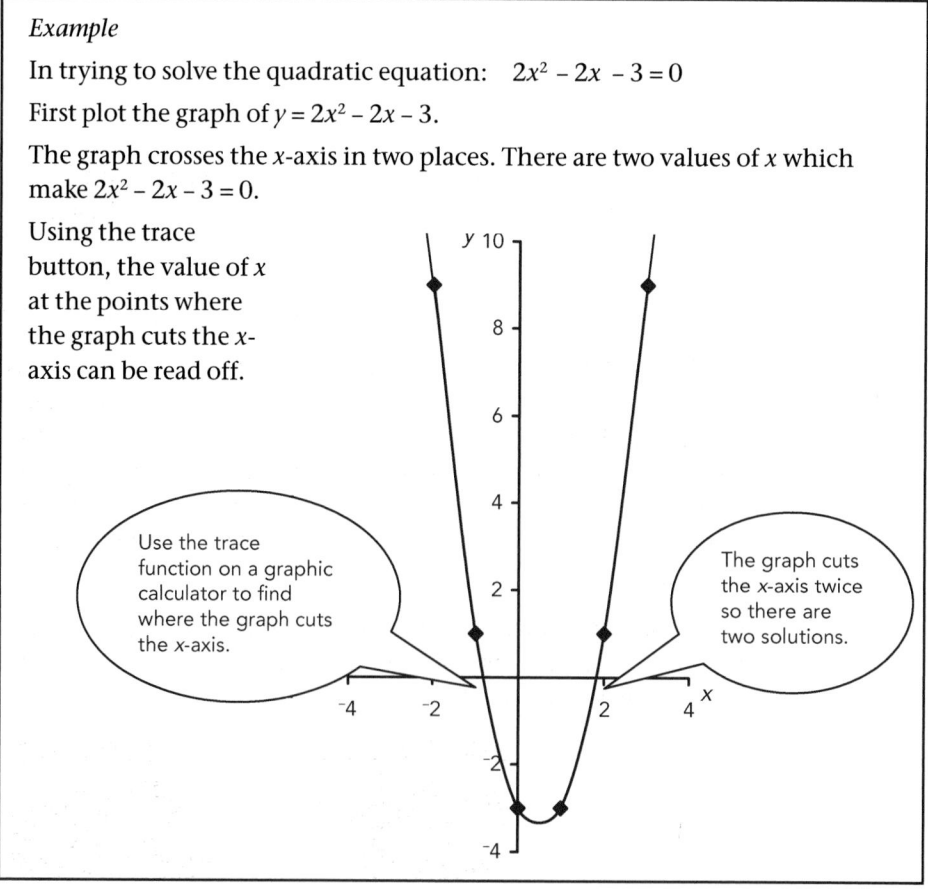
>
> Use the trace function on a graphic calculator to find where the graph cuts the x-axis.
>
> The graph cuts the x-axis twice so there are two solutions.

2.6 IMPLICATIONS FOR TEACHING PROPERTIES OF NUMBERS, NUMBER SEQUENCES AND ALGEBRA

By deepening your level of mathematical knowledge you can teach for understanding and respond confidently to children's questions. Some issues considered in this section could be helpful when you are planning your teaching in order to encourage children to explain their thinking and visualising.

Many young children reveal that they are developing algebraic thinking through their demonstrations and explanations of their methods. They may start by spotting patterns and using shortcuts based on pattern recognition.

For example Ryan, in Reception, worked out that 11 bears take away five bears left six bears. Next time he had 12 take away five and he said: 'Last time it was six so this time it is going to be seven'. He had spotted a pattern that may be stated as, 'If you increase the number you are taking away from by one and still take the same number away then you increase the answer by one.'

Although Ryan could not articulate this, he demonstrated an implicit understanding of a general rule. When this rule is articulated in words you can hear the algebra in it. Numerically Ryan's insight is shown like this:

$$11 - 5 = 6$$

$$(11 + 1) - 5 = 6 + 1$$

$$\text{so } 12 - 5 = 7$$

More generally if 11 is increased by any number then the answer will also increase by that number. This can be expressed using a symbol to represent the increase as:

$$(11 + x) - 5 = 6 + x$$

We can generalise this pattern even further by considering any starting number.

Algebra is the most succinct and sophisticated way of expressing the rules of generalised arithmetic which underpin the methods we use. There are many general rules about the way numbers behave that are implicit in children's shortcuts and the mental strategies we teach them. Encouraging children to express these methods in words helps their understanding. Primary school children don't need to manipulate symbols but teachers may recognise the beginning of algebra in the children's shortcuts.

Generalised arithmetic can also be expressed pictorially. For example you can see that two fives added together gives an even number by the use of visual images such as Numicon (Numicon Ltd).

From this it is easy to generalise that any two odd numbers will add to give an even number. Asking children to explain this rule encourages the beginning of algebraic thinking. Children may say something like, 'If you have two odd numbers there's two stickyout bits which go together to make an even number', which does not sound very like algebra, but the same rule can later be expressed with symbols and proved. Children could be asked to generalise other rules. For instance what happens with an even multiplied by an odd number (that is an even number of odd numbers), e.g. 4 × 5, 4 lots of 5.

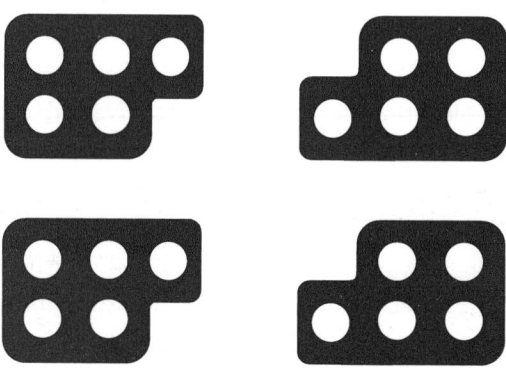

Operation signs are essential for expressing general relationships and are not just quick ways of presenting tasks to children. A symbol often misinterpreted is the equals sign. Recognising the equals sign in a number sentence as 'is exactly the same as' rather than seeing it as the prompt for an answer is important. The ability to rearrange equations in secondary level mathematics relies upon understanding the significance of this symbol. If teachers appreciate that a number sentence is essentially an equation they can help children develop to a more general understanding of the equals sign and its function in signalling equivalence. An important activity for children would be to ask them to make equations that balance, for example:

$$2 + 3 = 4 + \boxed{}$$

Older children could identify false equations such as:

$$2 + 3 \times 4 = 2 \times 3 + 4$$

and explore the difference brackets would make:

$$2 + 3 \times 4 = 2 \times (3 + 4)$$

which is a true equation since

left hand side (LHS) is $2 + 12 = 14$

right hand side (RHS) is $2 \times 7 = 14$

The idea of inverse is important in contexts where children are asked to find an unknown number or secret operation. 'Think of a number' problems can be set when children have a repertoire of mental strategies for the four operations. For example:

I am thinking of a number which when you add 3 to it you get 10. What is the number?

Children might use the inverse operation (subtraction of 3 from 10) to solve the problem.

The function machine is another idea that can be introduced early, especially if it is made into a concrete object (a box with 'in' and 'out' holes at either end). A stick of a small number of cubes, say 4, can be fed into the 'machine' where a child or adult does something to the stick such as 'add 2'. The new stick is pushed out of the 'out' hole and children have to work out what happened (the secret function). If this is done several times with the same secret function, children might spot the rule that each time the stick emerges with 2 more cubes added.

2.7 SELF-ASSESSMENT QUESTIONS Properties of numbers, number sequences and algebra

ALGEBRAIC NOTATION

1. In each of the sets of three expressions two are the same. Find the odd one out.

    a) $3x + 12$ b) $3(x + 2)$ c) $3(x + 4)$

    a) $7x + 2(x - 6)$ b) $9x - 6$ c) $3(3x - 4)$

NUMBERS AND NUMBER SEQUENCES

2. Use a spreadsheet to generate a large number of multiples of 99.

    Find as many patterns as you can.

3. Find an even multiple of 5 which is one more than a square number.

    Does this question have more than one answer?

4. Make the third triangle number out of multilink.

    Make another copy of the third triangle number and fit them together to form a rectangle. Note the size of the rectangle made .

    Repeat for a different triangle number.

    Can you predict the size of the rectangle which would be made by combining two copies of the 100th triangle number?

    Can you generalise and find a formula for the value of the nth triangle number?

5. Use divisibility tests and/or a calculator to test as efficiently as you can whether or not 211 is prime.

   If you would prefer a larger number try 30 031.

6. Find the sum of the first hundred odd numbers in as many different ways as you can.

EFFICIENT USE OF A CALCULATOR

7. To use a calculator efficiently you need to use the order of operations

   Brackets first

   Indices

   Division or multiplication

   Addition or subtraction

   You will also need to know how numbers are put in the memory on your calculator.

   Use these ideas to find:

   a) $35 + 17 \times 19$ b) $56 \times 32 - (2807 - 1814)$ c) $\dfrac{5.4 + 2.39}{6.8 + 2.4}$ d) $2.6 \div 3.1^2$

FUNCTIONS AND GRAPHS

8. Use a graphic calculator to find as many graphs as you can which go through the point with co-ordinates (1, 1).

DIFFERENCE METHOD

9. Use the difference method to find the formula for the nth term of the sequence:

   9, 11, 13, 15, 17, 19, . . .

   Plot the sequence as a graph by plotting the co-ordinates (1, 9) (2, 11) (3, 13) etc.

   Find the gradient and intercept of the graph and see how this links to the formula.

EQUATIONS

10. Solve this equation: a) algebraically b) using a graphic calculator or graph-plotting software.

    $6x - 4 = 2x + 13$

    Justify each stage in your solution.

    Can you invent a quite different equation which has exactly the same solution?

3 Handling data

Ideas of probability and statistics permeate every aspect of our life, from children's board games to the stock market, and the beginnings can be found very early in cultural history

PROBABILITY

The first recorded use of some kind of dice for Divination, Gambling and for Board Games dates from about 3000 BC. The earliest dice with six spots have been found in Iraq and also in Northern India and are made of pottery, but these were difficult to make without bias. Fortune telling is a very old practice, and was originally related to religious rituals. From very early times we also find people were interested in trying to predict the outcome of games of chance. When some kind of dice or stones were rolled, it was the outcome that was important, not the probability of getting a particular result, and this was the beginning of superstitions about 'lucky' and 'unlucky' numbers. In ancient times the 'dice' that were used were often the knuckle bones of sheep (astragali) which were rectangular with a roughly square cross section, and because of this, some outcomes happened more often than others. The astragali were probably used by the Roman soldiers who gambled to decide who would win Christ's clothes at the foot of the cross. Of course, the Church was against all forms of divination and gambling, but the 'pagan' practices prevailed; the Crusaders brought back the game of 'Hazard' ('al-zahr') played with two dice from the Middle East.

Later, in mediaeval times, when more regular (and hence fairer) dice began to be made, there are records of discussions about the number of ways two dice can fall to make up the numbers from 2 to 12. However, these results did not take into account the order in which the dice could fall (for example, for two dice coloured red and blue, there are two ways of throwing a three: red 2, blue 1; and blue 2, red 1). In 1526 the Italian mathematician Girolamo Cardano wrote a book on games of chance, showing that he had a clear idea of equally likely events, and he made systematic calculations about the probability of certain events. For example, he showed that for a single die the odds in favour of throwing a 1, 2, or a 3 were 3 to 6. Besides being an important mathematician, Cardano was well known for his drinking, and gambling, and he had clearly calculated the strategies that would be in his favour. Gambling was (and still is) the motivation for many mathematical questions about probability. The problem about how to divide the stakes in a gambling game if the game is stopped at any point was energetically discussed by Italian mathematicians in the fifteenth and sixteenth centuries, but the ground-breaking contributions to the problem came when the French mathematician, Blaise Pascal, started a correspondence with Pierre Fermat in 1654. In his solution to the problem, Pascal showed how to use the arithmetic triangle. This is often referred to as the 'Pascal Triangle', but this array of numbers had been known for at least 500 years, probably originating in China.

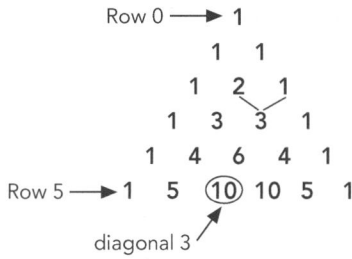

Having started from a problem about gambling, mathematicians began to develop the theory of modern probability. By 1812, when the French mathematician, Pierre Simon Laplace published his 'Analytical Theory of Probability', the foundations of modern probability had been established.

STATISTICS

The collection of data became important as soon as people began to organise themselves into towns and cities and to develop an agrarian society. Food had to be stored, supplies organised, and taxes levied. Data collection (and display) was important in early Middle Eastern cultures where rulers wanted to know (and show) their possessions. For example, the stone column of Hammurabi (1750 BC) shows the spoils of war and the numbers of prisoners brought back from his conquests. Fair wages were a concern even then, and the organisation of data in Mesopotamia from at least 2500 BC enabled the officials to work out how many hours a person had laboured in order to pay them a just wage. Probably the earliest example of collecting data in England was the Domesday Book (1086) where William wanted to know how many towns, farms, pigs and sheep were in the country he had just conquered, as a basis for his taxation system.

The question of 'how many?' has been important to people for a long time; how many things, how many people, how many times an event has occurred – all part of the human need to find out, and perhaps to predict what might happen next. In the seventeenth century in England, data on births, deaths and marriages, and other kinds of human behaviour like crimes, suicides and the incidence of diseases began to be collected. This, together with other data such as the value of cargoes and the number of ships lost at sea, began to be organised into the business of insurance.

This obsession with counting things prevailed right through to the nineteenth century, by which time data collection had become an enormous job – many people were employed by landowners and princes in just 'counting things' without much thought or organisation of purpose, just to show how much they possessed.

The essay by the radical politician Adam Smith *An Enquiry into the Nature and Causes of the Wealth of Nations* (1776) was an early example of social economics and relied on an awareness of the importance of collection of data to support rational scientific decisions. In the mid-nineteenth century, Florence Nightingale witnessed the tragic deaths of wounded soldiers in the Crimean war, and her use of statistics persuaded the government to organise field hospitals for the army.

By trying to analyse the kinds of data collected, the statistical laws were developed and used for explaining the course of events – both human and natural – hence 'laws of society' began to be proposed. The idea of averages and measures of spread brought about the concept of a normal person. One interpretation of the mass of data gave rise to statistical fatalism. Man is fated to act in certain ways; for example, a certain number of people will always be inclined to commit suicide. Predictions like this gave rise to disputes about personal freedom and free will, and thus began a more scientifically founded debate about what counts as evidence and what is objective knowledge. From the time of the French Revolution more emphasis was placed on rational and secular explanations for human conditions and in 1795 Marie Jean Condorcet published a social theory founded on analysis of statistical data. This approach to rational moral science also gave rise to theories of jurisprudence which considered the probability that a decision in a trial could be correct.

In 1835 Simeon Poisson applied probability to social matters and invented the notion of the law of large numbers which he referred to as 'a fact of experience which never goes wrong'. He used examples of rates of shipwrecks, of mortality, and of conviction in trials to show that if the numbers were large enough, the error involved in estimating what might happen would be very small. In 1844 Lambert Quetelet, using the Pascal Triangle, produced a bell-shaped curve and claimed that theoretical events could also be applied to human data, which included not only the height and weight of people but also moral characteristics like the propensity for criminality, drunkenness or madness.

The bell-shaped curve has the mean as a mirror line.

Data from the Paris courts for example, showed that over a given period there were the same number of murderers, poisoners, forgers, etc., and the bell-shaped curve nicely fitted the mass of empirical data and was used to predict the size of prisons that needed to be built. Since measurements were distributed around a mean then nature was aiming for an ideal type, and Quetelet applied this theory to 5732 Scottish soldiers to show that there was a normal or average soldier! The bell-shaped curve became named the normal law and was believed to be a true predictor of a wide range of natural and human phenomena.

In the late nineteenth century the English statistician Galton used Quetelet's ideas to mathematise Darwin's theory of evolution by looking at the way variations of characteristics were inherited in generations of sweet peas in the laboratory. He then collected similar data about the variation of characteristics between parents and children. Galton's application of statistical laws to human physiology and then to psychology, began the classification of human types which led to the idea of intelligence which was used in education by Cyril Burt and others for classifying adults and children.

Collecting data of all kinds has been a human preoccupation almost since we appeared on the planet; how we interpret that data and what we do with the results have changed over time. The manner of interpretation reflects the kinds of interests and passions, ideologies and ambitions of the human condition.

3.2 PROCESSING, REPRESENTING AND MAKING SENSE OF DATA

WHY COLLECT DATA?

Most questions in life do not have straightforward answers:

> What fraction of rush hour traffic can be attributed to 'the school run'?
>
> Is global warming really happening?
>
> How different are marriage patterns compared to 100 years ago?

Questions like these require information (or **data**) in order to find a plausible answer. Collecting data is time-consuming so it is important that you have a clear purpose before you begin.

- What are you trying to find out?
- What question do you want to answer?

The more tightly you define your purpose the easier it should be to decide how to collect your data.

Primary data is data you collect. It could involve measuring, counting, using a questionnaire etc.

Secondary data is data that someone has already collected. It could involve information on the internet or in a book or document. One of the problems with secondary data is that someone may have already begun to analyse the data and you cannot be sure how it was collected.

Posing the question or issue is the start of a process known as the **data-handling cycle:**

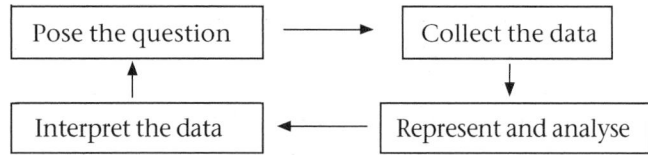

Once you have collected your data, you need to represent and analyse it in a helpful way that will allow you to interpret what the data is telling you about the situation and answer your original question.

COLLECTING THE DATA – SAMPLING

When collecting your own data there are some important decisions to bear in mind:

- Collect as much data as you can, because the larger your sample, the more reliable your conclusions are likely to be.
- It is usually impossible to use the entire population (i.e. all the children in the school or all the eligible voters in a town). You have to take a **sample** in order for your data collection to be manageable and to help ensure your results are representative.

Asking people who live in a particular part of town which political party they intend to vote for won't allow you to make predictions for the voting preferences of the whole town. This data would be **biased**.

The sample must be taken from the whole population that you are considering.

Sampling methods

- **Random sample** This means that each person in the population is equally likely to be chosen, e.g. put names into a hat on identical pieces of paper and then select names from the hat.
- **Stratified random sample** This means the original population is split into groups and a random sample is taken from each group, e.g. take a random sample of ten per cent of children from each year group in a school.

TYPES OF DATA

DISCRETE DATA

Discrete data are data that can be counted. Each item of data belongs to a single category, for example, 'Who will you vote for in the next election?'

The categories in England could be: Conservative, Labour, Liberal-Democrat, other, don't know.

- When collecting discrete data expect to have at least five categories.
- Too many categories make analysis difficult.

Some parties get a very small fraction of the total vote so these may be combined in the category of 'other parties'. Using too many categories can make it harder to present the findings clearly. For example a pie chart composed of tiny slices confuses the overall pattern.

Some other examples of discrete data are types of books, hobbies, car manufacturers.

Discrete data can also be numerical, for example, shoe size, the number of bedrooms in a house, the number of children in a family, etc. The data is numerical but only certain numeric values are possible.

CONTINUOUS DATA

Continuous data are data that are measured, such as height, weight, time, temperature, etc.

These all need to be recorded to a certain level of accuracy. In principle any value is possible and that is why this type of data is **continuous**.

Continuous data is often grouped into classes to make it easier to analyse and interpret.

SUMMARISING DATA

Values that are used to summarise a set of data are called statistics.

An average value is a statistic that best represents or typifies the data.

There are three different types of average: the mode, the mean and the median.

MODE

- The mode is the data value that occurs most frequently.

> *Example*
>
> Which size of shoe sells more than any other size?
>
> In a particular shop size 7 is the most common shoe size being sold. It is called the **mode**.
>
> This average is the easiest to determine and is useful when there are only a few categories or values.

The mode is easy to identify on a bar chart (look for the tallest bar) and on a pie chart (look for the largest slice).

Data is said to be **bi-modal** if there are two values which are most popular.

> *Example*
>
> Which letter occurs most in this example of written English?
>
> In the sentence above the letters 'e' and 't' each occur six times. This is an example of **bi-modal** data.

There is no mode when more than two values are equally highly popular.

When data has been grouped into classes the most popular class (i.e. most frequently occurring) is known as the **modal class**.

MEDIAN

- To find the median the data must be put in order; the median is then the middle value.

The highest daily temperatures during the first week in January were 8, 2, 2, 5, 0, 3, 4°C.

Putting these temperatures in order gives

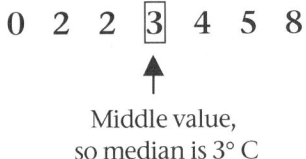

Middle value,
so median is 3° C

For an even number of data values the median is exactly half-way between the two central values, so if the temperatures are recorded for 14 days and put in order:

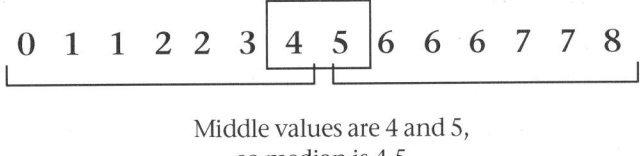

Middle values are 4 and 5,
so median is 4.5

The median value divides the data into two equal sized groups.

Remember that to obtain the median it is important to order the data first.

A possible misconception is that the median will be half-way between the smallest and the greatest values. The examples above show that this is not the case.

MEAN

- The mean is calculated by adding up all the data items and dividing by the total number of items.

To find the mean highest daily temperature for the first week in January:

Sum of temperatures for the week is $8 + 2 + 2 + 5 + 0 + 3 + 4 = 24$

There are seven days in the week, so mean temperature $\dfrac{24}{7} = 3.4°C$, to 1 decimal place.

You need to be careful when calculating the mean to ensure that you have the total of all the data values and that you divide by how many data values you actually have.

Note that the mean is calculated and so it is only possible to have a mean for numerical data.

A common misconception is to think that the mean should be one of the data values; in the example above 3.4° is not one of the recorded temperatures but it is the calculated mean. The statement, 'The average number of children per family is 1.7' does make sense. No family can have 1.7 children but the calculated mean number of children in a family can be 1.7.

Extreme values

For data which has extreme values, the mean does not give a good representative value for the data.

Example

Consider the salaries of the employees of a small business:

Proprietor	£55 000
Production manager	£25 000
Craftsperson 1	£15 000
Craftsperson 2	£12 000
Craftsperson 3	£11 000
Administrator	£14 000
Trainee	£8 000
TOTAL	£140 000

The mean salary is the total salary £140 000 divided by 7 employees which is £20 000.

This is not a particularly representative figure as most employees get paid quite a bit less.

The median salary is £14 000 which gives a better measure of central tendency in this situation.

(Note: to find the median salary first put the salaries in order of size.)

Using a spreadsheet

The mean is readily obtained using the AVERAGE command, and is often the value people think of when they hear the word, average.

However the mean, median and mode are all averages. They are single representative values for a set of data.

If you wish to compare sets of data you need to make sure the same type of average is used throughout.

RANGE

The **range** is a measure of spread. It provides additional information about the data.

Example

If two companies have the same mean salary would you expect individual salaries to be similar?

Company A: The mean salary is £20 000. The lowest salary is £7000 and the highest £55 000.

Company B: The mean salary is £20 000. The lowest salary is £15 000 and the highest £30 000.

The range of salaries is hidden when only the mean is given. These two companies have very different salary policies. To distinguish between these two companies the range is used.

The range is the difference between the lowest and highest data value.

The range for company A is £48 000 (£55 000–£7000)

The range for company B is only £15 000 (£30 000–£15 000).

REPRESENTING DATA

Data is represented using diagrams to make interpretation easier.

To produce a good representation:

- organise the data to enhance your understanding of what the data is telling you
- select an appropriate diagram
- give it a meaningful title
- use a key (if necessary)
- label the axes clearly.

FREQUENCY DIAGRAMS – BLOCK GRAPHS, PICTOGRAMS AND BAR CHARTS

These are the simplest diagrams that summarise a set of data.

The **frequency** is the number of times each data value occurs.

Block graph

To find out how many Smarties of different colours are found in a tube, the youngest children can actually line up the Smarties. The next stage is to draw a block graph.

- a block is used to represent each time a data value occurs.

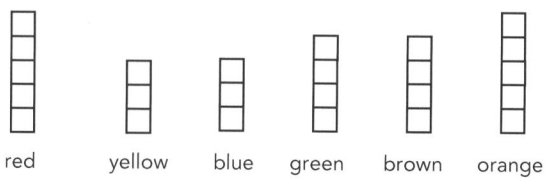

red   yellow   blue   green   brown   orange

Colour of Smarties in a packet

Pictogram

This is similar to a block graph.

- a symbol (or picture) is used to represent a certain frequency
- the symbols must all be identical within any particular diagram
- a key is used.

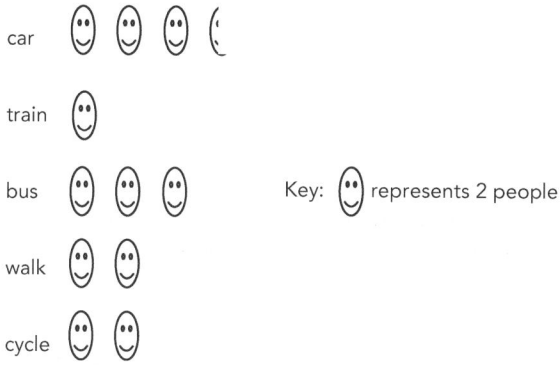

Methods of travelling to school for a class of 23 children

Bar chart

A bar chart shows the frequency plotted against the data value.

Bars can be:

- horizontal or vertical
- any width although they should all be of equal width in a given diagram
- they should **not** touch.

When the bars are simply lines the diagram is called a bar-line graph.

Bar charts are used for discrete data. The bars do not touch as there is no relationship between the data values; they are discrete.

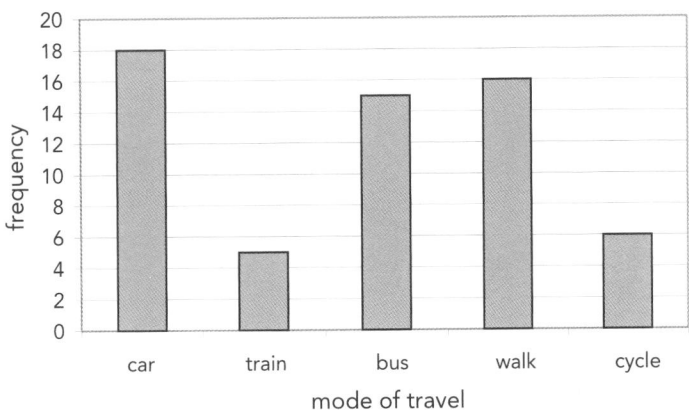

Bar chart for ways of travelling to school

Once data is grouped a histogram can be drawn – this looks like a bar chart but the bars touch and the horizontal axis is marked like a ruler (see the section on histograms).

OTHER TYPES OF DIAGRAMS

Other types of diagrams may be used for particular purposes: line graphs, pie charts, Carroll diagrams, Venn diagrams and binary trees.

Line graphs

This type of representation is used to illustrate trends in data (usually over time). The line graph below shows the average daily temperature month by month in a popular holiday resort.

The graph shows that the temperature is much higher in June and July than in December/January so the resort is probably in the northern hemisphere. However it is not possible to determine the likely temperature for a given date. Line graphs do not give information about values between the plotted points. For temperature, you might expect a reasonably smooth transition, on average, month by month. However the day-to-day variations are not taken into consideration.

Line graphs are often used in the media to illustrate trends in the economy, or academic standards. These need to be interpreted cautiously as it is rare that the changes have been linear over time, as the graphs imply!

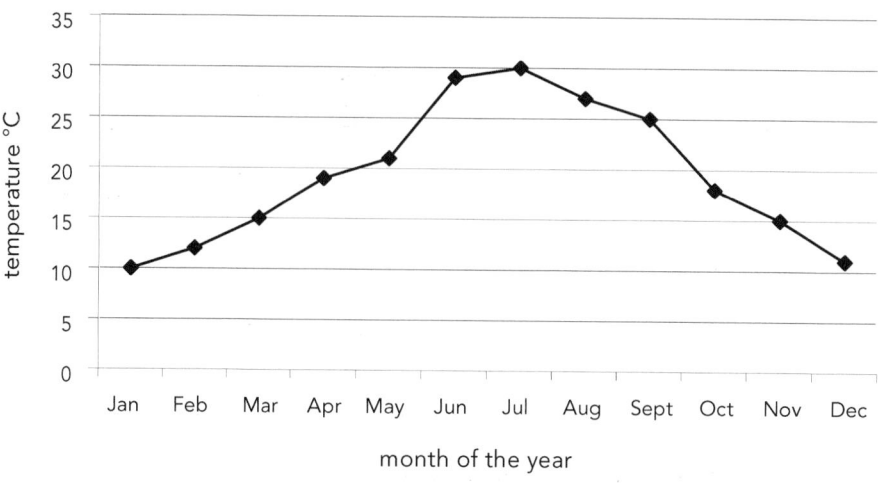

Average daytime temperature in each month of the year

Pie chart

A pie chart shows proportions and is easily obtained on a spreadsheet or database.

To construct a pie chart you need to consider what the whole pie will represent and then calculate the angle for each sector.

Example

This table shows the age of the children in Mr A's class.

Age of children	Number of children
9 years	10
10 years	8
11 years	2
	Total 20

There are 20 children altogether in the class so the 360° of the pie chart will represent 20 children.

Each child will be represented by a sector with angle 360° ÷ 20 = 18°.

Age of children	Number of children	Size of angle in pie chart
9	10	10 × 18° = 180°
10	8	8 × 18° = 144°
11	2	2 × 18° = 36°
	Total 20	Total 360°

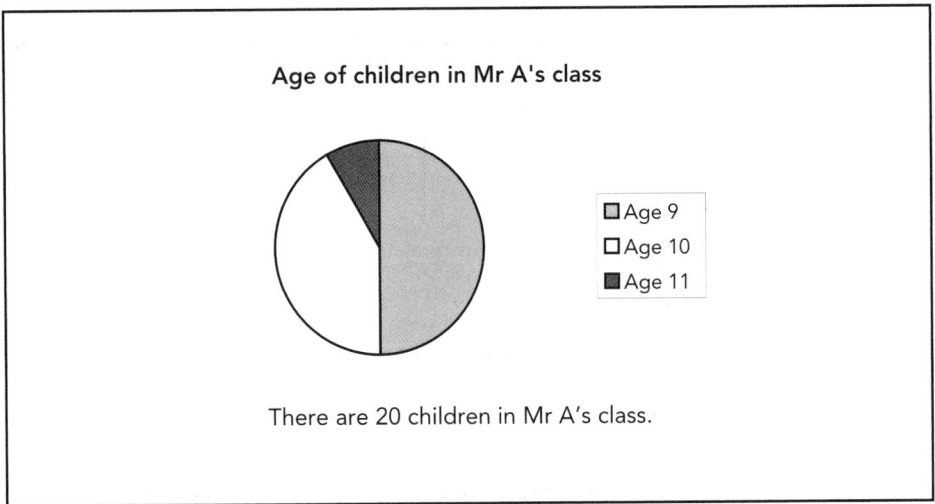

Age of children in Mr A's class

☐ Age 9
☐ Age 10
■ Age 11

There are 20 children in Mr A's class.

Comparing information in pie charts

The need to interpret and compare pie charts may well arise whilst using spreadsheets and databases.

The important question to consider is 'What does the whole chart represent?'

Consider the pie charts showing the age of children in Mr A's class and in Miss B's class.

Age of children in Miss B's class

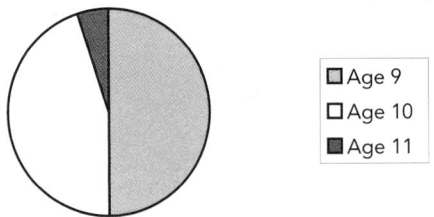

☐ Age 9
☐ Age 10
■ Age 11

There are 24 children in Miss B's class

Which of these statements is true?

There are the same number of 9-year-olds in Mr A's class and Miss B's class.

There is the same proportion of 9-year-olds in Mr A's class and Miss B's class.

The pie charts show that half the children in each class are aged 9.

There are 20 children in Mr A's class and so 10 of the children are aged 9.

There are 24 children in Miss B's class and so 12 of the children are aged 9.

There is the same proportion of 9-year-olds in each class.

Carroll diagrams

Carroll diagrams are named after Lewis Carroll who taught mathematics at Cambridge University and was the author of *Alice in Wonderland*.

A **Carroll diagram** is a way of sorting data with *two* attributes.

Example 1

Consider the set of numbers 1 to 10:

some are even, others aren't.

some are prime numbers (i.e. have just 2 factors: 1 and themselves), others aren't.

A Carroll diagram is a two-way table that allows you to sort the numbers using both criteria at once.

	Even	Not even
Prime	2	3, 5, 7
Not prime	4, 6, 8, 10	1, 9

This shows that there is just one even prime number.

Example 2

Consider a set of plane shapes:

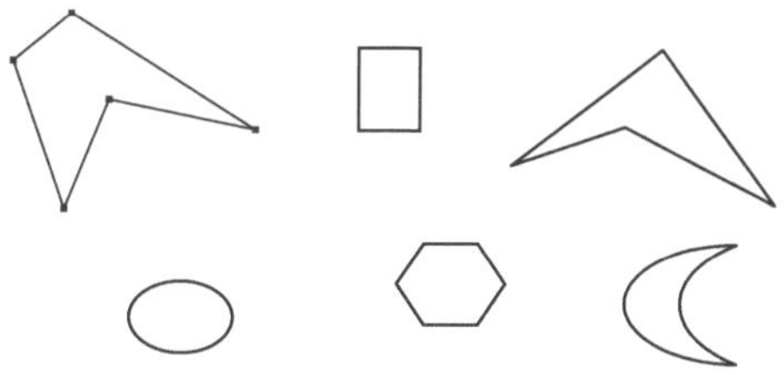

some shapes tessellate

some shapes have reflective symmetry

Sort the shapes into the correct section of the Carroll diagram.

	Shapes that tessellate	Shapes that do not tessellate
Shapes with reflective symmetry	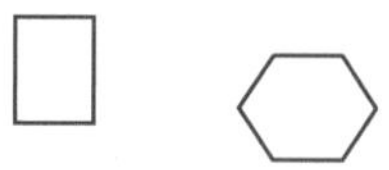	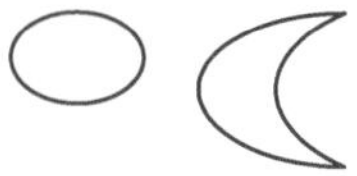
Shapes with no reflective symmetry	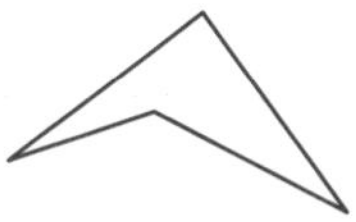	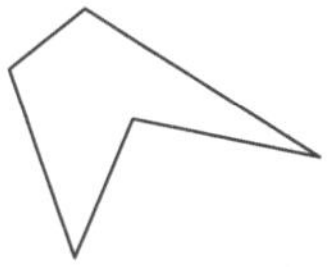

Note: See tessellation of an arrowhead in the Shape, space and measures chapter.

Venn diagrams

A **Venn diagram** is another way of displaying data with more than one attribute.

Example 1

Data with two attributes

Consider the set of numbers 1 to 10:

some are even, others aren't.

some are prime numbers (i.e. have just 2 factors: 1 and themselves), others aren't.

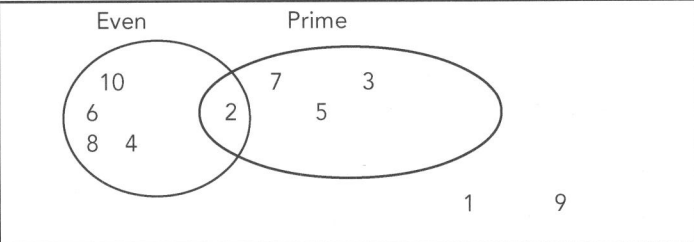

Set of numbers from 1 to 10

From this diagram it is easy to see which number/numbers are both even and prime (2) and those which are neither (1 and 9).

Compare this representation with the Carroll diagram above (Example 1).

Example 2

Data with more than two attributes

Consider a class of children who have different pets.

Group them into three categories: those who have a dog, those who have a cat, those who have another pet.

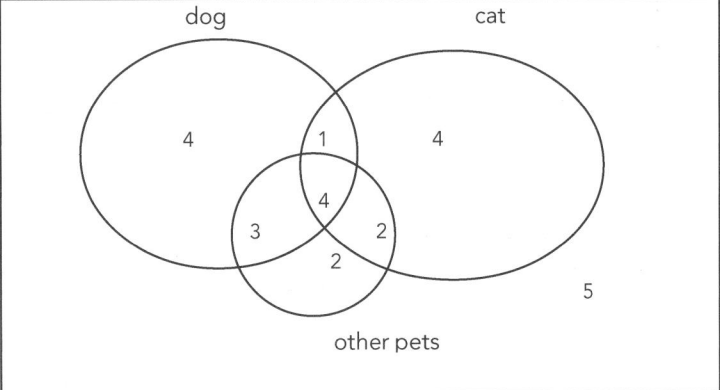

Type of pets

Now it is easy to see that one child has just a dog and a cat, and five children have no pets at all.

Binary trees

A binary tree is used to sort a set of objects (including numbers) into discrete categories.

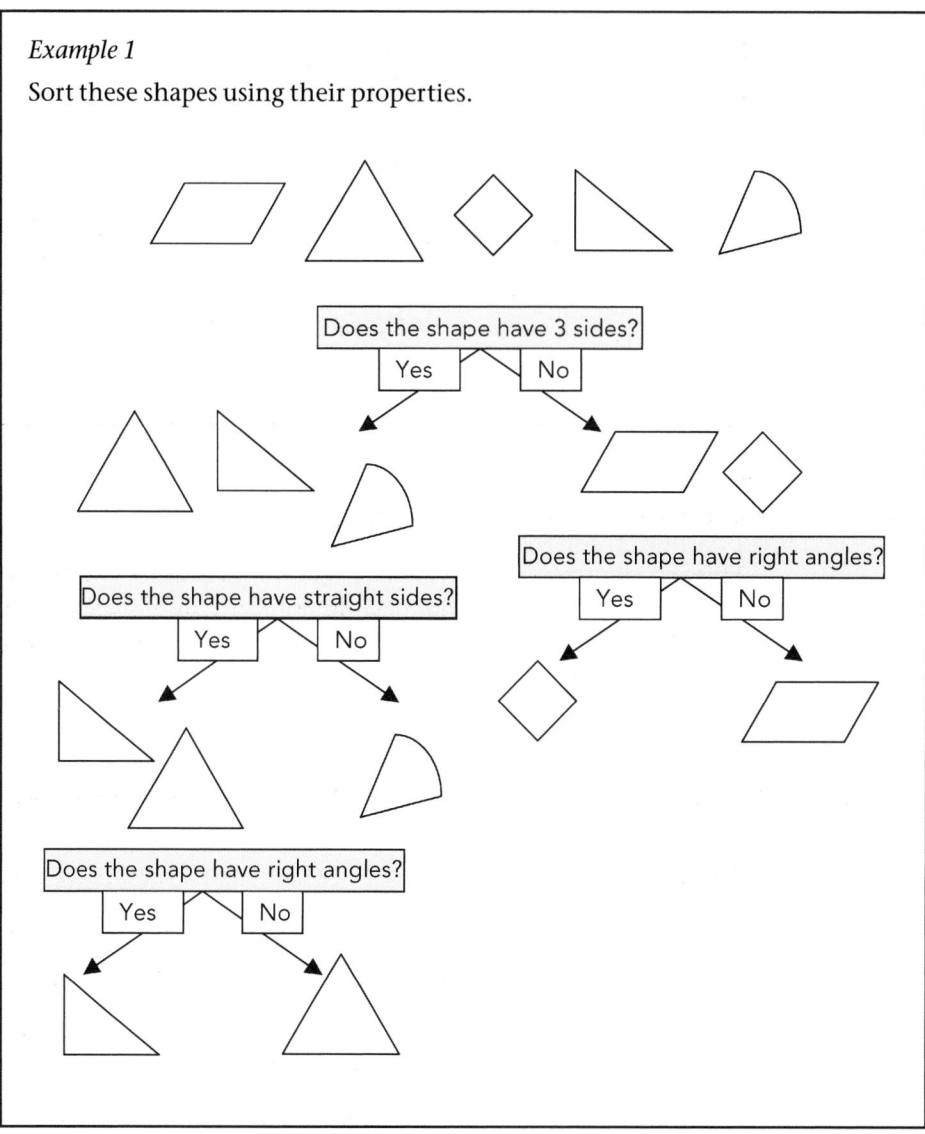

Example 1

Sort these shapes using their properties.

Example 2

Sort the whole numbers 1 to 4 using their properties.

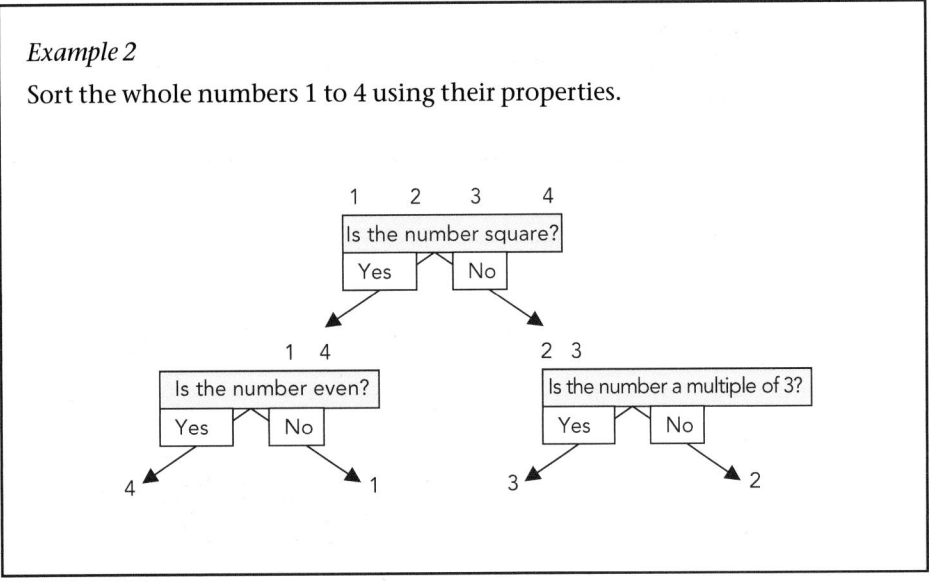

FURTHER STATISTICAL IDEAS

This section goes beyond what is needed to teach at Key Stage 2. It should help you to see how statistics develops beyond primary mathematics, assist you in knowing techniques for the QTS skills tests and also be helpful when working with computer databases, spreadsheets or larger sets of data.

ESTIMATING THE MEAN, MEDIAN AND RANGE FOR GROUPED DATA

The heights (to the nearest cm) of 30 children in a Y5 class are as follows:

158 137 147 153 152 150 149 153 170 168 144 146 146 164 156

163 168 158 139 143 130 167 176 163 147 157 153 144 135 150

You may want to calculate the mean, median and range (you should find they are 152.9 cm, 152.5 cm and 46 cm, respectively).

One way of analysing continuous data is to group the data. It is very important to define the limits of the group precisely. The groups are formally known as **class intervals**.

Normally you want at least five groups (or class intervals) but not too many more.

The frequencies can be found by completing a tally.

Each item is entered on the tally as you work through the list of data. This tally gives the frequency for each class.

Height of children	Tally	Frequency
130 cm up to but not including 140 cm ($130 \leq h < 140$)	IIII	4
140 cm up to but not including 150 cm ($140 \leq h < 150$)	HHT III	8
150 cm up to but not including 160 cm ($150 \leq h < 160$)	HHT HHT	10
160 cm up to but not including 170 cm ($160 \leq h < 170$)	HHT I	6
170 cm up to but not including 180 cm ($170 \leq h < 180$)	II	2

Once data is grouped only an estimated average is possible.

To estimate the mean you need to identify a representative value for each group; the convention is to use the midpoint of the class interval. The reason for this is that once you group the data you lose the detail of the data and so the safest assumption is that the data are evenly spread across the class. In practice this may not be the case, but if you are presented with grouped data it is the best approximation you can make.

Height of children	Representative value (cm)	Frequency
$130 \leq h < 140$	135	4
$140 \leq h < 150$	145	8
$150 \leq h < 160$	155	10
$160 \leq h < 170$	165	6
$180 \leq h < 190$	175	2

To estimate the mean we assume that we have 4 children whose average height is 135 cm, 8 children whose average height is 145 cm etc.

$$\text{The estimated mean} = \frac{4 \times 135 + 8 \times 145 + 10 \times 155 + 6 \times 165 + 2 \times 175}{4 + 8 + 10 + 6 + 2} = \frac{4590}{30} = 153 \text{ cm}$$

The estimated median is found by locating the value that cuts the data in half exactly. The median for grouped data is estimated by finding 50% of the way through the data. The easiest way to see this is on a **cumulative frequency graph**. The cumulative frequency is found by adding up all the frequencies below a given value as in this table:

Height of children	End of class interval (cm)	Frequency	Cumulative frequency
	130		0
$130 \leq h < 140$	140	4	4
$140 \leq h < 150$	150	8	12
$150 \leq h < 160$	160	10	22
$160 \leq h < 170$	170	6	28
$170 \leq h < 180$	180	2	30

12 = 8 + 4 gives number of children with height less than 150 cm

To estimate the median plot the graph and read off exactly half-way up the cumulative frequency axis, in this case at 15, across to the graph and then down to the height axis. Read off from this axis an estimate for the median. In this case the estimated median is 153 cm.

Cumulative frequency diagram for heights of children in class

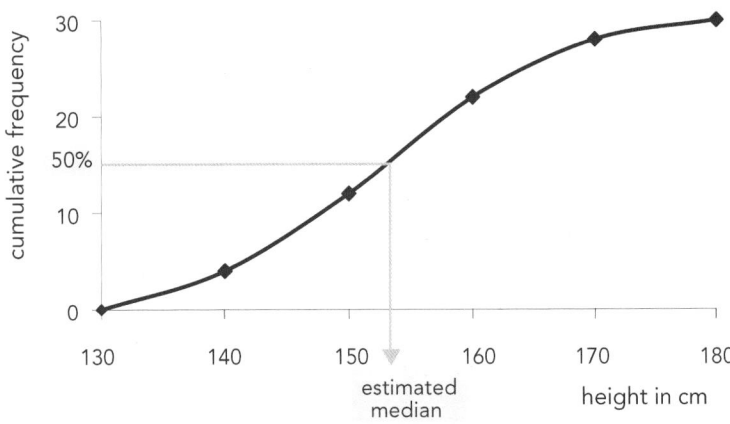

In this example the estimated value for the median of 153 cm and the true value of 152.5 cm (calculated from the original data before it was grouped) are similar because the data are fairly evenly distributed.

To estimate the range for the grouped data you have to use the extreme values of the lowest and highest class interval, i.e. 130 cm to 180 cm, which gives an estimated range of 50 cm.

Bar charts and histograms

Examples of bar charts and histograms in textbooks are not always consistent. The problem has been made worse by the use of spreadsheet packages which do not always give the option of choosing how scales are presented and whether bars touch. This table describes the most important distinctions between bar charts and histograms.

Bar chart for ways of travelling to school

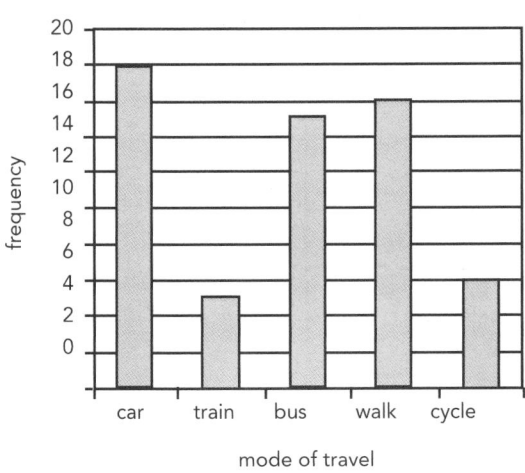

Bar chart

- Bars are of same width
- Bars do not touch
- On the horizontal axis each category is labelled
- The vertical axis shows frequency
- Used for qualitative or discrete data

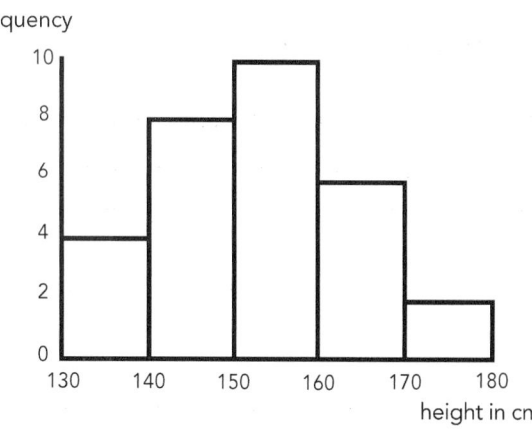

Histogram with equal class intervals

- Bars are of same width
- Bars touch
- Horizontal axis is marked 'like a ruler'
- The vertical axis shows frequency
- Used for continuous data

Note: A histogram is also used for grouped discrete data. Once you group the data you are considering not discrete values but all the values within a range of values, e.g. shoe sizes 4 and less than 6, 6 and less than 8 etc.

Histogram with unequal class intervals

You may need to interpret a histogram where the class intervals are of different sizes. In that case you need to look at the area of the bars and not just their height.

Example

Waiting time for buses (min)	Frequency
0 and less than 10	5
10 and less than 20	4
20 and less than 30	2
30 and less than 50	2

This information on the length of time waiting for a bus is in unequal class intervals.

To give an accurate impression that the wait time was between 30 and 50 minutes for only 2 buses the area of the bars represents the number of buses.

- Widths of bars depend on class interval
- Bars touch
- Horizontal axis is marked 'like a ruler'
- It is the area not the height which shows frequency so the vertical axis is marked 'Frequency density'
- Used for continuous data and grouped discrete data

Frequency = frequency density × class width

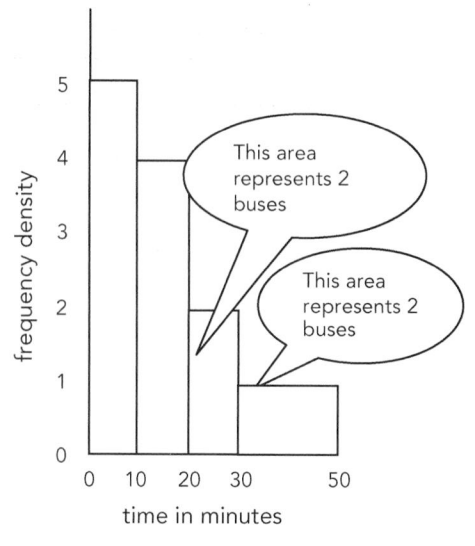

OTHER MEASURES OF SPREAD – INTERQUARTILE RANGE

So far just one measure of the spread of a set of data has been considered, the range.

Just as extreme values can distort the mean they can also distort the range.

Example

Company A: The mean salary is £20 000. The lowest salary is £7000 and the highest £55 000.

Range of salaries = £48 000

However if you exclude the highest salary, that of the proprietor, the range is just £18 000.

More sophisticated measures of spread are not affected by extreme values to the same extent.

The measure of spread associated with the median is called the **interquartile range**.

The interquartile range is based on dividing the ordered data into quarters. The median splits the ordered data into two halves. The median is not included in either half of the data. The median for each half of the data is found and these are called the **lower** and **upper quartiles** respectively:

ordered data

lower half of ordered data	median	upper half of ordered data

	lower quartile		median		upper quartile	

The interquartile range is the difference between the lower and upper quartiles.

Example

Salary details for company A:

Proprietor	£55 000
Production manager	£25 000
Craftsperson 1	£15 000
Craftsperson 2	£12 000
Craftsperson 3	£11 000
Administrator	£14 000
Trainee	£8 000

The mean salary is £20 000 (£140 000 divided by 7).

The median salary is £14 000 (from ordered data).

The ordered data: £8000, £11 000, £12 000, *£14 000*, £15 000, £25 000, £55 000

The lower quartile is the median of £8000, £11 000 and £12 000

      i.e. £11 000

The upper quartile is the median of £15 000, £25 000 and £55 000

      i.e. £25 000

So the interquartile range is £25 000 – £11 500 = £13 500.

For grouped data the quartiles can be estimated using a cumulative frequency diagram in a similar way to the median.

Box and whisker plots

These are used to summarise a set of data and compare sets of data.

A box and whisker plot is a diagrammatic representation of the five key values for numeric data:

- the minimum
- the lower quartile
- the median
- the upper quartile
- the maximum.

This means the diagram illustrates the range (maximum to minimum) and the interquartile range (upper quartile to lower quartile).

Drawing a box and whisker plot:

- must be to scale
- can be horizontal or vertical.

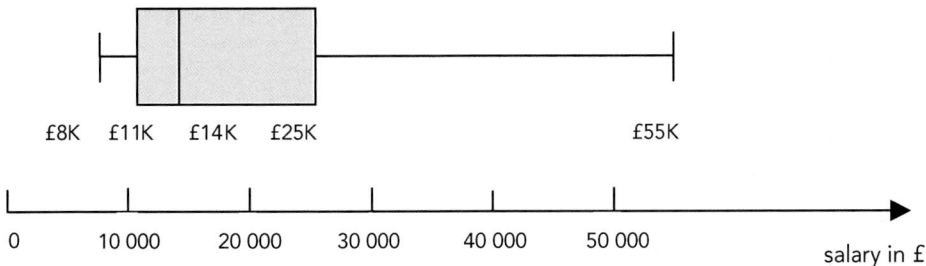

Box and whisker plot to show the distribution of salaries for company A

Points to remember:

- the box is drawn to illustrate the range of data values taken by the central half of the data (i.e. the interquartile range).
- the median is the line drawn across the box which makes it possible to see how the central half of the data is distributed about the median.
- the whiskers are the lines extending beyond the box to the minimum and maximum values (they should not be drawn through the box).
- the scale is included.
- the five key values are marked on the diagram.

Scatter diagrams (or scatterplots)

Are longer babies heavier?
Do children who do well in English do well in mathematics?
Do countries with a low gross national product (GNP) have a higher rate of infant mortality?
Is the rate of heart disease related to the consumption of cigarettes?
Do countries that cover large areas have larger populations?
Do people consume more alcohol in countries with higher rates of adult literacy?

Here you are looking for a relationship. This requires **paired-variable data** (i.e. two types of data per person or country).

A scatter diagram (or scatterplot) allows you to look for this relationship.

Each data pair is represented by a point on a grid.

Correlation This is the arrangement of points on the grid which gives an indication of the extent to which the variables are related. It is an indication of a mathematical trend in the data. It can be positive, negative or there might be no correlation.

Example 1

Do countries with a low gross national product (GNP) have a higher rate of infant mortality?

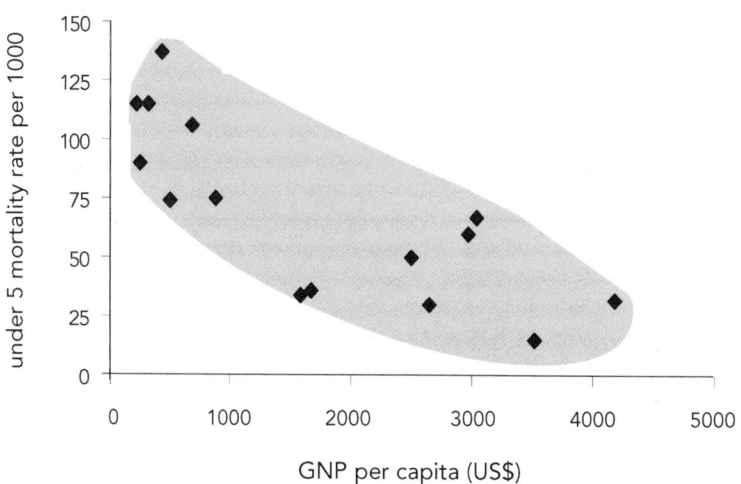

This scatterplot shows negative correlation because one variable decreases as the other increases. The shading on the diagram illustrates the trend in the data. Low values of GNP are associated with high under-5 mortality rates. High values of GNP are associated with low under-5 mortality rate.

Example 2

Do people consume more alcohol in countries with higher rates of adult literacy?

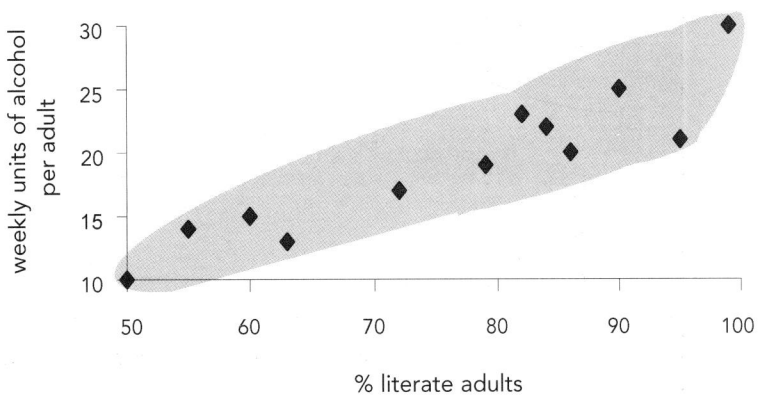

Alcohol consumption v. adult literacy

This scatterplot shows positive correlation because one variable increases as the other increases. The shading on the diagram illustrates the trend in the data. Higher adult literacy is associated with greater alcohol consumption.

Remember correlation is only an indication of a mathematical trend. It does not imply that one thing causes another.

For example, the positive correlation between levels of adult literacy and alcohol consumption does not imply that education leads to drinking! There are many factors that could be responsible for this, e.g. more affluent countries tend to have higher rates of both adult literacy and alcohol consumption.

Example 3

Do countries that cover large areas have larger populations?

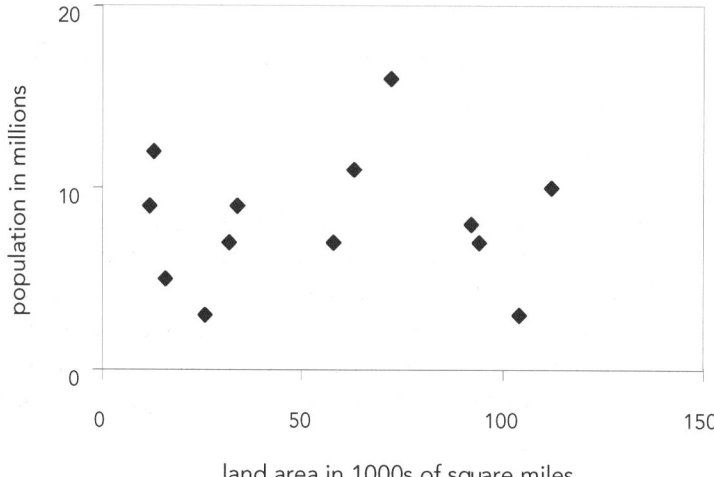

Population v. land area

This scatterplot shows no correlation because there is no obvious trend.

3.3 PROBABILITY

THEORETICAL PROBABILITY

Probability deals with how likely something is to happen.

Probability can be described qualitatively using words such as certain, likely, unlikely, possible.

In some cases it is possible to give a numerical value to a probability somewhere on a scale from 0 to 1, where 0 represents an impossible event and 1 an event which is certain. Probabilities can be written as fractions, decimals or percentages.

When you toss an unbiased coin you can get either a head or a tail. These events are equally likely.

We say that the probability of a head is $\frac{1}{2}$ and the probability of a tail is $\frac{1}{2}$ (or 0.5 or 50%).

You are certain to get either a head or a tail so the two probabilities sum to 1 ($\frac{1}{2} + \frac{1}{2} = 1$).

When you throw an unbiased dice there are six possible outcomes 1, 2, 3, 4, 5 or 6. These six events are all equally likely, so the probability of just one of them, such as throwing a three, is $\frac{1}{6}$.

These probabilities, decided by a logical examination of all the equally likely outcomes, are called **theoretical probabilities**.

EXPERIMENTAL PROBABILITY

How could you decide the probability that it will rain tomorrow?

A common misconception is that tomorrow it can either rain or not rain so the probability of rain is $\frac{1}{2}$.

You can see how wrong this is by imagining you are trying to decide the probability of rain when you are standing in the middle of the Sahara Desert. In an area where there is no rain for months on end it is clearly not true that the probability of rain is $\frac{1}{2}$. To make a sensible estimate of the probability of rain you would need to look at records of rainfall in a particular season and area of the Sahara. If it has rained on three days out of 200 for which records are kept, then an **experimental probability** of rain is $\frac{3}{200}$.

MUTUALLY EXCLUSIVE EVENTS

If you know the probability of an event happening, then it is easy to work out the probability of that event not happening. The two probabilities cover all the possible outcomes and they therefore must add up to 1.

> *Example*
> The probability of getting a score of six on a dice is $\frac{1}{6}$, and the probability of not getting a six is $1 - \frac{1}{6} = \frac{5}{6}$.

We say events that cannot occur together and whose probabilities add up to one are **mutually exclusive** events. Some examples of mutually exclusive events are:

- throwing an even number on a dice and throwing an odd number
- raining tomorrow and not raining tomorrow.

INDEPENDENT EVENTS

If I toss a coin and it comes up heads ten times in a row, is it more or less likely to come up heads on the eleventh throw?

Many people will argue strongly that after a string of heads the probability of a head on the next throw is not $\frac{1}{2}$. Some people will argue that it is more likely to come up heads because of the trend (sometimes called positive recency), others will argue that a tail is more likely as change must come soon (sometimes called negative recency). The belief that what has happened in the past does affect the outcome of purely random processes (e.g. throwing dice, tossing coins, drawing cards etc.) is known as the gambler's fallacy.

Each time a coin is tossed, or a dice is thrown the probabilities of the different possible outcomes are unchanged. Events like these are said to be **independent**. Whatever has happened in the past has no effect on the next experiment. It may help to imagine someone outside the room who has no knowledge of how the coin has fallen. They will argue logically that heads and tails are equally likely so the probability of a head next time is still a half.

DEPENDENT EVENTS

Sometimes the result of one experiment will affect the result of the next experiment. In this case the two events are not independent.

Example

If you have a bag containing 4 green and 2 red sweets, the probability of taking a red sweet is $\frac{2}{6} = \frac{1}{3}$.

If you eat this red sweet and take another, will the probability that the sweet is red still be $\frac{1}{3}$?

There are now 4 green and 1 red sweets in the bag so the probability of a red sweet is only $\frac{1}{5}$. The event of taking a sweet and eating it has influenced the next event of taking and eating a sweet. The probability of the second event is **dependent** on the outcome of the first event.

COMBINING EVENTS

Throwing two dice

It is rare that we are concerned with just single events. In many board games two dice are thrown to give a combined score. So what events can happen in this situation and what are the probabilities?

The easiest way to see what can happen is to draw up what is known as a **possibility space**. This is a two-way diagram which shows all the different possibilities. This table shows the score on the first die added to the score on the second die giving 36 possible outcomes although several totals are repeated.

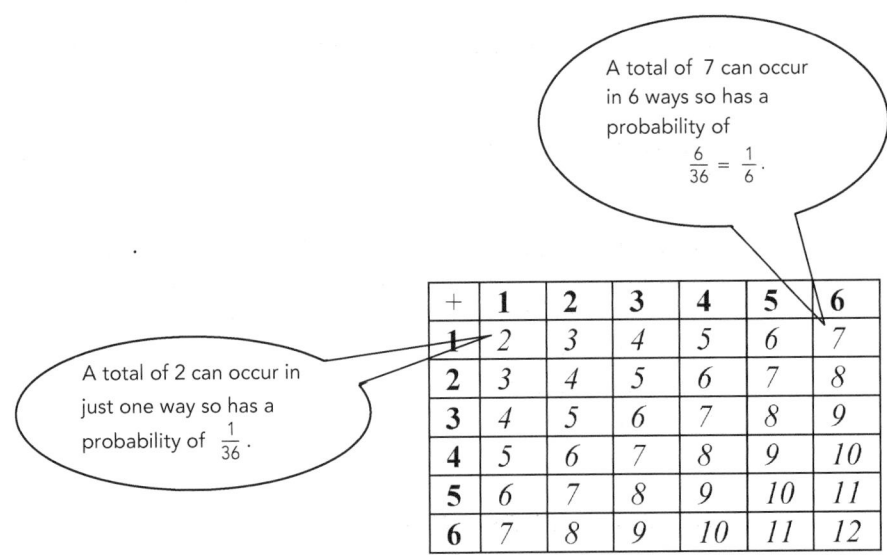

Tossing two coins

Two coins were tossed 100 times and the results recorded for two heads, two tails and one of each. The results are shown in the bar chart.

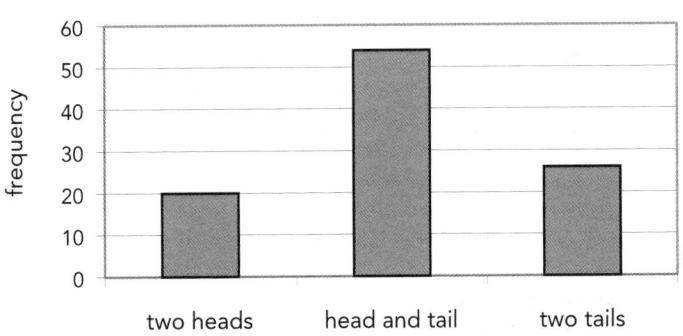

The results for two heads and for two tails are roughly similar as you would expect for a fairly large number of throws.

But why should there be so many more cases of a head and a tail?

The following possibility space shows all the possible outcomes when two coins are thrown:

		Second coin	
		H	**T**
First coin	**H**	*HH*	*HT*
	T	*TH*	*TT*

The category one head and one tail blurs the fact that there are two ways of getting a head and a tail, either a head on the first coin and a tail on the second or a tail on the first coin and a head on the second. So although there is a probability of $\frac{1}{4}$ that two heads will be obtained there is a probability of $\frac{2}{4}=\frac{1}{2}$ that one head and one tail will be obtained.

TREE DIAGRAMS

A tree diagram is constructed by drawing a branch for each possible event. They can be used when many events are combined. Consider a family with three children. What is the probability that all the children will be of the same sex? We will assume that the probability of a girl is $\frac{1}{2}$ and the probability of a boy is $\frac{1}{2}$ although statistical information about births suggests that the probabilities are not exactly equal. The first child can be either a boy (B) or a girl (G) and then the branches of the tree show the various possible families.

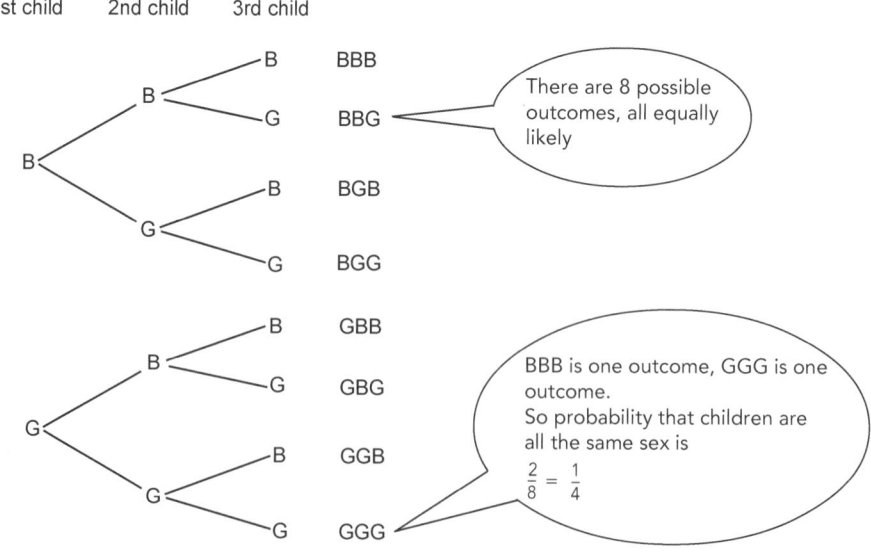

How sure can you be?

One of the most important things to understand about probabilities is that probability deals with what is likely to happen over a large number of trials. If I toss a coin once I do not know whether it will turn up head or tails. If I toss it a thousand times I know that it is likely to turn up heads about 500 times. I still can't know what will happen for any particular thousand throws. Extreme and unusual events can occur. The line graph below shows how the proportion of heads might vary over time for just 100 throws.

Proportion of heads when tossing a coin 100 times

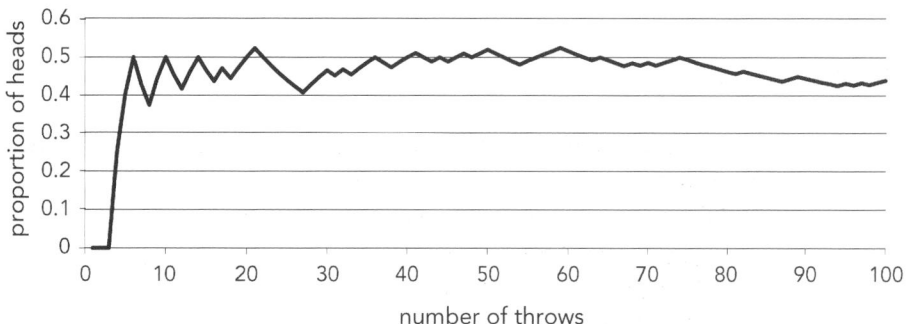

3.4 IMPLICATIONS FOR TEACHING HANDLING DATA

By deepening your level of mathematical knowledge you can teach for understanding and respond confidently to children's questions. Some issues considered in this section which could be helpful when you are planning your teaching are starting with a question, designing a survey, emphasising the importance and the complexities of collecting the data, and the language of probability.

Young children in school can begin to employ techniques of the data handling process, in order to make sense of situations. This begins with sorting, organising and classifying data. At this stage children seem to be fascinated by rearranging their personal collections of cards and toys, according to their own questions and criteria. Techniques for representing the data may range from ordering, comparing and making physical arrangements of objects, to beginning to draw up lists, tally charts and simple graphical representations. The ability to discuss and explain results is very relevant at this stage. Adults, who work or live with children, are constantly aware of the changing nature of these collections and the development of the latest craze. Manufacturers exploit this childhood enthusiasm by developing collectable sets of toys, action figures, spinning or moving toys.

Classically, the data handling cycle begins with a question or an idea for an investigation. Teachers may embark on a data handling project in the hope of producing an eye catching display or of using specific software packages. In such instances the original question or investigation can assume less importance than the mode of representation. Some familiar examples are over used and the resulting conclusions may not capture the imagination of the children. How relevant, for example, is it for young children to know the distribution of eye colour, or favourite crisp flavour of children in the class? When the context seems irrelevant to children, most of the initial questions, the organisation of data collection and interpretion of questions tend to come from the teacher. The resulting findings may appear to have little impact on children's lives. The most fruitful lines of enquiry for children are those to which they want an answer themselves. In school, issues such as, fair distribution of playground equipment or equal access to popular food at lunchtime offer more potential interest and consequently ensure that children will become engaged with the data. Surveying and voting techniques of data collection can stress the value of making collaborative decisions. Analysis and interpretation of such data emphasises the importance of reaching a consensus.

The topic 'Ourselves' occupies a perennial position in many school curricula. The following example illustrates how one extended investigation, within the ourselves topic, developed from a simple chance occurrence.

In a Year 3 class one day a child lost a tooth, generating a lively discussion in general about the children's teeth. Children demonstrated their acute awareness of the number of teeth they had lost to date. The teacher, realising the potential in this investigation, made links with the study of teeth and bones in science and arranged a simple data collection activity. Children soon realised that they faced a dilemma in entering data on the chart because many of them had already started to grow replacement teeth in the original position. The original question of 'How many teeth have you lost?' needed refining and developing in order to include this new aspect of the data. Data collection related to the dental status of tooth loss and growth then carried on over a prolonged period. From this wealth of primary data, further questions arose during the course of the investigation including:

Is there a difference between the number of teeth lost by boys and girls?

Have the oldest children in the class lost the most teeth?

This last question led some of the children to begin to look for relationships involving correlation between age and number of lost teeth. From this analysis, children were able to interpret and conclude that most children would begin to lose teeth between their seventh and eighth birthdays. The children waited confidently for the youngest child in the class to lose his first tooth. He came to school one day towards the end of the summer term just before his eighth birthday brandishing his first lost tooth like a trophy, much to the delight of the class, who had used their knowledge and understanding of the data handling process and applied it to make this prediction!

One day in the same class a child came in with her arm in plaster . . .

Opportunities for the teaching and learning of data handling are often presented in other areas of the curriculum. It is important to maximise these opportunities for meaningful investigations and problem solving by integrating data handling techniques, e.g.

A Year 4 class were studying the local environment in geography and giving consideration to the current issue of whether the high street should be closed to traffic.

In a variation on the familiar traffic survey, study groups of children adopted the character of users of the high street, e.g. the delivery truck drivers, the local resident, the local worker, the shopkeeper. They then devised questionnaires from their own point of view and went out into the high street to interview passers-by and to collect opinions on the current local issue.

Opportunities to design, collect and then use such questionnaires gave the children an insight into the practical realities of eliminating bias from data collection and of predicting categories of likely responses. This is a much more refined level of data collection than that of completing a survey chart which has already been designed by the teacher.

When children working in a relevant context are given the opportunity to pose their own questions and develop their own modes of representation, meaningful analysis, interpretation and prediction can ensue.

PROBABILITY

Children's misconceptions and hazy notions of probability are often apparent in their vocabulary and use of language. Initially, children's ability to predict can seem very inflexible and they may want to know with certainty, whether or not an event will occur. So when young children hear adults using the language of probability in social context, e.g. 'Take a coat. It *might* rain', or 'We will *probably* go to France for our holiday this year', 'It is *unlikely* that we will have time to go to the cinema': they are likely to respond by asking for affirmation, e.g. 'Will it rain?' or 'But will we go?'

In school, learning about probability is as much about developing an understanding of the subtle nuances of the mathematical vocabulary as it is about understanding the outcome of events.

A typical context in which young children begin to develop the notion of probability is in playing games. Children may need a lot of persuading that there is an equal chance of rolling any number on a die. Remarks such as 'If I am lucky I will get a six' or 'I will roll a six soon' indicate that notions of fairness are more likely to be linked to the general desirability of an outcome rather than any mathematical consideration. Children may claim, 'it is not fair' that their friend won a game rather than themselves.

Playing games provides a meaningful context in which to develop and refine an understanding of this vocabulary, especially those with an element of the unpredictable such as snakes and ladders in which fortunes can change on the rung of a ladder or fang of a snake!

3.5 SELF-ASSESSMENT QUESTIONS   Handling data

PROCESSING, REPRESENTING AND MAKING SENSE OF DATA

1. For which of the following sets of data would it not be appropriate to calculate a mean?
   a) Daily maximum temperatures for a month
   b) Examination grades for a school
   c) Heights of children in a class
   d) National Curriculum levels for a school at the end of a key stage
   e) Examination grades for a school
   f) Colours of cars passing the school gate in a 30-minute interval
   g) Times for 30 children to swim 10 lengths of a pool

2. It is easy to produce graphs with little meaning. What, if anything, is wrong with the following representations of data?

a)

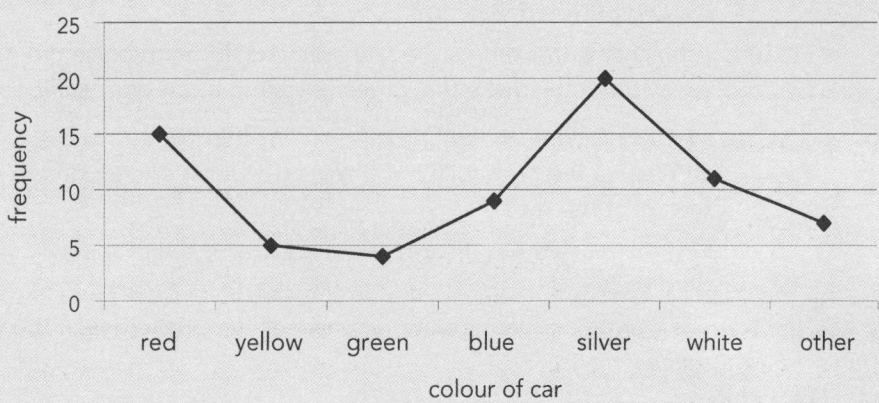

Colours of cars passing the school gate

b)

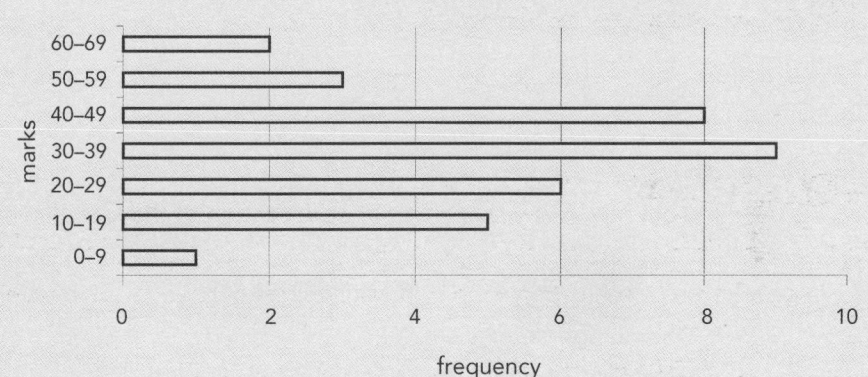

Test results for class 6B

c)

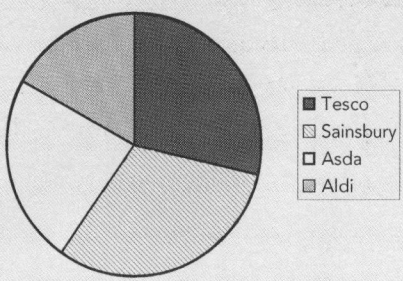

The price of baked beans

PROBABILITY

3. Determine the probabilities in the following situations:

   a) The probability of buttered toast landing buttered side down is determined by experiment to be 0.6. What is the probability of the toast landing buttered side up?

   b) A teacher is throwing a die and asking children to place the digits in such a way that they make the largest possible three-digit number.

   i) What is the probability of throwing three sixes?

   ii) What is the probability of throwing at least one six during the three throws of the die?

   iii) If the teacher has thrown two sixes what is the probability of throwing a third six?

   c) The Carroll diagram below summarises the properties of the following shapes:

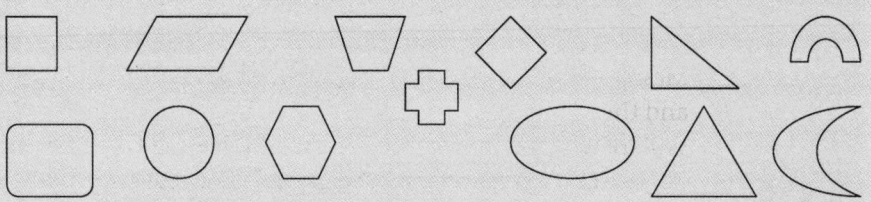

   Find out how many shapes go in each section of the Carroll diagram.

	Straight sides only	Not straight sides only
Some right angles		
No right angles		

   What is the probability that one of the shapes has no right angles and not straight sides only?

4 Shape, space and measures

Shape, space and measures is the phrase in use in our schools to identify ideas more widely known as geometry. The term comes from two Ancient Greek words meaning 'earth' and 'measure' and this gives us the clue to some of the origins of this branch of mathematics. The ideas themselves, however, pre-date even the Ancient Greeks.

There is material from ancient civilisations which records evidence of people's knowledge and use of such ideas. Perhaps the oldest of these civilisations was that of Mesopotamia (present-day Iraq) which was centred on the river valleys of the Tigris and the Euphrates. Development here began before 3500 BC. People developed the skills of writing and recorded onto clay tablets. It is in the translation of these tablets that we find evidence of mathematical knowledge and its use. Many of these tablets are dated to around 1700 BC when Babylon was the dominant city in Mesopotamia and so the mathematics is often referred to as 'Babylonian'.

The Egyptians studied and made practical use of mathematical ideas as shown by the Rhind Mathematical Papyrus and the Moscow Mathematical Papyrus, both of which were created in approximately 1850 BC. Aspects of Egyptian society were driven by reliance on the River Nile and the deposits of rich soil left behind after annual flooding. Tax was levied according to the area of land worked by individuals, hence the need to be able to measure accurately. This is an excellent example of the need for mathematics and its application in a real and practical situation. Also well known are the amazing achievements of the Egyptians in their building, of which the pyramids are the most striking example. Once again the application of mathematical ideas was vital to these achievements; right angles were created and heights established in order to generate the form and shape of these impressive structures. A knotted rope with equal spacing, in the arrangement of a 3, 4, 5 triangle, was used to create a right angle (an idea later formalised as 'Pythagoras' Theorem'). The Egyptians also knew about the relationship between the circumference and diameter of a circle and were able to establish approximate values for its area: their standard approximation was eight-ninths of the area of the surrounding square, as illustrated below.

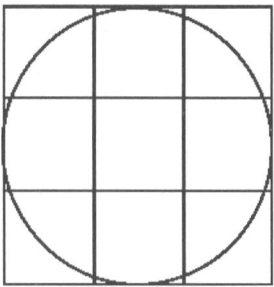

The Ancient Greeks, however, are probably the people most closely associated with the development of mathematics in general and of geometry in particular. Indeed it has been argued by many that it was the Greeks who changed the nature of the approach taken to mathematics. The accident of their geographical position and their creation of empire saw these people being exposed to the cultural and social backgrounds of many different societies. This exposure, allied to the emergence of an elite or leisured class within their own society, prompted the Greeks to question. Crucially, they 'began to ask and to try to answer, "why?" ' (Katz 1998). They moved beyond the application of mathematics, used merely to solve practical problems. The Greeks actively sought proof that ideas were correct and the leisured elite had the motivation and opportunity to pursue that proof. Katz argues that it is this idea of needing to prove which forms the basis of modern mathematics and, by extension, of our modern technological civilisation. This is indeed a major contribution to human development.

Thales (c.600 BC) is credited with beginning this development of geometry as an intellectual pursuit and the names of many who followed him are familiar to us. We have already referred to Pythagoras. The great philosopher Plato was very clear concerning the importance of geometry as an integral part of our thinking. The three-dimensional shapes made from only one type of regular polygon, bear his name (the five Platonic solids – can you identify them?). Archimedes has the semi-regular polyhedra named after him. Archimedean solids have wonderful names: try 'great rhombicosidodecahedron' (made from 30 squares, 20 regular hexagons and 12 regular decagons)! Euclid tackled the huge task of gathering together and adding to many of the ideas explored by his fellow mathematicians and philosophers. His great work, known as the *Elements*, is still regarded as a major contribution to our collection of mathematical knowledge and thought and as such formed the basis for the teaching of geometry in schools for over two hundred years. Thinkers such as those identified above, and many others like them, took geometry into areas such as astronomy, music and geography; their attempts to explain nature by rational argument 'became the model for virtually the whole of mathematics discourse up to the twentieth century' (Royal Society/JMC 2001).

The Greek period stretched from about 640 BC to AD250. Arab scholars, in North Africa, developed its achievements and it was they who transmitted these ideas, and those of Jewish and Christian scholars, to western Europe (Royal Society/JMC 2001). Such was the contribution of the Greeks, allied to the nature of European societies during the mediaeval period, that what was known became the focus for the sciences in general. The Middle Ages 'devoted itself to time-tested and authoritative works . . . the spirit of the times forced minds to follow trusted, prescribed and rigid ways' (Kline 1972). Hence important developments in geometry were few. Later, during the Renaissance, the trend towards realism in art fostered renewed interest in geometry. Brunelleschi's interest in mathematics, Vasari tells us (cited in Kline), 'led him to study perspective and . . . he undertook painting just to apply geometry'. Leonardo da Vinci (1452–1519) 'believed that painting must be an exact reproduction of reality and that mathematical perspective would permit this' and Kline identifies Albrecht Dürer (1471–1528) as the best mathematician of all the Renaissance artists.

Geometry has contributed to a wide variety of human experience. There are many examples, in early civilisations, of the use of simple geometric forms as ornament on pottery and in textiles. These same forms were used in architecture in many parts of the world and across centuries on monuments and buildings, including those with religious significance. The beauty of buildings themselves rests in part on their proportions. Extensive use has been made of what appears to be our instinctive appreciation of symmetry – a fine example is offered below.

University of Surrey Roehampton   Photographer: David Rose

Looking further to the Taj Mahal, in India, and the Nasrid Palace in the Alhambra in Spain, consider the beauty (as well as the religious significance) of the patterns used in Islamic art. Stunning examples of these are to be found, again in the Alhambra, in the Patio de los Leones and the Patio de los Arrayanes. The natural world too is filled with the beauty of geometric form from the structures of snowflakes to the leaf arrangements of plants to the elliptic paths of the planets.

We can pursue geometry across cultures, find it in human creativity and aesthetics, in the wonderful abstractions of the intellect and as part of the natural world. As an ancient and important branch of mathematics it has contributed much to our practical, intellectual and cultural development and it continues to do so today in a wide variety of disciplines. Importantly and unsurprisingly, it also continues to be a major area of research within mathematics itself.

Further reading

Katz, V.J. 1998 *A History of Mathematics: an introduction* Harlow: Addison-Wesley

Kline, M.1972 *Mathematics in Western Culture* Harmondsworth: Penguin

Royal Society/JMC 2001 *Teaching and Learning Geometry 11–19* London: Royal Society

4.2 PROPERTIES OF SHAPE

Much of the power of mathematics comes from making statements that are true for a whole set of objects such as all even numbers or all quadrilaterals. An important stage in the process is agreeing on useful ways of classifying types of shapes and types of numbers.

Consider the shapes below: these are **plane** shapes.

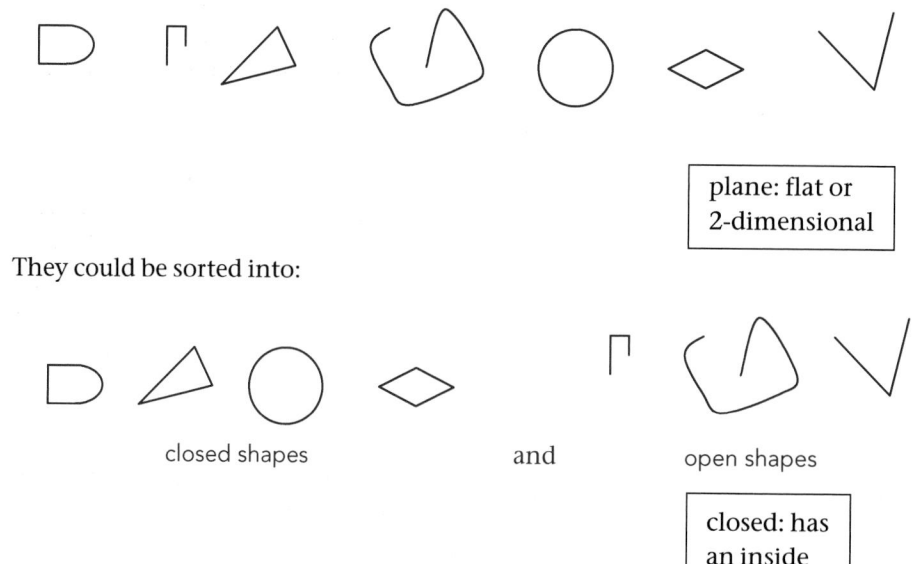

plane: flat or
2-dimensional

They could be sorted into:

closed shapes   and   open shapes

closed: has
an inside

They could also be sorted into:

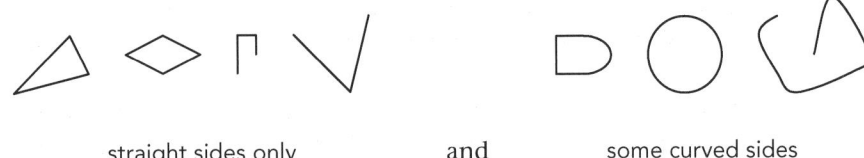

straight sides only   and   some curved sides

POLYGONS

The closed shapes that have only straight edges are known as **polygons**. 'Poly' means many and 'gons' means knees or angles. One way of classifying polygons is by the number of sides they have:

Sides	Name	Root (these roots are from Greek or Latin)
3	triangle	tri as in tricycle, tripod
4	quadrilateral	quad as in four children born together
5	pentagon	pent as in pentathlon
6	hexagon	hex German for 6 is sechs, English is six
7	heptagon	hept September rather confusingly used to be the seventh month of the year until the Roman Emperor Augustus inserted the months of July (for Julius) and August (named after himself)
8	octagon	oct as in octopus
9	nonagon	non as in November
10	decagon	dec as in decade or December
11	hendecagon	hendeca one and ten
12	dodecagon	dodeca two and ten

> polygon: a closed plane shape with straight sides

When there are more than twelve sides the polygon can be named informally, for example a polygon with 15 sides can be referred to as a 15-gon.

There are many ways of sorting polygons:

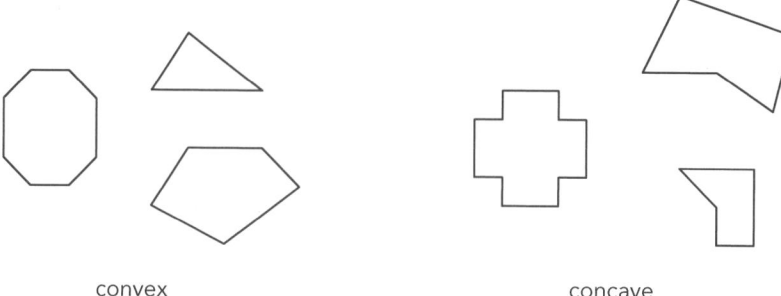

convex   concave

All the concave shapes have at least one of their interior angles greater than 180°.

Polygons with all interior angles less than 180° are convex.

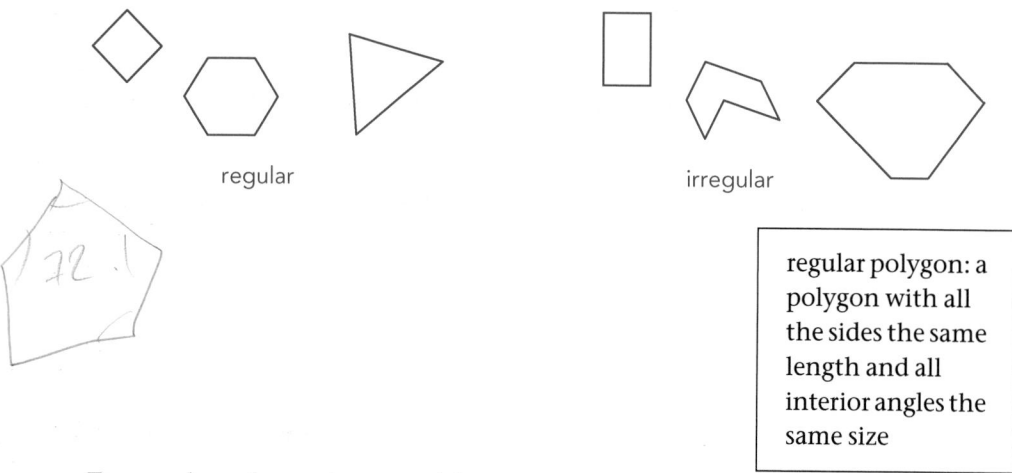

regular   irregular

> regular polygon: a
> polygon with all
> the sides the same
> length and all
> interior angles the
> same size

Two regular polygons have special names:

    a regular triangle has three equal sides and three equal angles, it is called an equilateral triangle

    a regular quadrilateral has four equal sides and four equal angles, it is called a square.

PROPERTIES

The properties of any geometric shape are those features which remain **invariant** for that shape. For example a triangle always has three sides and the sum of the interior angles is 180°. The lengths of the sides and the sizes of the interior angles can vary.

> invariant: always
> stays the same

TRIANGLES

Triangles, with just three sides, are the simplest polygons, they can be classified:

either by the size of the largest angle

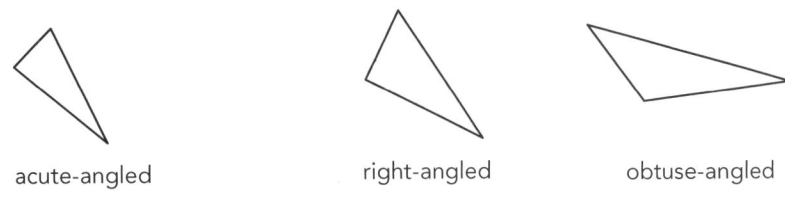

acute-angled   right-angled   obtuse-angled

or by the lengths of their side

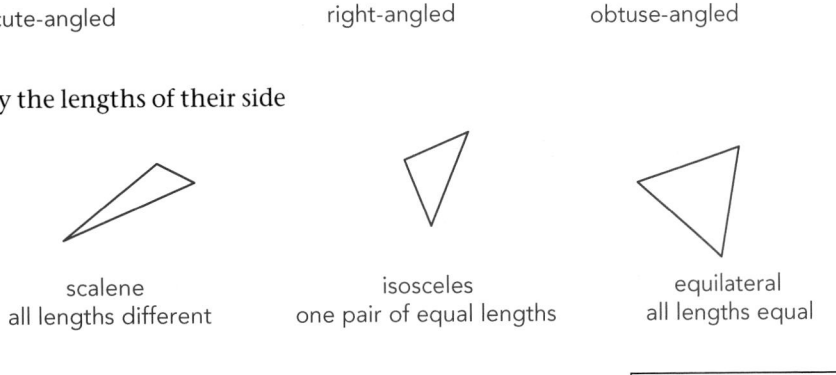

scalene
all lengths different   isosceles
one pair of equal lengths   equilateral
all lengths equal

An equilateral triangle is an example of a **regular** polygon.

> Naming triangles: you need a name for side lengths and a name for the largest angle

Two shapes which may differ in size but are otherwise identical are called **similar.**
E.g. all equilateral triangles are similar. All isosceles right-angled triangles are similar.

> similar: shapes may differ in size but are otherwise identical

QUADRILATERALS

There are a number of four-sided polygons which have special names.

A regular quadrilateral has four equal sides and four equal angles and is called a **square**.

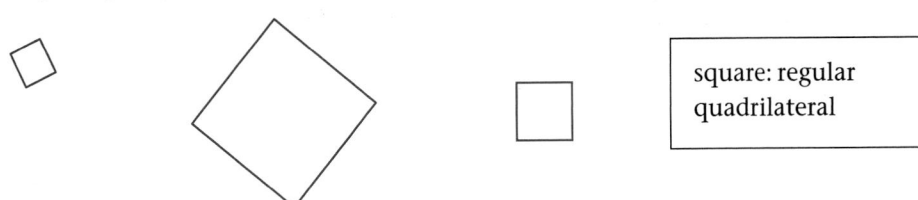

> square: regular quadrilateral

A quadrilateral with four equal sides is a **rhombus**. A square is a special rhombus.

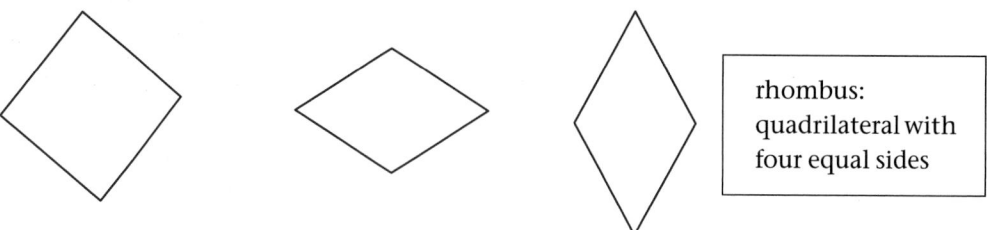

rhombus:
quadrilateral with
four equal sides

A quadrilateral with four right angles is a **rectangle**. The name, rectangle, means right angles.

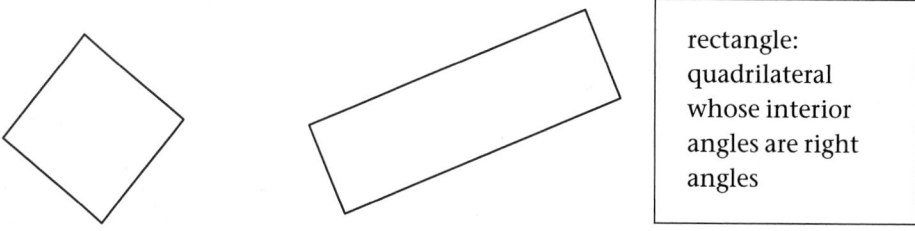

rectangle:
quadrilateral
whose interior
angles are right
angles

To distinguish squares from rectangles the word **oblong** can be used which means that the length of one pair of parallel sides exceeds the length of the other pair of parallel sides.

Note that a square is both a special rhombus and a special rectangle.

oblong: a
rectangle that
is not square

Rectangles and rhombuses also have opposite sides parallel and are special cases of quadrilaterals called **parallelograms**. Because there are two pairs of parallel sides, opposite sides are equal in length.

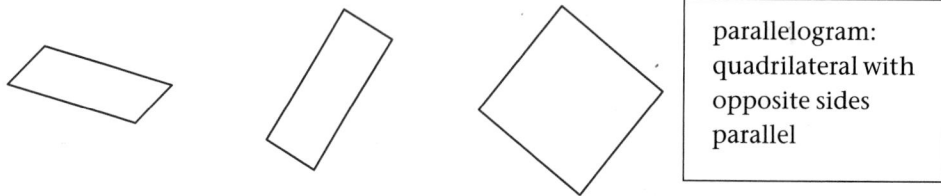

parallelogram:
quadrilateral with
opposite sides
parallel

A quadrilateral with one pair of parallel sides is a **trapezium**.

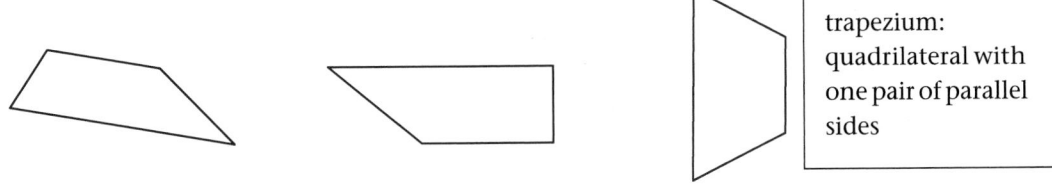

trapezium:
quadrilateral with
one pair of parallel
sides

A kite has two pairs of adjacent sides equal in length.

The diagonals of a kite meet at right angles.

A rhombus (and hence a square) is a special kite since all four sides are equal in length.

A concave kite is sometimes called an arrowhead.

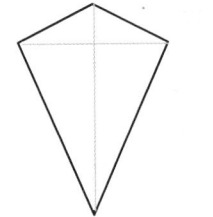
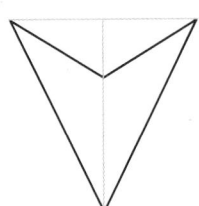
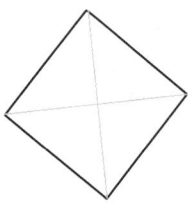

kite:
quadrilateral with
two pairs of
adjacent sides
equal in length

THREE-DIMENSIONAL SHAPES

We live in a three-dimensional (3-D) world so it is not surprising that children are often more familiar with 3-D shapes than they are with plane shapes. It is also not uncommon for children to use the names for plane shapes when describing 3-D objects (e.g. square instead of cube, and rectangle instead of cuboid).

3-D objects have faces, vertices and edges. We do not use the word side when describing 3-D shapes as it can be confusing. (We often use sides in 2-D when we mean the outer edge of a polygon; in 3-D the outside is made up of surfaces.) In mathematics a face is any surface of the 3-D object, an edge is where two faces meet, and a vertex (plural vertices) is a point where edges meet.

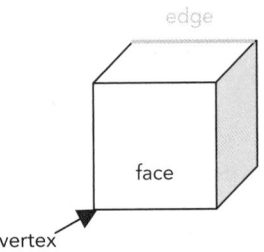

A solid with plane (or flat) faces only

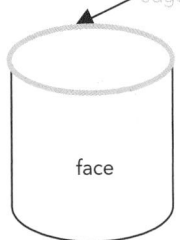

A solid with a curved face and two plane faces

Think about 3-D shapes you know. Can you think of a shape that has no edges or vertices?

A shape that has no vertices? How many edges does it have?

Can you think of a shape that has just one edge?

A **sphere** has just one curved face, with no edges or vertices.

If you cut through the centre of a sphere you will get a hemisphere – one flat face, one curved face and just one edge.

A **cylinder** has one curved face, two plane faces which are circles and two edges.

A **cone** has one vertex, one edge, a curved face and a flat face.

In general an edge is formed wherever two faces meet.

POLYHEDRA

Polyhedra are 3-D shapes that have flat or plane faces only; this means that the faces are polygons. Cubes and cuboids are everyday examples, as are prisms and pyramids. Cardboard shapes and materials like Polydron or Clixi are excellent for exploring polyhedra. The naming for polyhedra is similar to that for polygons. 'Poly' means many and 'hedron' means surface (or literally seat).

> polyhedron: a 3-D solid with polygons as faces
> polyhedra is the plural of polyhedron

Look at the vertex of a polyhedron. You will see that there must be at least three faces at a vertex of a polyhedron.

A **tetrahedron** has four triangles as faces and can also be called a triangle-based **pyramid**.

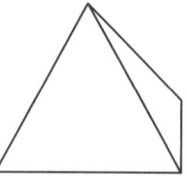

> pyramid: any polygon as the base with triangles from each edge of the polygon that meet at a point

Can you think of any solids with five faces?

You may be familiar with a square-based pyramid (with one square and four triangular faces) or a triangular (triangle-based) **prism** (with two identical triangular faces and three rectangular faces).

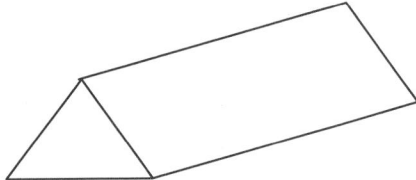

A rectangle-based prism is called a cuboid. When the faces are all squares we have a cube.

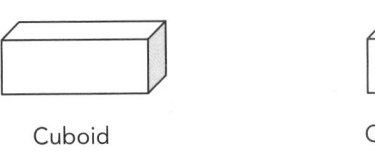

Cuboid   Cube

> prism: two identical polygons that are parallel with corresponding edges joined by rectangles

Regular polyhedra have one type of regular polygon as the face and the arrangement at each vertex is identical. By considering first triangular, then square then pentagonal faces etc. we will try to establish how many regular polyhedra exist.

How many regular polyhedra can you make with triangular faces?

You can't have just two triangles at a vertex so try three triangles.

Three equilateral triangles at each vertex gives a **tetrahedron**.

All the vertices are identical.

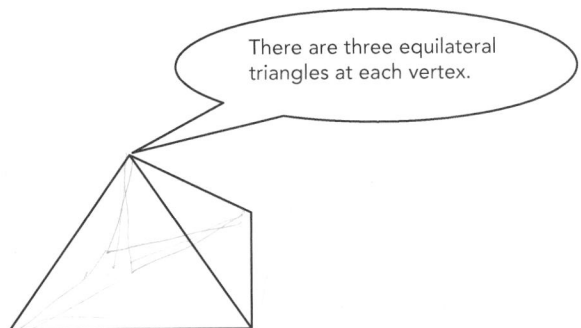

There are three equilateral triangles at each vertex.

> 1. A regular tetrahedron has four equilateral triangles as faces.

With six triangles you can make a **hexahedron** that looks like two tetrahedra (triangle-based pyramids) stuck together.

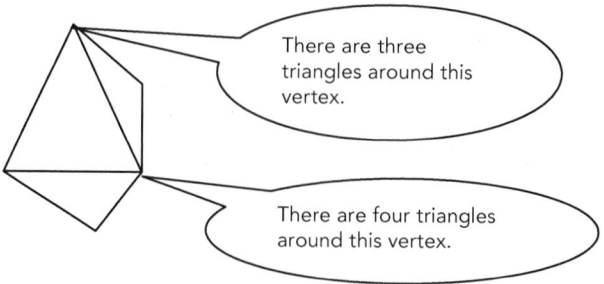

This is **not** a regular polyhedron, because the vertices are not identical.

What about four equilateral triangles at each vertex?

With eight equilateral triangles you form an **octahedron** that looks like two square-based pyramids stuck together. In this case there are four equilateral triangles around each vertex so the octahedron is regular.

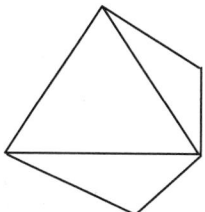

2. A regular octahedron has eight equilateral triangles as faces.

It is possible to make a shape with five triangles at every vertex using 20 equilateral triangles. The shape is called an **icosahedron**.

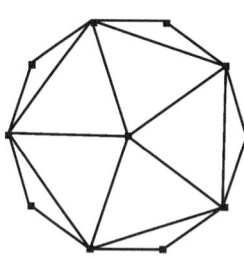

3. A regular icosahedron has 20 equilateral triangles as faces.

If we try using six equilateral triangles at a vertex we will not make a solid but a pattern that covers the plane called a regular tessellation.

How many regular polyhedra can you make with square faces?

To make a 3-D solid we must have at least three squares around each vertex. The **cube** is precisely such a shape.

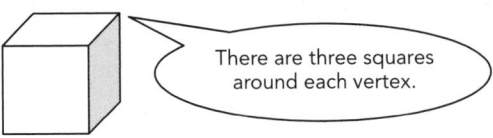

There are three squares around each vertex.

4. A cube is a regular polyhedron with six square faces.

With four squares around a vertex we end up with something that is flat, so there is only one regular polyhedron with squares as the faces.

How many regular polyhedra can you make with pentagonal faces?

We know that three pentagons around a point have an angle sum of less than 360° because the interior angle is 108°. The diagram below shows that it is impossible to tile the plane with regular pentagons.

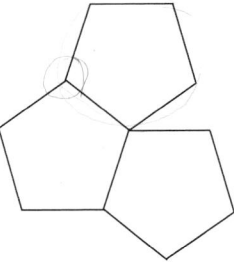

However with three pentagons at each vertex you can create a regular polyhedron. As you will need 12 pentagons to do this: the polyhedron is a regular **dodecahedron.**

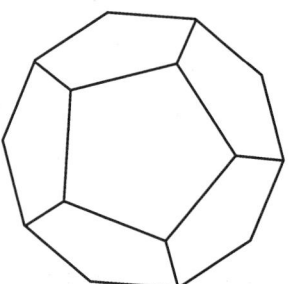

5. A regular dodecahedron has 12 regular pentagons as faces.

It is not possible to form a regular polyhedron with four pentagons around a point because the angle sum exceeds 360°, so there is just one regular polyhedron with pentagons as faces.

How many regular polyhedra can you make with hexagons as faces?

Regular hexagons form a regular tessellation with three hexagons around each vertex. There is no space to fold up to make a solid. It is impossible to make a regular polyhedron with hexagons.

The interior angles in regular polygons with more than six sides are greater than 120° so it will not be possible to make regular polyhedra using them as faces.

This means there are just five regular polyhedra, their properties summarised below. They are sometimes called the **Platonic solids**.

Polyhedron	Polygon used	Polygons at each vertex	Faces	Vertices	Edges
regular tetrahedron	equilateral triangle	3	4	4	6
regular octahedron	equilateral triangle	4	8	6	12
regular icosahedron	equilateral triangle	5	20	12	30
cube	square	3	6	8	12
regular dodecahedron	regular pentagon	3	12	20	30

Notice that the sum of the number of faces and the number of vertices is two more than the number of edges. This is always the case for polyhedra and is known as Euler's Rule.

Euler's rule:
The sum of the
number of faces
(F) and the number
of vertices (V) is
two more than
the number of
edges (E) for any
polyhedron.
$F + V = E + 2$

Semi-regular polyhedra use more than one type of regular polygon as faces and all the vertices must be identical. There are 13 semi-regular polyhedra sometimes called the Archimedean solids which include truncations of all the regular polyhedra (this is where the vertices are sliced off and replaced by an equilateral triangle), e.g. imagine a tetrahedron and remove the vertices by making a slice one-third of the way along each edge; you are left with a shape that is made of four regular hexagons and four equilateral triangles – a truncated tetrahedron, with two hexagons and one triangle around each vertex.

Two other semi-regular polyhedra are the icosidodecahedron and the cuboctahedron.

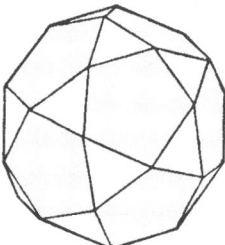

icosidodecahedron
pentagons and triangles

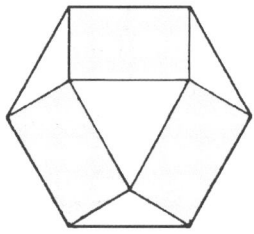

cuboctahedron
squares and triangles

There are also two infinite sets of semi-regular polyhedra:

- Prisms which have regular polygons for the two identical faces and squares for the rectangular faces (for example a cube).
- Anti-prisms which are made of two regular polygons whose centres are aligned but whose vertices are not. The polygons are joined by equilateral triangles (a regular octahedron is an example of an anti-prism).

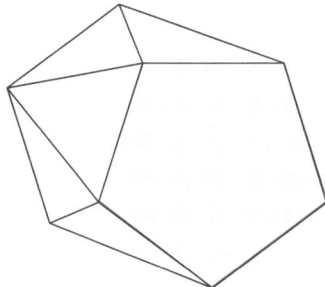

pentagonal
anti-prism

NETS

The two-dimensional arrangement of polygons that can be folded up to make a polyhedron is called a **net**.

The net of a solid is not unique and it is often worth exploring different nets to see which is the easiest to assemble. Polydron and Clixi make it very easy to explore nets. The solid can be carefully pulled apart so that possible nets can be explored. You can also use packaging to explore nets. How were the nets designed? How much waste will there be when the net is cut out from a large piece of card?

There are 11 different nets for a cube – can you find them all? You will need to work systematically and take care not to include rotations or reflections. Remember that, mathematically speaking, shapes are identical (i.e. congruent) even when their orientation is different.

Here are three of the possible nets for a cube. If you were going to make them out of card where would you add the tabs?

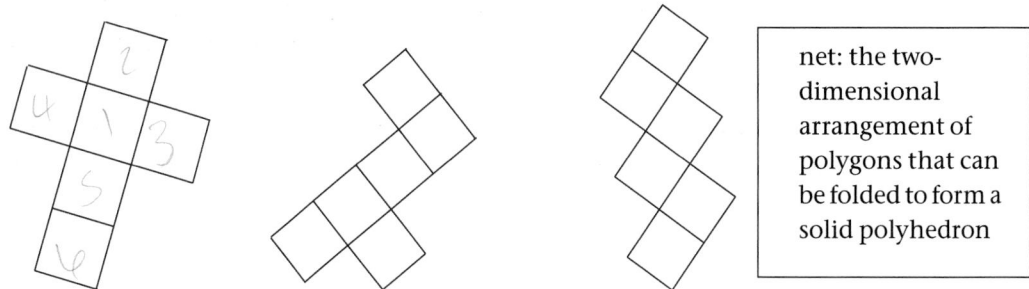

net: the two-dimensional arrangement of polygons that can be folded to form a solid polyhedron

If you were going to make them into dice where would you write the numbers (opposite faces sum to 7)?

How do you design the net of a cuboid? Look at the nets below; will they fold up to make cuboids – if not why not?

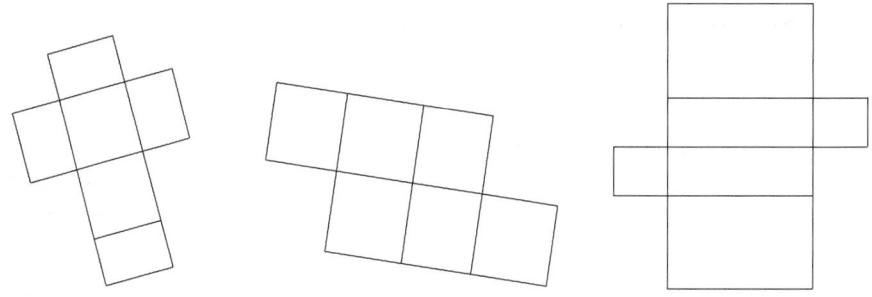

Visualisation is an important part of net design. Recognising which edges join together can be quite challenging.

Which of the nets below will form a tetrahedron?

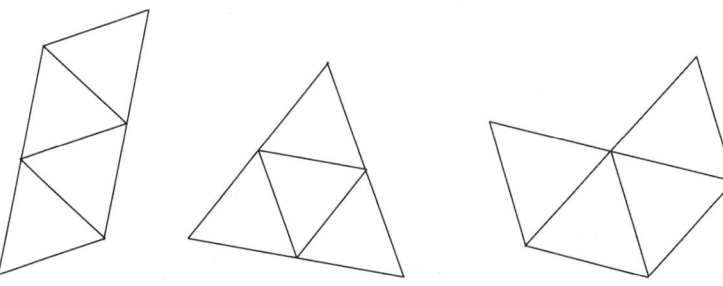

You might like to try making shapes out of multilink and designing nets for them.

Adding tabs to a net

Two edges on the net will join to make one edge on the solid, therefore adding tabs to half the edges of the net will be sufficient. In fact adding tabs to every alternate edge of the net will do.

Every net of a cube has 14 edges, which means that seven tabs are needed. In the nets below tabs should be added to all the blue edges of the net or to all the black edges.

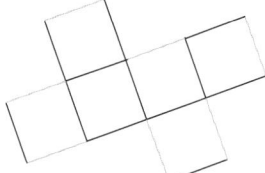 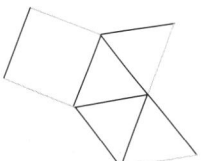

SYMMETRY

SYMMETRY PROPERTIES OF 2-D SHAPES

There are two types of symmetry:

- Mirror or reflective symmetry in 2-D
  For 2-D shapes this is most easily illustrated using the shape cut out of paper – in how many different ways can you fold the shape in half so that the pieces fit exactly on top of each other?

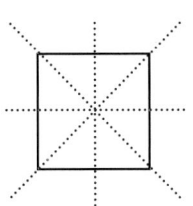 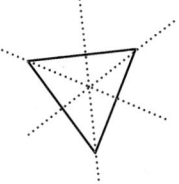

> reflective symmetry: the number of distinct fold lines that can be made so that each half matches is the number of lines of reflective symmetry

Regular polygons always have the same number of lines of symmetry as they have sides.

For irregular polygons this is not the case:

an isosceles triangle and a kite each have one line of symmetry

a rectangle and rhombus each have two lines of symmetry (except when they are squares)

a parallelogram has no lines of symmetry (except when it is a special case e.g. a rectangle or rhombus).

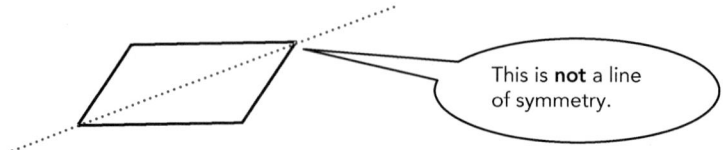

This is **not** a line of symmetry.

A circle has an infinite number of lines of reflective symmetry that pass through its centre.

- Rotational symmetry in 2-D

  Again using a paper cut-out of the shape is helpful, but this time draw an outline of the shape, and mark one corner. Turn the shape around its centre. How many times does it fit inside the outline exactly, before you get back to where you started? The number of times that the shape fits inside itself is called the order of rotation.

  Clearly any shape will eventually fit back inside itself after a full turn of 360° so any shape has order of rotation at least 1. A shape has rotational symmetry if the order of rotation is greater than 1.

> rotational symmetry: the number of times a shape fits exactly into an outline of itself during a complete turn is its order of rotation

An equilateral triangle has rotational symmetry, order 3.

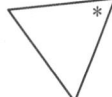 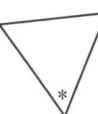 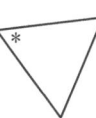 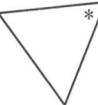

120°   120°   120°

Regular polygons with n-sides have order of rotational symmetry n.

A rhombus, rectangle and parallelogram have order of rotational symmetry 2.

SYMMETRY PROPERTIES OF 3-D SHAPES

- Reflective symmetry in 3-D

  3-D shapes also have reflective symmetry but rather than lines of symmetry there will be planes of symmetry.

A plane of symmetry defines where a cut could be made through the solid to give two identical halves.

It is worth experimenting with solids made from playdough to identify the planes of symmetry.

- Rotational symmetry in 3-D

An axis of symmetry defines a line around which the solid could be spun so that it fits exactly into the same space before having completed a full turn.

What symmetry does a triangular prism have?

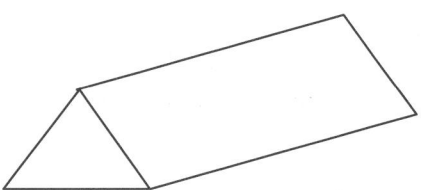

This triangular prism has equilateral triangles at each end and three identical rectangular faces.

There are three planes of symmetry that pass through the mirror lines of the equilateral triangles. There is one plane of symmetry that is parallel to the triangular faces and passes through the centre of the rectangles.

There is one axis of rotational symmetry order 3 which passes through the centre of the triangular faces. There are three axes of rotational symmetry order 2 that are parallel with the mirror lines of the equilateral triangle and pass through the centre of the prism. As a challenge you might like to try and identify the symmetry properties for a cube or cuboid.

TILING THE PLANE

Fitting shapes together to cover the plane without leaving any gaps is dependent on the properties of the shapes used. If the tiling pattern is identical wherever you look and can be continued for ever in any direction you have a tessellation. (From Latin: the Romans called the little pieces used to make mosaics *tesserae*).

REGULAR TESSELLATIONS

Think of tiling patterns that you see around you everyday:

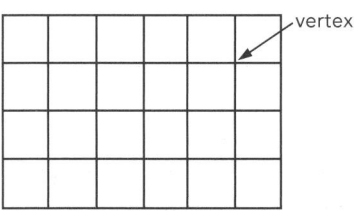

This pattern of squares could be continued indefinitely to cover the plane. It is an example of a **regular tessellation** as identical regular polygons are joined edge to edge in such a way that every **vertex** or **node** is identical.

> vertex: the point on a tiling at which corners of the shapes meet

The vertex in this tessellation can be classified as a 4.4.4.4 (or 4^4) vertex because there are four 4-sided polygons at each vertex.

> regular tessellation: identical regular polygons are joined edge to edge to cover the plane without leaving any gaps

What other regular polygons form regular tessellations?

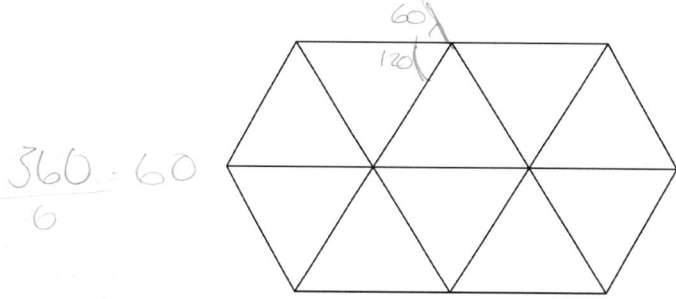

This pattern of equilateral triangles could be continued indefinitely to cover the plane. The vertex type is 3.3.3.3.3.3 (or 3^6) as six equilateral triangles meet at each vertex.

You may be familiar with honeycomb, another regular tessellation, but this time of regular hexagons. How many hexagons meet at a point? From the diagram of equilateral triangles you may notice that six equilateral triangles form a regular hexagon. At each corner of the regular hexagon there are two equilateral triangles. This means that the interior angle of a regular hexagon is 120° = 2 × 60°. For a tessellation the angle sum at a vertex needs to be 360° (squares 4 × 90° = 360° and equilateral triangles 6 × 60° = 360°) so three hexagons will meet at a vertex 3 × 120° = 360° and the vertex type will be 6.6.6 (or 6^3).

If you investigate other regular polygons you'll find it is impossible to use them on their own to form a tessellation. The angles simply don't work!

Interior angles

In order to check whether or not regular polygons will tessellate you need to check the sum of the angles at a vertex. This means you need to know the interior angle of the polygon. You know that the angle sum of a triangle is 180°. See the section on proof for how to show this is the case. Given this fact you can find the angle sum of any polygon (not necessarily regular) by finding out the least number of triangles that the polygon can be split into.

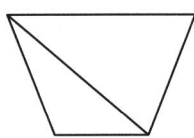

A trapezium can be split into 2 triangles

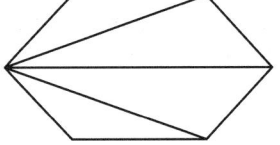

A hexagon can be split into 4 triangles

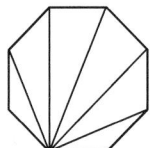

An octagon can be split into 6 triangles

Using the results above we can complete the table below to show the sum of the interior angles in a polygon of any number of sides. We can find the size of the interior angle in the regular polygon because all the interior angles must be equal in this case.

Polygon	Number of sides	Least number of triangles	Angle sum of polygon degrees	Interior angle for a regular polygon
Triangle	3	1	180	$180 \div 3 = 60°$
Quadrilateral	4	2	360	$360 \div 4 = 90°$
Pentagon	5	3	540	$540 \div 5 = 108°$
Hexagon	6	4	720	$720 \div 6 = 120°$
n-sided	n	$n-2$	$180(n-2)$	$180(n-2) \div n$

In any polygon the least number of triangles is two less than the number of sides.

The interior angle sum for the polygon is 180° multiplied by the least number of triangles.

In a regular polygon the interior angles are all the same size. The interior angle for a **regular polygon** is the angle sum divided by the number of sides.

The results in this table help us to understand why there are only three regular tessellations.

An equilateral triangle has an interior angle of 60°.

60 fits into 360 exactly 6 times.

So six equilateral triangles will fit around a point.

Four squares with angles of 90° will fit around a point.

Three regular hexagons with angles of 120° will fit around a point.

For polygons with more sides than a hexagon the angle will be larger than 120° and so at each point there will be only two polygons and a gap.

SEMI-REGULAR TESSELLATIONS

Using regular polygons with the same edge length (ATM MATs are a good resource for this) it is possible to form tessellations which have the same cyclic arrangement of polygons at each vertex.

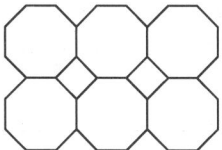

This arrangement of regular octagons and squares is popular for tiling. At each vertex there are two octagons and one square. The vertex type is 4.8.8 (or 4. 8^2); checking with the interior angles we find that $2 \times 135° + 90° = 360°$. This is an example of a **semi-regular tessellation**.

> semi-regular tessellation: more than one type of regular polygon is used edge to edge to form a tessellation in which each vertex has the same cyclic arrangement of polygons

You may want to investigate other semi-regular tessellations for yourself. Altogether there are eight distinct semi-regular tessellations. One of these ($3^4.6$) can be in two forms which are mirror images of one another.

The regular and semi-regular tessellations are sometimes called the Archimedean tilings.

TESSELLATION DUALS

Every tessellation has a dual which can be found by joining the midpoints of the tiles via the shortest route. Equilateral triangles are the dual of regular hexagons as shown in the diagram below.

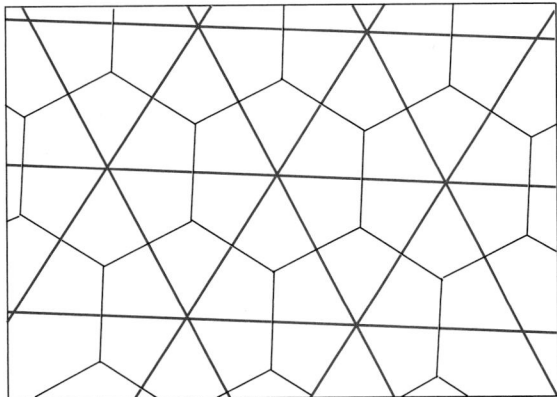

A tiling of right-angled isosceles triangles (half squares) is the dual of the semi-regular tessellation with regular octagons and squares.

Other tessellations

Any triangle will tessellate because edges can be matched in such a way that the angle sum of the triangle can be made twice. The following tessellation is of an acute-angled scalene triangle. Can you see how it might be made?

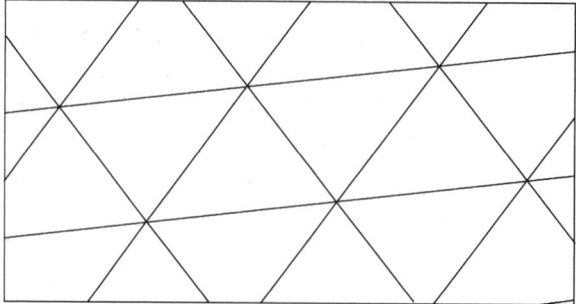

You can tessellate with any quadrilateral:

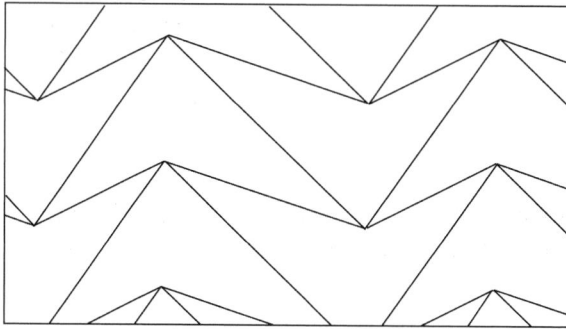

As well as tiling patterns that we see all around us many fabric and wallpaper designs are based on tessellations.

If you relax the condition of fitting edge to edge and having every vertex identical you can come up with some very exciting designs. M.C. Escher based much of his art work on distortions of tessellations.

CONSTRUCTIONS AND THE CIRCLE

The symmetry properties that shapes possess can be used to construct them accurately.

If you make a point on a piece of paper and then draw points exactly 1 cm away from that point, what shape will you get?

A circle, radius 1 cm!

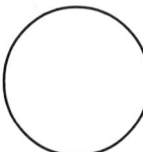

A circle is a special shape and the fact that drawing the set of points a fixed distance away from a given point is a circle is the basis of geometric constructions with a straight edge and a pair of compasses.

Properties of the circle

The distance from the centre of the circle to the edge (the **circumference**) is called the **radius**. Any line that goes from one point on the circumference to another is called a **chord**. It divides the circle into a **major segment** (the larger part) and a **minor segment** (the smaller part of the circle). The longest chord in a circle passes through the centre of the circle and is called the **diameter**. The diameter is twice the radius. A small section of the circumference is an **arc**. Part of the circle bounded by two radii and an arc is a **sector** (a sector looks like a piece of a pie chart and a common error is to call a sector a segment – the only sector that is a segment is a **semicircle**).

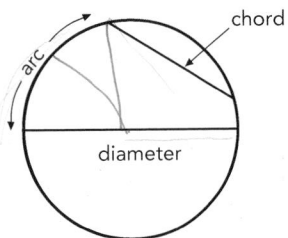

Imagine two crosses on a piece of paper. Where could you place a counter so that it was exactly the same distance from both crosses?

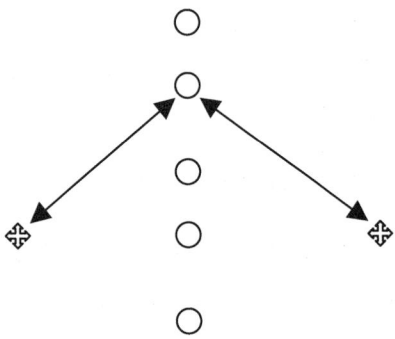

The counter could go in the very middle of the line segment joining the two crosses but there are many more possible places.

All of the counters lie on a line that passes through the midpoint of the line segment and is perpendicular to it.

This line is known as the **perpendicular bisector** of the line segment joining the original two points (perpendicular because it is at right angles to the line segment and bisector because it cuts the line segment into two equal pieces).

CONSTRUCTING THE PERPENDICULAR BISECTOR

Start with a line segment AB.

Construct a circle with centre A.

Construct a circle with centre B and the same radius. The radius must be greater than half the length of the line segment or your circles won't meet!

Where the circles cross the points must be exactly the same distance from A and B.

Joining the intersection points gives the perpendicular bisector of the line segment.

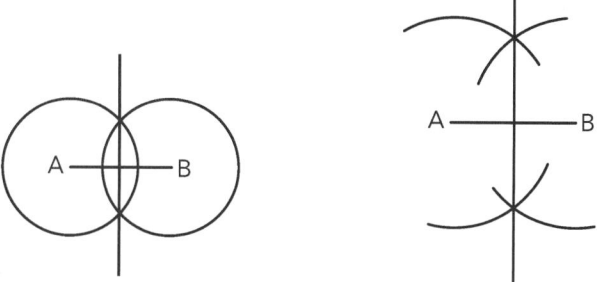

The perpendicular bisector is used as the basis for constructing midpoints and right angles.

> Note: You don't need to draw in the whole circle – just two arcs will do to fix the points of intersection.

CONSTRUCTING AN ANGLE BISECTOR

Given an angle with vertex O, draw a circle with centre O and mark the points A and B where the circle cuts the lines defining the angle. These points will be the same distance from O.

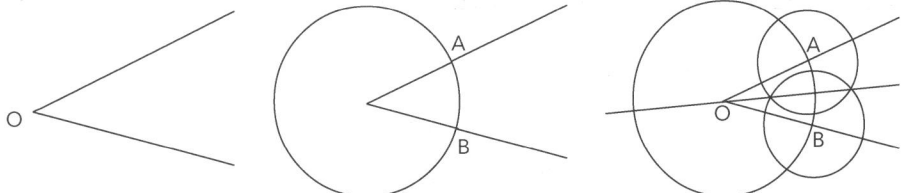

Draw two circles with the same radius, one circle centre A, the other centre B.

Join the points where these circles cut to the point O to get the angle bisector.

These construction techniques can be used to construct polygons, reflections and many attractive geometric designs.

Your pair of compasses is used to transfer lengths so it is not necessary to measure with a ruler.

Try constructing an equilateral triangle and a square. Once you have your square you could bisect all the sides to get a regular octagon . . .

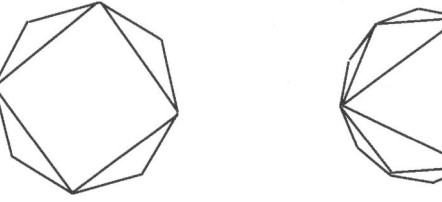

Software like Cabri and Logo allow you to explore constructions.

CONSTRUCTING POLYGONS IN LOGO

Logo is a simulation of a programmable floor turtle. To get the floor turtle to draw a regular polygon you need to get the turtle to complete a 360° turn whilst drawing the entire polygon. The angle the turtle turns is known as the **exterior angle**.

The sum of the interior and exterior angles is always 180°.

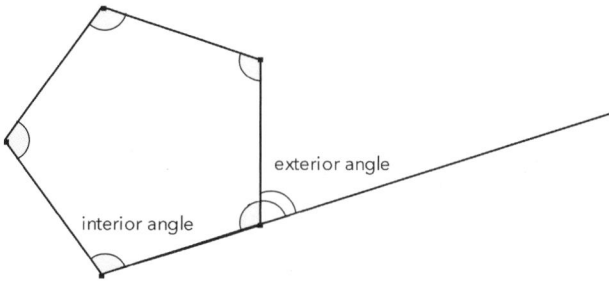

Logo can be used for exploring many aspects of shape and space including angles of turn. Precise instructions can be given to manoeuvre the turtle around the screen to create particular designs or travel through a maze (for example). A floor turtle allows children to experience the principles of Logo before working in the computer environment.

4.3 POSITION AND MOVEMENT

DEFINING YOUR POSITION: CO-ORDINATES

Defining your position exactly is much easier if you can define it relative to a given reference point. Grid references allow you to locate a place or landmark relatively accurately. In mathematics the precise position of a point on a plane or even in space can be defined using co-ordinates. On a plane, given a reference point, usually called the origin, your position can be defined by saying how many units you have to move in one direction and how many units you need to go in another direction. The convention is to use x- and y-axes that are perpendicular to one another. These are known as Cartesian co-ordinates after Rene Descartes (1596–1650).

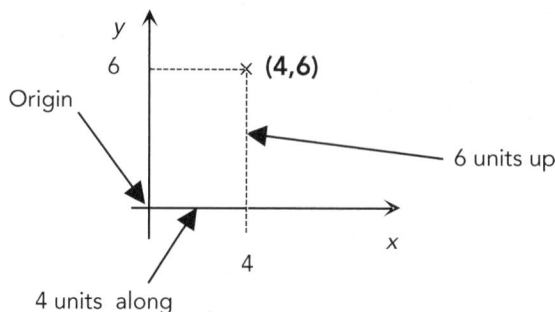

TRANSFORMATIONS

In the following tessellation it is possible to move the individual shapes so that they lie on top of one another.

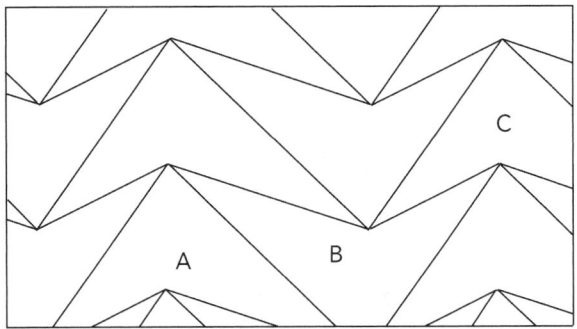

Congruent shapes are identical in both size and shape.

How would you move A onto B, or A onto C or C onto B or ...?

The mathematical processes of moving shapes in the plane are called **transformations**.

We will consider three transformations that do not alter the size or shape of the starting object, i.e. the image is **congruent** to the object. These transformations are **translation**, **reflection** and **rotation**.

Enlargement is also a transformation but the image can be larger, smaller or the same size as the object.

TRANSLATION

The object is moved so that its orientation is unchanged. In the tiling pattern above, A onto C is a translation.

On a set of co-ordinate axes a translation is usually defined using a **vector** which neatly records the amount to be moved in the positive x-direction and the amount to be moved in the positive y-direction. In the diagram below the object is translated to the image by the vector $\begin{pmatrix} 5 \\ 3 \end{pmatrix}$. To move the image back to the object would need the translation $\begin{pmatrix} -5 \\ -3 \end{pmatrix}$.

A translation needs a vector to describe how to move the object.

A vector gives information about how much to move
$$\begin{pmatrix} x\text{-direction} \\ y\text{-direction} \end{pmatrix}$$

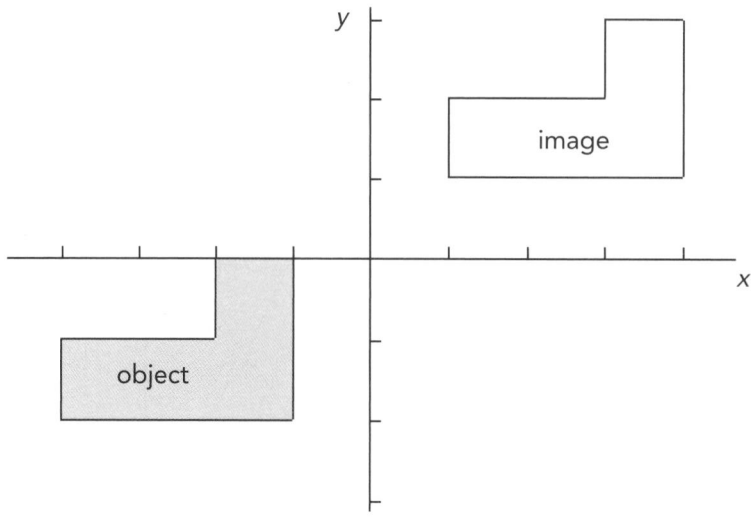

REFLECTION

The object is reflected in a given mirror line to produce an image. Together the object and image have reflective symmetry. In the diagram below the triangle has been reflected in the mirror line.

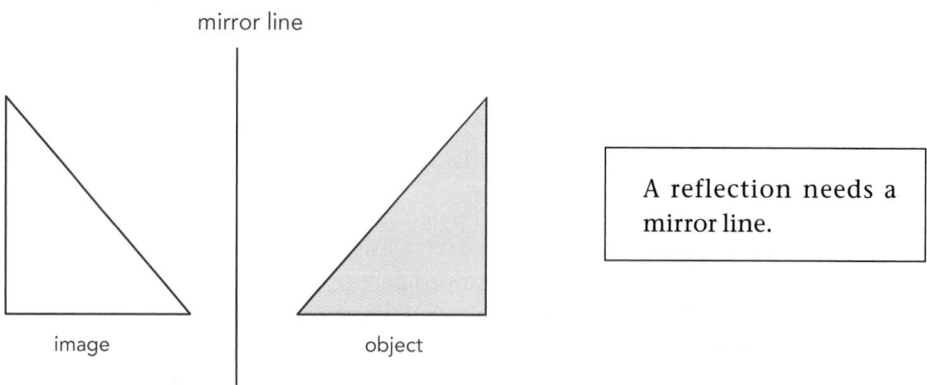

A reflection needs a mirror line.

Two common difficulties with reflection are reflecting in lines that are neither vertical nor horizontal and reflecting when part of the object overlaps the mirror line.

A reflection can be undone by reflecting the image in the mirror line back to where it started.

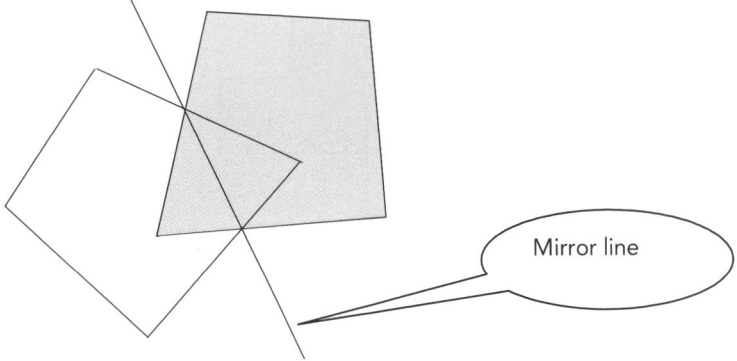

Mirror line

ROTATION

In the quadrilateral tessellation, page 185, triangle A could be moved onto triangle B by rotating it a half turn (180°) about the midpoint of the common side.

To describe a rotation you need to give an angle through which to turn, a direction and a centre of rotation. The flag has been rotated through 90° clockwise about the point A.

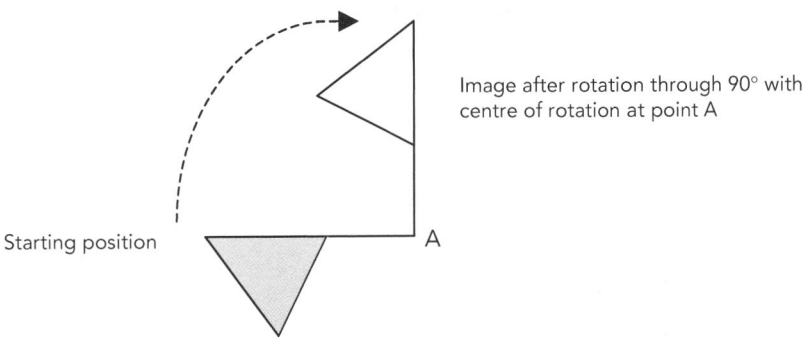

Image after rotation through 90° with centre of rotation at point A

Starting position

A

It is not necessary for the centre of rotation to be on or within the object. In the following diagram the centre of rotation is the origin (0, 0) and the angle of rotation is 90° clockwise. Tracing the image and then rotating the tracing can help to locate the position of the image.

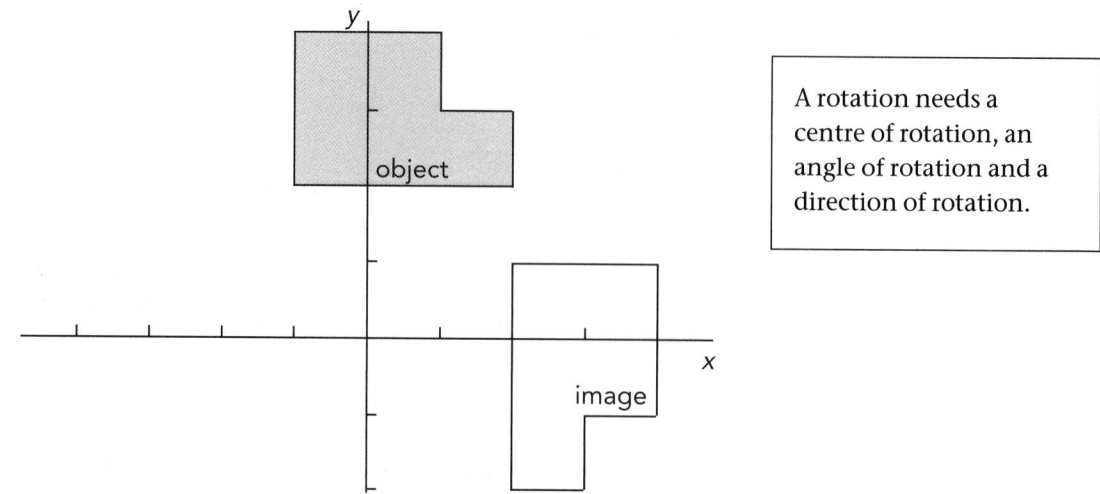

A rotation needs a centre of rotation, an angle of rotation and a direction of rotation.

How would you undo a rotation?

ENLARGEMENT

An enlargement is a transformation. Both of the images below represent enlargements of the smaller square with scale factor two. One enlargement has centre of enlargement O the other has centre A.

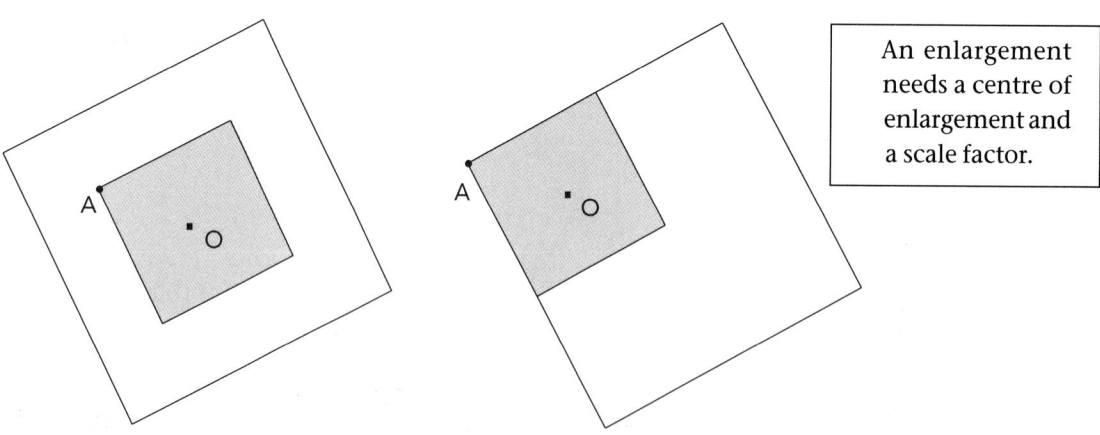

An enlargement needs a centre of enlargement and a scale factor.

In fact any arrangement of image and object is possible depending on the centre of enlargement. In the following diagram the scale factor is still 2.

In all the images the lengths have doubled.

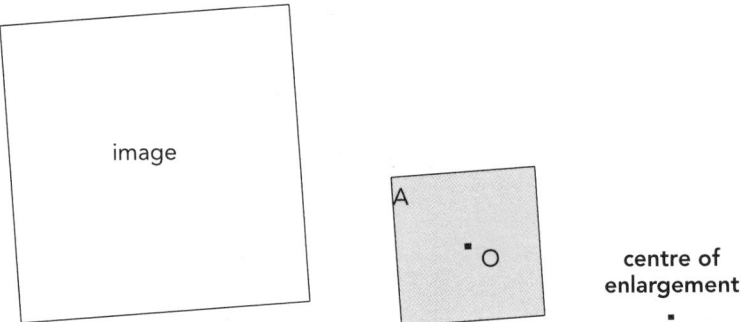

What has happened to the area?

It is four times larger as four of the original squares will exactly fit into the enlarged square.

What would happen to the lengths and areas if the scale factor was 3 or 4 or any number?

The scale factor tells you what to multiply the lengths by – the scale factor must be squared (i.e. multiplied by itself) to find out the scale factor for the area.

Enlargement always results in an image that is **similar** to the object.

> Similar: similar shapes may differ in size but are otherwise identical.

How do you construct an enlargement when the centre is outside the object?

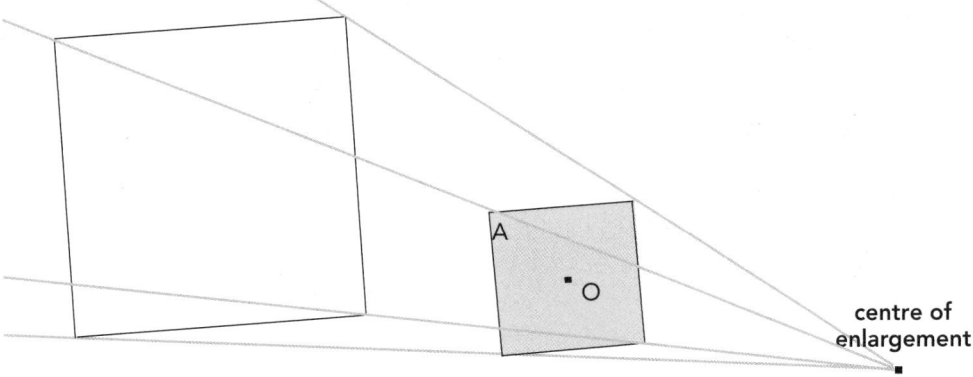

The blue lines are construction lines. Draw lines from the centre of enlargement to the object and extend them so that they are the *scale factor* times as long.

Is it possible to have an enlargement with a fractional scale factor?

The diagram below shows an enlargement scale factor a half with centre the origin (0, 0).

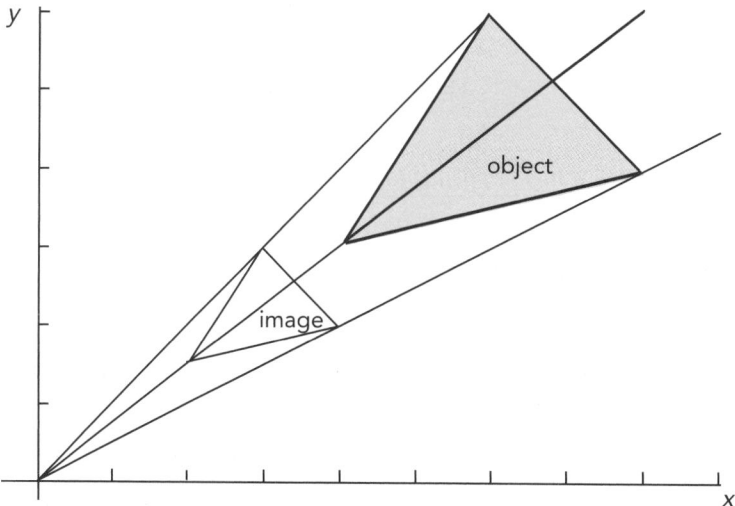

How would you undo an enlargement?

Other transformations

The transformations described above are the most common. Other transformations you might come across are a glide reflection which is a translation parallel to a mirror line followed by a reflection, and a stretch which is a one-way enlargement relative to a fixed line.

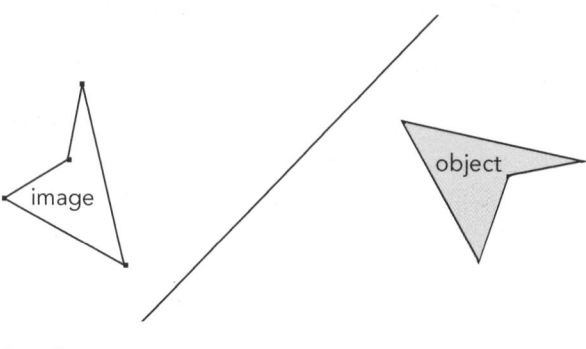

Glide reflection

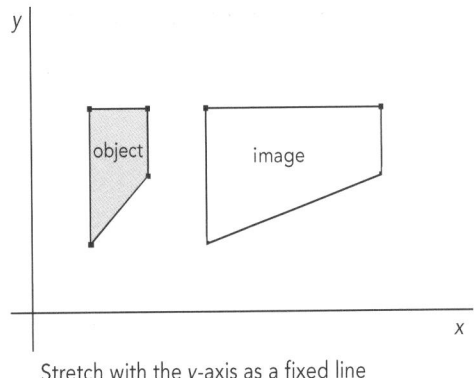

Stretch with the y-axis as a fixed line

UNDOING TRANSFORMATIONS

The transformation that undoes a transformation is called the **inverse transformation**, in the same way that the operation that undoes an operation in arithmetic is called the inverse operation (e.g. the inverse of addition is subtraction).

To undo a translation of 3 units in the x-direction and 2 units in the y-direction $\binom{3}{2}$:

you need a translation of ⁻3 units in the *x*-direction and ⁻2 units in the *y*-direction $\binom{-3}{-2}$.

To undo a reflection:

you need to reflect again in the same mirror line.

To undo a rotation of 50° clockwise about point A:

you need to rotate though 50° anticlockwise about the same point A.

To undo an enlargement of scale factor 2 with centre of enlargement A:

you need an enlargement with scale factor ½ from the same centre A.

4.4 MEASURES

COMPARISONS

Two people can compare their heights by standing next to one another but comparing relative sizes of planets would be trickier. It is not easy to compare the capacity of containers by eye because there are three dimensions to consider at once. Standing containers next to one another can mislead because one might be wider but shorter than the other. Therefore, to compare objects that cannot be brought physically together or do not lend themselves to easy comparison, some sort of indirect approach is required.

Indirect comparison can be achieved without using numbers – consider the use of an unmarked rod to compare a piece of furniture with a space in a room, where furniture and space are compared with reference to a point identified on the rod – but for most purposes measurement involves a numerical comparison including some unit of measurement.

UNITS OF MEASURE

STANDARD AND NON-STANDARD UNITS

Units are a human creation and can take any form as long as there is consistency and widespread agreement on them. If we wished to compare the size of two rooms in our house, counting footsteps along the length of each would be good enough to see which was longer but in communicating measures there needs to be a common understanding to allow transactions to be made. If we need to buy a carpet the shop will want to know the size in standard units. Measuring with foot lengths is an example of non-standard measure while using recognised units is using standard measure.

Standard units can be traced back to some original physical representation, for example there was a yard measure in England which was destroyed by fire in the nineteenth century. Metric units were first introduced in eighteenth-century France and were required to have a scientific basis. A metre was defined as a ten-millionth part of the distance from the equator to the North Pole. The modern scientific definition of a metre is the distance light travels in 1/299 792 458 of a second. A gram was defined as the mass of one cubic centimetre of water. The kilogram mass is different from the other measures in that it relates back eventually to a cylinder of platinum iridium alloy and the UK kilogram is kept at the National Physical Laboratory (more information can be found at www.npl.co.uk). The metre, kilogram and second are commonly known as SI units (International System of Units), recommended by the Conference Generale des Poids et Mesures in 1960. In the UK both imperial and metric measures are still used in everyday life but it is the metric system which is explicitly taught in schools.

IMPERIAL UNITS

The equivalence of imperial units has a historical base so there are no easy ways of remembering them. The table below shows some relationships.

length	12 inches (ins) in 1 foot (ft)
	3 ft in 1 yard (yd)
	1760 yds in a mile.
area	144 square ins in a sq. ft
	9 sq. ft in a sq. yd
	640 acres in a sq. mile

volume	1728 cubic ins in a cu. ft
	27 cu. ft in a cu. yard
capacity	5 fluid ounces in a gill
	4 gills in a pint (pt)
	two pts in a quart
	eight pts in a gallon or 4 quarts in a gallon
mass	16 ounces (oz) in a pound (lb)
	14 lbs in a stone (st)
	8 st in a hundredweight (cwt) and
	20 cwt in a ton

METRIC UNITS

Metric units are much easier to work with than imperial units because they are all based on powers of ten.

The basic units are metre, litre and gram. The prefixes tell you the multiple of the unit you require. How many grams in a *kilo*gram? 1000. How many metres in a *kilo*metre? 1000.

A tonne is 1000 kg. There are 100 hectares in a square kilometre. One of the great things about metric units is the relationship between volume and capacity: a volume of 1 cubic centimetre is equivalent to 1 millilitre.

> The volume of the solid is the amount of space it occupies. The capacity is the amount that can be contained within the shape.

Things get a bit more complicated with relationships between units for area and volume.

An area of 1 square centimetre (cm²) actually measures 1 cm by 1 cm which is 10 mm by 10 mm. So in 1 cm² there are 100 mm². How many square centimetres in a square metre?

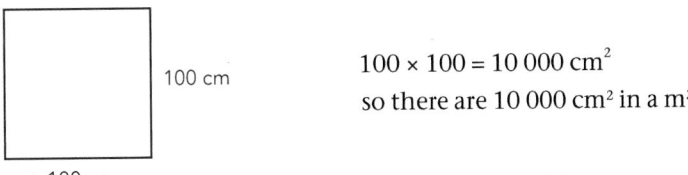

100 cm

100 cm

$100 \times 100 = 10\,000 \text{ cm}^2$

so there are 10 000 cm² in a m²

For area, as there are two dimensions, the scale factor for length must be squared (see the section on enlargement and similar shapes, earlier in the chapter).

The volume of a three-dimensional shape is the amount of space it takes up and is measured in cubic units. You could imagine the volume made of up of identical cubes. A volume of 1 cubic centimetre is very small (a multilink cube has a volume of almost 8 cubic centimetres) but that is 1000 cubic millimetres!

How many cubic centimetres in a cubic metre?

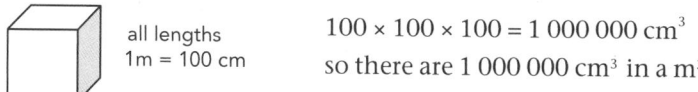

all lengths
1m = 100 cm

$100 \times 100 \times 100 = 1\,000\,000 \text{ cm}^3$

so there are $1\,000\,000 \text{ cm}^3$ in a m^3.

The table below summarises the most common units of measure and meanings of prefixes in the metric system which are from Latin and Ancient Greek (usually Latin prefixes denote fractional parts e.g. centi means hundredth, while Greek prefixes denote multiples e.g. hecto means hundred).

Measure	Imperial units	Metric units	Prefixes
Length	inch, foot, yard, mile	millimetre (mm), centimetre (cm), metre (m), kilometre (km)	milli – thousandth of a metre centi – hundredth of a metre kilo – a thousand metres
Area*	sq. inch, sq. foot, sq. yard, acre, sq. mile	mm^2, cm^2, m^2, hectare, km^2	hectare – 100 metres × 100 metres
Volume*	cu. in., cu. ft, cu. yd	mm^3, cm^3, m^3	see length above
Capacity	fluid ounces, gills, pints, quarts, gallons	millilitre (ml), centilitre (cl), litre (l)	millilitre – thousandth of a litre centilitre – hundredth of a litre
Mass	ounce, pound, stone, hundred-weight (cwt), ton	milligram (mg), gram (g), kilogram (kg), tonne	milligram – thousandth of a gram kilogram – a thousand grams

* Note that in the imperial system square and cubic units are usually written as sq. inch, cu. in. etc. but in the metric system the notation is cm^2 (read as centimetre squared).

CONVERTING UNITS

Imperial units linger in everyday life as the metric system is being introduced more widely and so it is necessary at times to be able to convert between the two. Many people in the UK will be more familiar with their heights and weights in imperial measure and milk is still bottled in pints. To convert from imperial to metric units and vice versa you need to have some reference points or key facts. With height if I want to convert my height in feet and inches to metres and centimetres it is helpful to know that one inch is equivalent to about two and a half centimetres (often suggested as 1 inch is about 2.54 cm).

To convert a height of 5ft 3inches into its metric equivalent:

> use knowledge of the relationship between feet and inches (12 inches = 1 foot)
>
> convert firstly into inches only (5 × 12 = 60 so 5 feet is the same as 60 inches)
>
> add on 3 inches to reach 63 inches
>
> multiply 63 by 2.54 which gives 160.02 i.e. just over 160 cm
>
> Using the relationship between metres and centimetres (100 cm = 1 m), this value becomes 1.6 m or 1 metre and 60 cm.

Everyday metric-imperial equivalences

Measure	Metric	Imperial
Length	1 metre	1.1 yard
Length	2.5 cm	1 inch
Length	8 kilometres	5 miles
Area	m²	1.2 sq. yd
Area	25 acres	10 hectares
Volume	16 cm³	1 cu. in.
Capacity	1 litre	1.75 pints
Capacity	568 ml	1 pint
Mass	1 kg	2.2 lb
Mass	28 g	1 oz
Mass	1 tonne	1 ton

Individuals may have their own key points based on personal experience so that people who make clothes may be confident in converting metres and yards for buying fabric while those who are keen on DIY may have developed confidence with metres/millimetres and yards/inches.

CHOOSING APPROPRIATE UNITS

The selection of units appropriate to what is being measured is an important part of measuring. Personal body measures *could* be expressed as kilometres but are more appropriately related to metres and centimetres. Sometimes there are different forms of expression which arise in different countries or regions. For example, in the UK body weight in imperial measures is usually given in stones and pounds (14 pounds in a stone) while in the USA only pounds are used. In the UK someone might be 9 stones and 2 pounds in weight while in the US their weight would be expressed as 128 pounds. Different forms may also depend on what are seen as more easily understood numbers, for example wine bottles may be labelled as 75 centilitres rather than 0.75 litre. Perhaps it depends on the impression of quantity given by a whole number or a fraction!

Often there is more than one way of measuring a particular attribute but some units might aid more efficient calculation. In measuring area (surface) the approach is to visualise the surface as a grid of squares which can be counted. In fact any tessellating shape will do because these cover the surface without gaps, ensuring all the surface is accounted for. However, squares are generally considered more convenient because they produce clear rows and columns, which means any shape can be thought of as a sum of rectangles, and the area of a rectangle can be calculated using multiplication.

SCALES

Nearly all aspects of measure involve the reading of some kind of scale, such as rulers, graded containers or kitchen scales. The continuous nature of measure is explicit on an analogue scale like a ruler and when reading scales the subdivisions of units are seen to be important in determining levels of approximation and accuracy. They are read 'to the nearest . . .'. More sensitive scales which can represent very small units such as milligrams might be needed in some circumstances such as weighing out medicines while in others, such as buying food, weighing to the nearest 25 grams might be sufficient. With digital displays, however, the need to interpret scales is removed and the continuous nature of measure is less explicit because a discrete value is displayed. If a shopper asked for 500 g of fish at the supermarket the amount weighed will never be exactly that. It might show as 478 g on a digital display and cause the pointer on an analogue scale to move close to the 500 g mark and the shopper will need to decide whether they want fish a little over 500 g or a little under for their purposes.

Mathematicians have devised methods of measuring the length, area and volume of increasingly complicated shapes.

MEASURING DISTANCE

PERIMETER

The **perimeter** of a closed shape is the total distance round the edge of the shape.

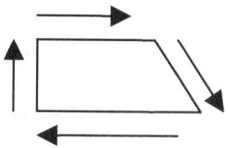

Perimeter of a circle

The distance around a circle is known as the **circumference**.

1. Take a 1 × 1 square.

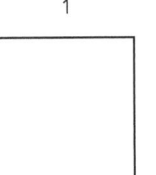

2. Fit a circle inside.

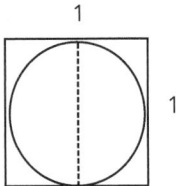

3. The length of the diameter is 1.

4. The perimeter of the square is 4.
   The circumference of the
   circle is less than 4.

5. Half of the circumference (A to B) is clearly more than 1 so the circumference is
   more than 2.

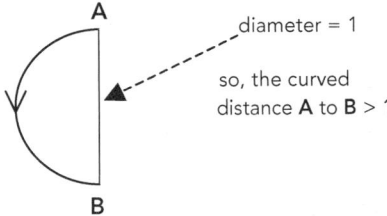

So the circumference is greater than 2 units and less than 4 units.

6. The circumference is a bit more than three times the diameter.
   The ratio of the circumference to the diameter for any circle is pi (π).
   π is an irrational number that cannot be expressed exactly as a fraction.
   It is approximately 3.14159 (to 5 decimal places). It has a fascinating history as
   approximations for π have been sought for thousands of years.

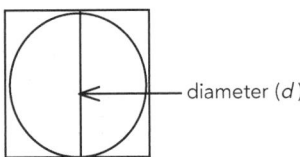

Circumference (C) of a circle is the diameter (d) multiplied by π

$C = \pi d$ or $C = 2\pi r$

(or two lots of the radius multiplied by π)

Reminder: radius is half the diameter.

MEASURING AREA

The area is the space contained within a plane shape. The area of any shape can be estimated by making a copy of the shape on squared paper and counting the squares.

RECTANGLES

Calculating the area of these two rectangles is convenient because the squares covering them are arranged in columns and rows. In the first rectangle there are 3 columns of 4 squares and a counting or multiplication (3 × 4) can be carried out to reach an answer of 12. Turning the rectangle around gives 4 columns of 3 squares and an area of 12 again (4 × 3).

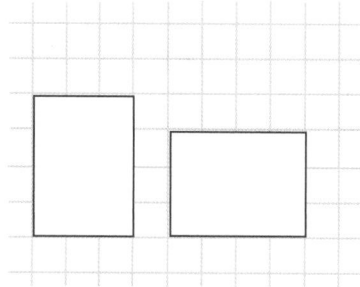

The number of rows in the rectangle is equivalent to the length of one of its sides and the number of columns is equivalent to its breadth so we can say that the area of a rectangle can be calculated by multiplying length by breadth.

TRIANGLES

The area of triangles, parallelograms and trapezia can be related to the area of rectangles.

To find the area of a triangle construct a rectangle with one side of the triangle as base. The rectangle needs to be high enough to enclose the triangle . . .

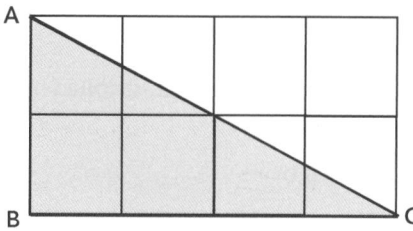

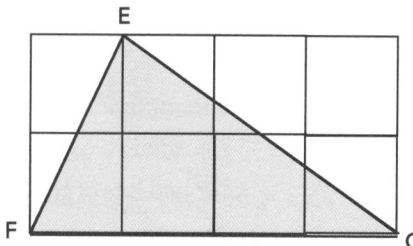

Triangles ABC and EFG have the same area: 4 square units, half of the smallest rectangle they fit into.

With the triangle below it is easiest to take GK as the base. The area of the triangle is half that of the 6 × 2 rectangle.

The base of the triangle is 6 units, the perpendicular height is 2 units.

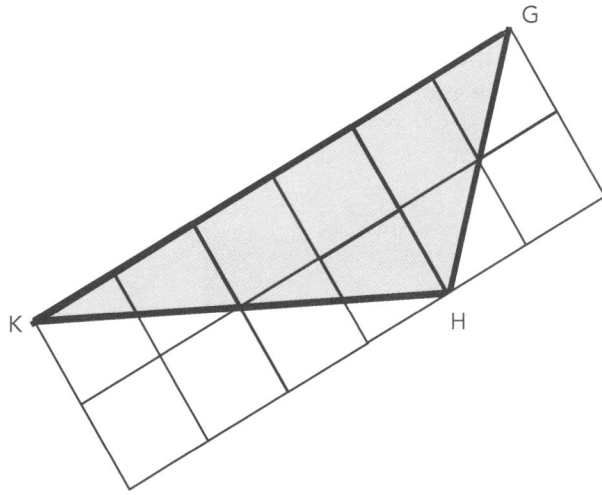

- The area of a triangle is half the base multiplied by the perpendicular height.

Parallelograms and trapezia can be changed to rectangles with the same area:

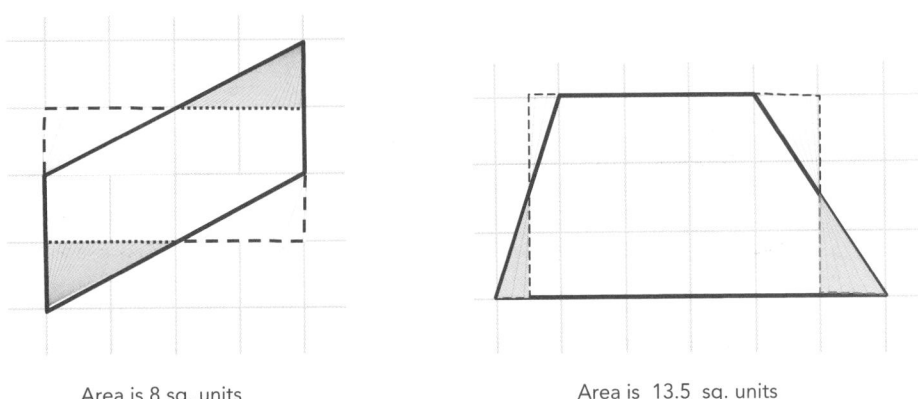

Area is 8 sq. units   Area is 13.5 sq. units

The shaded triangles can be moved into the triangles outlined.

Areas of polygons can be calculated using the areas of rectangles and triangles as a basis.

PYTHAGORAS' THEOREM

(Note the name is a misnomer as this result was known by the Babylonians and Chinese long before Greek mathematicians. However, the Greeks are believed to be the first to prove the result.)

It is unlikely you have got through school without having heard of Pythagoras' theorem. The theorem concerns right-angled triangles and the squares that can be drawn on their sides.

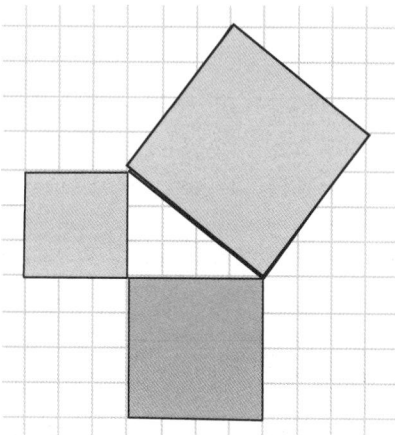

In a right-angled triangle the sum of the areas of the squares on the two shorter sides is equal to the area of the square on the longest side (called the hypotenuse).

The diagram shows a special case where all the lengths of the sides of the right-angled triangle are whole numbers: 3, 4 and 5. They form a Pythagorean triple (3, 4, 5) and

$$3^2 + 4^2 = 5^2$$

Any set of multiples of 3, 4, 5 will also work since the triangles are similar to this one.

There are infinitely many Pythagorean triples, but these are only a small subset of all right-angled triangles.

If you try adding squares to the sides of non right-angled triangles they will not have this property. If you add similar shapes to the sides of a right-angled triangle (e.g. semicircles) Pythagoras' theorem will still be true.

The semicircle opposite the right angle is equal in area to the sum of the other two semicircles.

You might like to check this yourself if the lengths of the sides are 6, 8 and 10 (another Pythagorean triple). You can then calculate the areas of the semicircles.

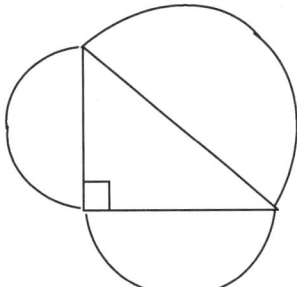

Area of a circle

For a given perimeter the greatest area that can be enclosed is a circle. The circle is the most compact plane shape there is.

Imagine cutting a circle up into many identical slices and rearranging them. As the pieces get smaller and smaller they can be arranged in a shape which becomes closer and closer to a rectangle with one side the radius and the other side half the circumference.

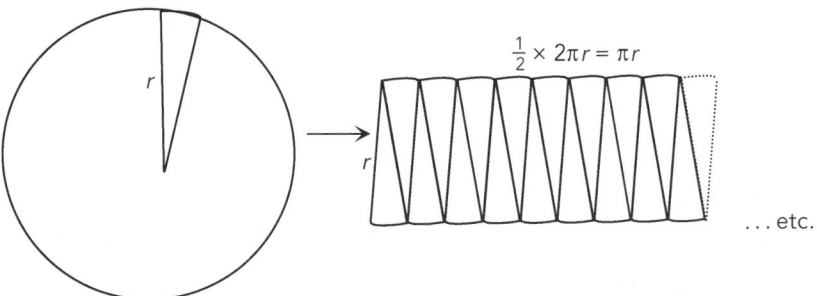

Area is half the circumference multiplied by the radius.

The circumference is $2\pi r$

So, half the circumference is πr

So the area of a circle, A, is

$$A = \pi r \times r \text{ or } \pi r^2.$$

Possible misconception. To calculate the area of a circle you need to first square the radius and then multiply by π. Working out $\pi \times r$ and then squaring will give $\pi^2 r^2$ which is not what is required.

AREA AND PERIMETER

Area is not dependent on perimeter. A long thin shape will have a large perimeter. A compact shape of the same area will have a smaller perimeter.

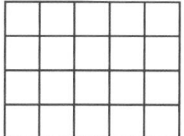

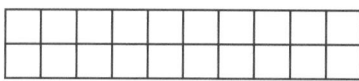

Area of a 4 by 5 rectangle is
20 sq. units.
The perimeter is 18 units.

Area of a 2 by 10 rectangle is also 20 sq. units.

The perimeter is 24 units.

MEASURING VOLUME

The 3-D space that a shape occupies is its volume. Volume is measured by comparison with a unit cube. Space within the shape (i.e. what it can hold) is its capacity.

CUBOIDS

Making solids out of centi-cubes (cubes that are exactly 1 cm³) can help to develop children's understanding of volume. The cubes can be seen as building up in layers.

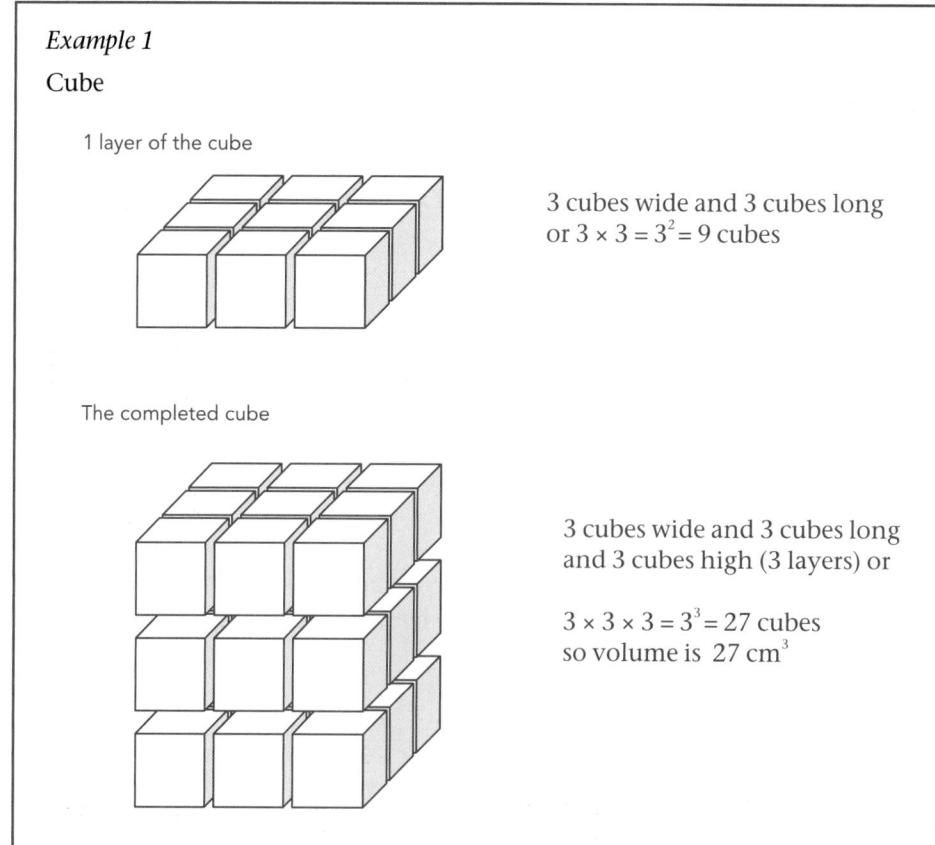

Example 1

Cube

1 layer of the cube

3 cubes wide and 3 cubes long
or $3 \times 3 = 3^2 = 9$ cubes

The completed cube

3 cubes wide and 3 cubes long
and 3 cubes high (3 layers) or

$3 \times 3 \times 3 = 3^3 = 27$ cubes
so volume is 27 cm^3

Example 2

Cuboid

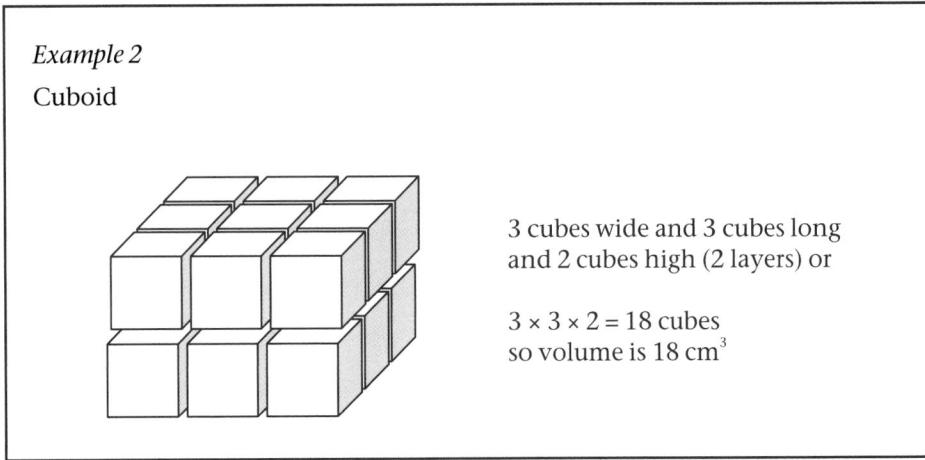

3 cubes wide and 3 cubes long and 2 cubes high (2 layers) or

$3 \times 3 \times 2 = 18$ cubes
so volume is 18 cm^3

The rectangular face of each layer of the cube or cuboid has rows and columns representing the length and breadth of the rectangle. The number of layers is also the height of the cube or cuboid. Thus:

• The volume of a cuboid (or a cube) can be calculated by multiplying length by breadth by height.

This is the same as the area of the base multiplied by the height.

PRISMS

Take a prism with a right-angled triangle as its base. Slide two of these prisms together and you have a cuboid. The volume of the right-angled triangular prism is half that of the cuboid.

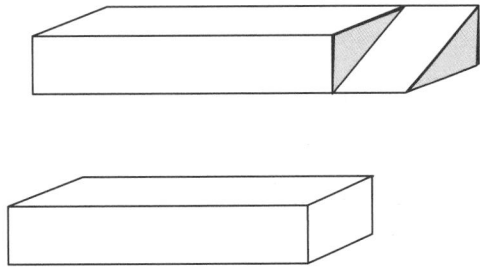

This idea can be extended to triangular prisms with any type of triangle as base.

The area of a triangle was found by drawing the smallest possible rectangle around the triangle with twice the area of the triangle.

The volume of a triangular prism can be found by fitting it into a cuboid whose volume is twice that of the triangular prism.

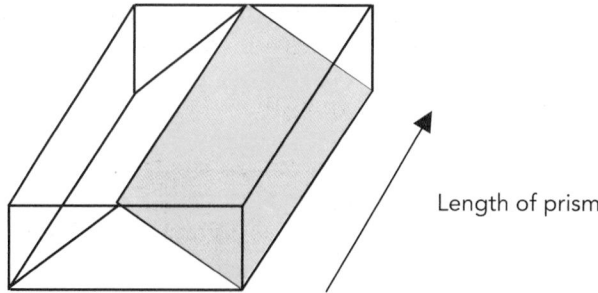

Length of prism

The volume of the cuboid is the area of the rectangular cross-section times the length.

The volume of the triangular prism is half the area of the rectangular cross-section (that is the area of the triangular face) times the length.

It is possible to show that for any prism:

- Volume of the prism = area of cross-section × length.

MEASURING SURFACE AREA

Surface area is the total area of all the surfaces of a solid. So the surface area of a cube of side 2 cm is found by calculating the area of one square face as 2 cm × 2 cm = 4 cm². As there are six faces the total surface area is 24 cm². Surface area can also be thought of as the area of the net of the solid.

MEASURING CAPACITY

To measure the volume of some materials, such as a quantity of water, it is necessary to contain them. The volume of the water is then compared to the space within a container, or how much it holds (its capacity). Markings on the container may represent metric (litres/millilitres etc.) or imperial (fluid ounces/pints/gallons etc.) measures of capacity.

In metric measures there is a convenient equivalence between units of volume and capacity; one millilitre is equal to one cubic centimetre. This means that a 10 cm × 10 cm × 10 cm cube will contain exactly one litre of liquid.

MEASURING MASS

MASS AND WEIGHT

In everyday language we might say 'How much did the baby weigh when it was born?' or 'Mike Tyson weighed in at 225 pounds'. In both cases we would say we are interested in heaviness. We are alluding to two different, but related, concepts: mass and weight. Weight can vary depending on context while mass is a constant value. For example, a person's mass is the same whether they are measured on earth or in space, while their weight will vary because there are different forces acting upon them. In everyday language, however, we usually say we 'weigh' objects rather than 'find their mass'.

MEASURING ANGLES

Angles are a measure of turn and can be measured as a fraction of a whole turn or in degrees, a whole turn being 360°. It is much easier to use an angle measurer, which has a moving pointer, rather than a protractor to measure angles. Angles can be measured clockwise or anticlockwise.

Name	Size of angle
Acute	between 0° and 90°
Right	90°
Obtuse	between 90° and 180°
Straight	180°
Reflex	greater than 180°

Bearings are used to indicate the direction in which you need to travel to move from one point to another. To find the bearing of B from A imagine standing at the point A. Start by facing due North. Turn clockwise until you are facing in the direction of the point B. The angle you have turned through is the bearing of B from A.

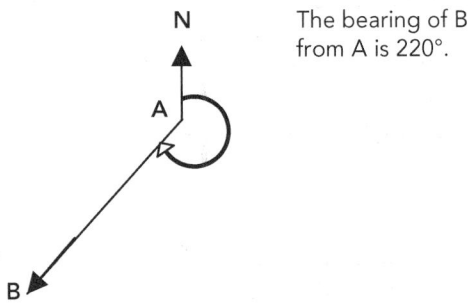

The bearing of B from A is 220°.

PROPERTIES OF ANGLES

A complete turn is defined as 360° and so . . .

- Angles at a point sum to 360°.

- Angles at a point on a straight line make up half a turn and so sum to 180°.

  They are called supplementary angles.

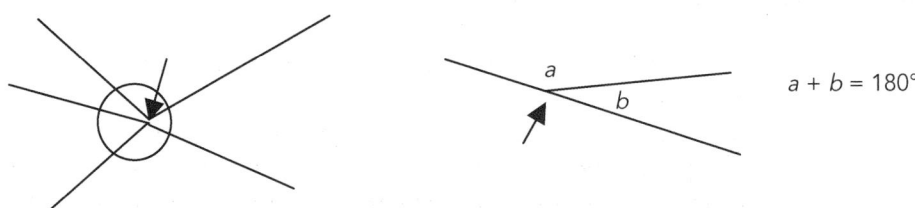

$a + b = 180°$

Vertically opposite angles are equal. Think about opening a pair of scissors: the angle between the blades is always the same as the angle between the handles. When two lines meet, the angles opposite one another (known as vertically opposite angles) will always be equal.

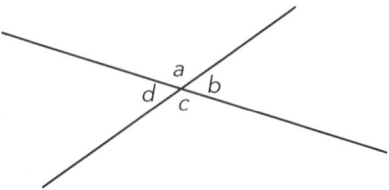

Because the angles meet at a point on a straight line each pair must be equal to 180°, which means that opposite angles must be equal.

$a + b = 180°$, $a + d = 180°$ implies $b = d$

Similarly $a = c$.

Alternate (Z) angles and corresponding (F) angles
In the diagram below there are two parallel lines and a line crossing them. Angles of the same size are marked with the same letter.

- Alternate angles are equal
  (Z-shape around the two angles)

- Corresponding angles are equal
  (F-shape around the two angles)

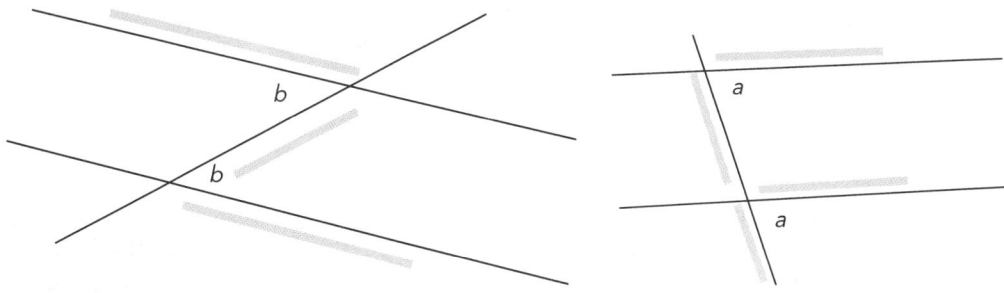

MEASURING TIME

While the measurement of time involves the same principles as other measures, there are some differences. Time can be measured in standard or non-standard units (days, hours, minutes or the time interval measured by water dripping through a water clock). It can be represented both on a dial and digitally (analogue and digital clocks) and it has a system of related units. However, the system of units does not use ten as a base but a mixture of bases developed from early observations of the cycles of day and night and the year. The Babylonians (about 3000 BC) are usually credited with the measure of 360 days for the earth's orbit of the sun. Although this required adjustment in the development of calendars historically, 360 has remained a significant number in measurement (also the number of degrees in circle). Base 60, used by the Babylonians in their counting system, also remains in the units of time, 60 seconds in a minute and 60 minutes in an hour. The result of this is that in calculating time there is not a consistent base to which we work. This can sometimes cause difficulties for children in reading digital representations of time:

12:03   means 'three minutes past twelve' not 12 and three-hundredths

3:59   one minute later is not 3:60 but 4:00 or 'four o'clock'

this could also represent a time interval on a timer – 3 mins and 59 secs

Another issue with time is that of scale. The dial of an analogue clock is marked in intervals similar to the dial on weighing scales or on a ruler. It can be seen as a linear scale wrapped round into a circle. The complexity of the scale used on the analogue clock is not always recognised and it is sometimes assumed that teaching 'telling the time' is straightforward. The following points need to be acknowledged in developing understanding of measuring time:

- The scale on the clock shows hours numbered but minute intervals are not numbered.

- A number may be read in different ways depending which hand is pointing at it. 7 may be read as the hour or '35 minutes past' or '25 minutes to'.

- 15, 30 and 45 minutes past the hour are often read as fractions e.g. 'quarter to or past'.

- The clock face below can be read as '3 o'clock', '3 pm', '3 am', or 03.00 or 15.00 hours, depending on whether it is in the middle of the day or night.

The difference arises when we wish to compare points on the scale. Looking at a ruler, 12 cm represents a quantity which is twice that represented by the 6 cm mark. This is known as a ratio scale. On a clock dial 12 o'clock does not represent 'twice 6 o'clock'. Thus, while the interval of 6 hours can be calculated like the interval of 6 centimetres on the ruler, the actual points on the scale do not relate to each other in the same way as they do for distance. In reading the clock dial we are using an *interval* scale rather than a *ratio* scale. For the other measures discussed the scale is *both* interval and ratio.

International time

Because different parts of the earth are facing away or towards the sun at different times of the day and are at different distances from it at different points in the year, different places in the world have day and night and seasons at different times from each other. In school children may have experience of time changes when they travel or contact friends and family overseas.

Greenwich, because of its position in maritime travel in the nineteenth century, was chosen as the common starting point from which to calculate times across the globe. A line is envisaged from the North to South Pole running through Greenwich, that is a line of longitude. When it is 12 noon along that line the time is later or earlier by equal intervals along successive lines of longitude. These intervals form time zones and times around the world can be worked out using their distance from the original line of longitude. In addition there are seasonal variations such as British Summer Time (BST). Some examples are given below:

London (GMT)	Rio de Janeiro (3 hours behind)	New Delhi (5.5 hours ahead)
8 am	5 am	11.30 am
12 noon	9 am	5.30 pm
10 pm	7 pm	3.30 am (the next day)

COMPOUND MEASURES

Compound measures involve the use of more than one measure in their calculation.

The **density** of an object is calculated by dividing mass by volume. Different materials have different densities so that, for example, a block of polystyrene of the same volume as a block of stone will be lighter and its density therefore less.

$$density = \frac{mass}{volume}$$

If mass is measured in grams and volume is measured in cm^3 then the units of density are grams per cubic centimetre, written gcm^{-3} or g/cm^3.

Speed is the distance travelled in unit time.

$$speed = \frac{distance}{time}$$

Common units for speed are $m\ s^{-1}$ (metres per second or m/s) and mph (miles per hour).

Example 1

To calculate speed:

You walk for 2 hours and cover 5 miles.

speed = distance divided by time = 5 ÷ 2 = 2.5

Speed is 2.5 mph.

Example 2

To calculate journey time:

You travel 180 miles at 60 mph

time = distance divided by speed = 180 ÷ 60 = 3

Journey time is 3 hours.

By deepening your level of mathematical knowledge you can teach for understanding and respond confidently to children's questions. Some issues considered in this section which could be helpful when you are planning your teaching are tactile exploration, classifying, similarities, technical language, context for measurement, reasoning and communicating.

PROPERTIES OF SHAPE

From an early age, children notice similarities between shapes and the properties that help them fit together. Very young children will select a circle to represent a face and build models by choosing shapes with flat surfaces.

Children learn about shapes and spatial relations from birth: they have to synthesise perceptions from seeing, touching and moving around to create an understanding of their 3-D environment. From a partial view of a ball or a staircase they become able to visualise how these will feel and appear from other viewpoints. Later they create and interpret 2-D representations of 3-D shapes and spaces. This will develop into the skill of using drawings, plans and diagrams to visualise objects, buildings and spaces and the way they fit together.

Investigating and classifying are part of the process of organising learning about shape and space properties and relationships. According to Piagetian theory, tactile exploration helps develop visualisation, so for instance, construction and pattern making activities are important. As children get older, they progress from recognising whole shapes to become increasingly analytical, identifying properties and reasoning from definitions.

Children will learn a lot through creative activities, such as making pictures or models with shapes. They may comment spontaneously on similarities, such as the clock being the same shape as a badge. Usually, however, the relations and properties they are noticing and using will be far in advance of their ability to articulate these. Teachers can help children to consolidate their learning by talking about what they are doing; this involves encouraging the children's own informal language, like 'pointy bits' and 'box-shaped' as well as introducing more precise mathematical vocabulary. Deciding when and how to do this is a matter of professional judgement. Referring to 'sides' of 3-D shapes can be confusing and is clarified by distinguishing 'edges' and 'faces'; the more technical mathematical vocabulary is usefully precise. However, is 'sphere' more useful than 'ball-shaped' when they mean the same thing and young children have difficulty saying the word and pronounce it as 'sofia'? Similarly it is up to teachers to decide which young children will relish terms like 'triangular prism' and which may get confused with triangular prisons.

Many of the complexities of the concepts of shape and space are tied to language. As well as the Greek and Latin vocabulary, there are the alternative meanings of common words like 'regular', so that mathematically, a rectangle uncomfortably becomes an irregular shape. If teachers are familiar with the mathematical classification system then they can understand these complexities, such as how shapes can be simultaneously rectangles and squares. Without understanding the basis of the classification system they may incorrectly teach children for instance, that shapes must be either rectangles *or* squares. Teachers need this awareness to make professional judgements about whether to bring in finer distinctions, such as an oblong being a non-square rectangle. In order to classify shapes children need the language of properties as well as the names of shapes and teachers need to plan activities which stimulate children to discuss properties. Teachers who are confident with the terminology are more likely to use it unselfconsciously and appropriately, and so help children become familiar with mathematical language in an unpressurised way.

Therefore activities that involve children in physical exploration of shape and space and the opportunities to reason and communicate their ideas and thoughts enable them to develop their geometric thinking.

One example of an activity designed to develop and connect tactile and visual perception and the language and the properties of shape is the 'feely bag'. A shape is put into a bag. Feel the shape with both hands without looking at it and describe it to your partner. After listening to the description and posing questions to gain further information your partner then has to find the matching shape from a selection. The challenge can be increased by the complexity or unfamiliarity of the hidden shape or by the similarity in the range of shapes provided from which to choose a match. (The more similar the shapes, the more discriminating and precise the language needs to be.) A variation on this activity is to sit back to back and describe arrangements of shapes for partners to make or draw; these can range from models with five multilink cubes to complex geometrical designs. There is always a moment of suspense before the partner's version is compared with the original, provoking some discussion of the accuracy of the description and the listening!

These activities involve visualisation which provides a way for children to think about properties of shapes. You can tell children stories about shrinking and walking inside 3-D shapes, for example:

> You are inside a cube which starts to tilt so you slide into a vertex. If you look up what do you see above you? How many edges meet at the vertex?

You could ask children to imagine combining 2-D shapes, for instance:

> Imagine an equilateral triangle then another one the same size touching it along a whole side. What shape do you get? If a third one is joined along a whole side what is your new shape? Can you draw it?

In creative activities with shapes, such as construction or picture making, you can observe children selecting shapes according to their properties. For instance if they choose straight sided shapes for legs and circles for wheels, this indicates that they can discriminate straight from curved. Combining shapes to make models or patterns can involve them in finding relationships, such as fitting four right angles round a point, or making a hexagon from six equilateral triangles. Seeing what shapes you can make from other shapes can be open-ended or more structured, and will provoke descriptive language. For instance, from just two isosceles triangles you can make a rhombus, a parallelogram, a kite and, if you allow overlaps, shapes with six, seven and more sides.

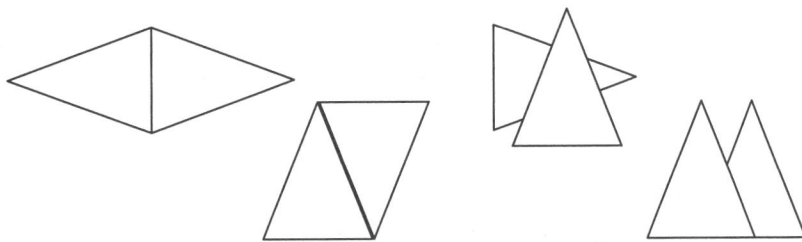

Seeing how many 3-D shapes you can make with six polydron will stimulate discussion of solid shapes. Geostrip investigations can lead to identification of relationships between properties; two pairs of equal geostrips can produce shapes with different properties in terms of equal angles, right angles, parallel sides and axes of symmetry. Asking which properties go together, and which cannot go together, will encourage children to spot relationships and to reason. When children are investigating in open-ended ways, teachers need to be confident in identifying a range of learning which may be going on, and also in spotting when children are mathematically incorrect, so that they can make decisions about how to extend or redirect children's thinking.

MEASURES

The activity of comparing occurs early on in children's experiences. Their own growth means that clothes become too small. They like to compare their height with others in seeing how tall they are. When constructing with materials they build tall towers or make houses for small world figures. The comparison is mostly carried out by examining objects in direct physical proximity like standing next to each other to 'see who is the biggest'.

At this stage language is important and it is probably 'big' and 'small' and 'more' which feature most often in young children's comparisons. Even these words, though they have their comparative versions (bigger, smaller) imply comparison as 'bigness' can only really be judged against something else. In the early stages in school, children's play and practical experience will, in the main, consist of comparing things directly, extending language (heavy, light, heavier, lighter) and trying to see whether things fit, for example 'this apron's too big for me'.

Much of this will be addressed in children's play, especially in building and creative activities and adults will support development of perception and language through their interaction with children. In addition, adult-led activities such as cooking can offer contexts for measuring.

Children are often misled in their thinking when some attributes of what is being measured change. The water that nearly filled one container now seems to only just cover the bottom of another. Surely there must be less water? They will need experiences which tackle this idea, conservation, through the provision of 'tricky' examples, e.g. comparing the lengths of curved objects as well as straight, containers which are tall and thin and short and fat, material which is distorted in shape but retains its mass like different shapes moulded from the same size balls of plasticine, and cutting up and rearranging paper shapes into different patterns.

Indirect comparison, or what might be called true measuring, becomes necessary when objects cannot be placed side by side or on top of each other. How might you compare the height of your tower to your friend's? If the tower is built from large bricks you could count the bricks, count your friend's bricks and see who has the larger number. In this way the idea of units of measure is introduced, at first possibly as non-standard and later as standard units, such as metres and centimetres. In addition it is important that units are uniform, whether non-standard or standard, so that we know the comparison is a 'fair' one. Once comparison of three or more objects is encountered the concept of transitivity is needed to help with ordering. For example, if the apple weighs more than the pear and the pear weighs more than the plum, then the apple weighs more than the plum. Giving children sets of objects (Which is the longest? Can you put them in order of . . . length, mass . . . ?) or sets of containers (Which holds the most? Can you put them in order?) to compare and giving them the problem to solve of how to do this, offers the opportunity for discussion of whether direct comparison can be used, and of estimation and choice of units. This sort of activity can reveal children's understanding of measuring through the observations they make and the strategies they use.

When standard units are used children will begin to notice that measuring is not exact. When tracking the growth of plants in the classroom, perhaps to study optimum growing conditions, they might mark changes on a chart on the wall behind the plant and observe 'This week the plant is nearly two centimetres taller than last week'. When cooking they might notice that the spoonful of flour they put on the weighing scales measures 'a little bit more' than 50 g. The need for subdivisions of units becomes apparent and the idea that we are always measuring approximately (to the nearest . . .) is brought out in teaching about measurement.

As children learn about units the main focus will be on metric units and these require an understanding of the base-ten system and place value. Decimal notation will be met quite early on in, for example, recording the height of a person as 157 cm, 1 m 57 cm or 1.57 m. This can also be a good reinforcement of place value showing that in 1.57 m, 1 is a whole unit (m), 5 is 5 tenths of a metre (50 cm) and 7 is 7 hundredths (7 cm). This is a very good example of the interconnections in the mathematics curriculum and the awareness teachers need to identify both the knowledge and understanding children need to have to move forward in particular mathematical topics and the ways in which particular contexts can offer the opportunity to apply knowledge and understanding.

Children will have knowledge of imperial units and at the later stage in primary school they can begin to be taught about useful conversions so that when they encounter these units in other contexts they will have some idea of them. In studying food rationing in the Second World War children will encounter imperial units in looking at documents from that time. Before children can think about how they would cope with restrictions on what one can eat they will need to be able to make sense of the weights.

To be meaningful measuring must have some context and purpose for children. In school, links with other subjects provide a range of problems for which skills and understanding are required and where they can be rehearsed and developed. Science is one subject where measuring is frequently required; for example, in studying materials children might test the strength of different types of shopping bag by loading them with increasing weights (which bag holds the greatest weight?). They could test how waterproof fabrics are by seeing how many millilitres of water will soak through them. In design and technology measurement is an important skill and physical education provides opportunity for timing skills development or measuring heart rates during exercise.

In these contexts children will need to have their attention drawn to the approximate nature of measurement and the reading of scales. Accurate measuring can be difficult. In using a ruler children need to understand that you start from zero (which is not necessarily at the beginning of the ruler or tape) and to understand what measure the marks represent. Some rulers are marked in centimetres, others millimetres, others inches and some in all three. Whilst this might be a useful resource for equivalence it is potentially confusing. The various units are likely to be subdivided. Millimetres are not usually subdivided (as they are very small anyway). A centimetre is likely to have ten subdivisions (into millimetres). An inch may be divided into tenths, or quarters, or eighths or even sixteenths.

Understanding of fractions, decimals and rounding are examples of number concepts children will need to have to be able to read and interpret scales, in addition to the knowledge of the units and their interrelationships mentioned earlier. Discussion of the meanings of the prefixes (centi for hundredth and so on, see p. 194) will help with the latter and experience with number lines will support skills in rounding to the nearest appropriate 100, 10, 1, tenth and so on.

Problem solving with measures provides many possibilities for applying and learning skills and developing understanding in measures. Some starting points could be:

- stories involving giants or small people where children can calculate the size of (and make) things for the characters such as beds for the Borrowers or an envelope for a giant to send a birthday card

- best value researches – is the 2-litre bottle of water better value than the 33 cl one?

- adapting recipes for different numbers of people
- making a set of nesting boxes.

Depending on the age and experience of children these problems can be tackled in various ways and children can be offered a variety of equipment, such as standard or non-standard units, different measuring apparatus, and calculators or computers where numbers are cumbersome or a spreadsheet would help in dealing with a set of calculations.

In relation to particular aspects of measures, questions and interventions of teachers will help in addressing some of the common difficulties and misconceptions. This can often be thought of in terms of providing 'tricky examples'.

With weighing, children could be given small heavy objects as well as large light ones so that they can begin to disconnect mass and volume. With containers children could be given examples which are difficult to compare by eye.

With older children, exploring rectangles with the same areas or perimeters is a fruitful investigation. How many different rectangles can you find with an area of 12 squares? Do they all have the same perimeter? Try the reverse, finding rectangles with the same perimeters but different areas. For a given perimeter which one has the greatest area? There is plenty of opportunity for discussion here about what changes and what stays the same.

With the measuring of time, as well as reading dials and digital displays which requires interpretation of numerical values, children need experience of timing intervals. Children can read times from clocks without having much understanding of the passage of time. Young children can try timing a variety of activities – running, skipping, writing their names or threading beads – and record the different results for the different activities. They can think about why the results are different and they can work at improving timings for skills in PE. Real analogue and digital clocks should be referred to as part of everyday classroom activities and compared at particular key times of the day. Geared clocks should be used for demonstrations as they show the way the hour hand moves between the hour markings as the minute hand is rotated and a clock with only the hour hand is good for showing how time can be read by its position alone while a minute hand only clock would not be useful!

Measuring involves some sophisticated ideas and techniques but it also provides some purposeful experience, involving large numbers and decimals, and contexts for problem solving.

4.6 SELF-ASSESSMENT QUESTIONS   Shape, space and measures

PROPERTIES OF SHAPE

1. A polygon has sides of equal length. Is it a regular polygon?

2. Decide which of the shapes below are polygons.

a)   b)   c)   d)   e)   f)

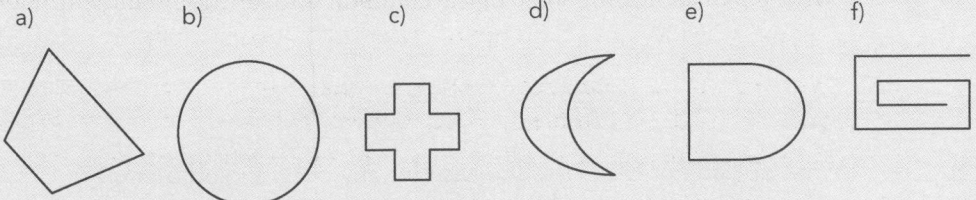

3. What are the symmetry properties of the shapes below?

a)   b)   c)

d)   e)   f)

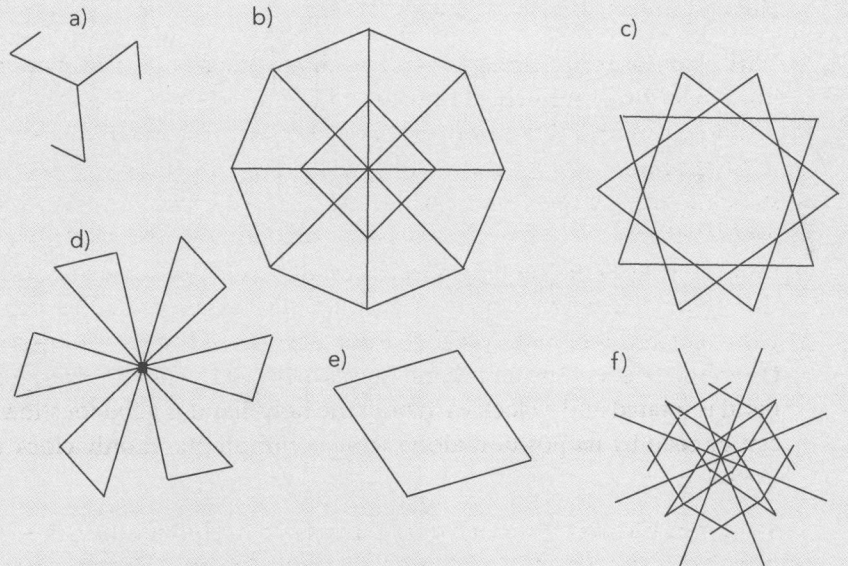

4. Which of the following vertex types will form a semi-regular tessellation:

4.4.8,   3.3.6.6,   3.3.3.4.4,   4.6.12,   3.3.12?

MEASURES

5. Design a net for a cuboid with a volume of 24 cm³ which will fit on a sheet of card measuring 20 cm by 30 cm.

6. Find the perimeters and areas of the two right-angled triangles below:

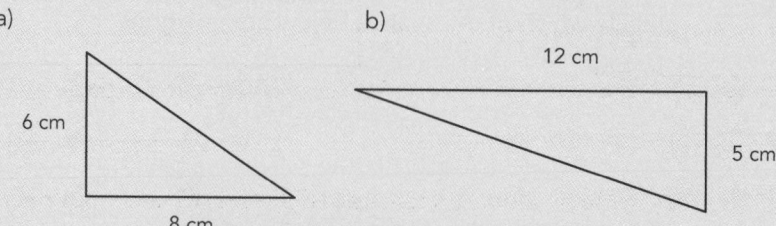

a)

6 cm

8 cm

b)

12 cm

5 cm

What do you notice? Is this the case for any right-angled triangle?

7. Put these objects in order of volume and then in order of surface area.

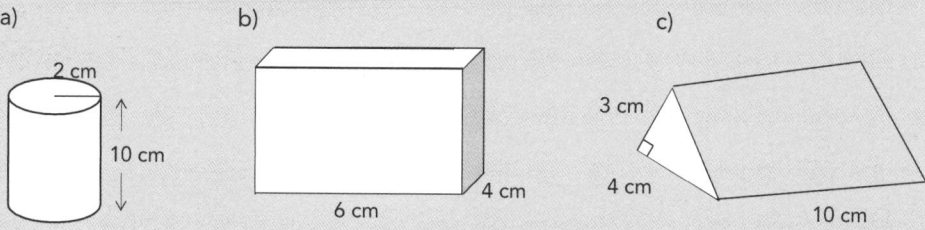

a)

2 cm

10 cm

b)

6 cm

4 cm

c)

3 cm

4 cm

10 cm

8.

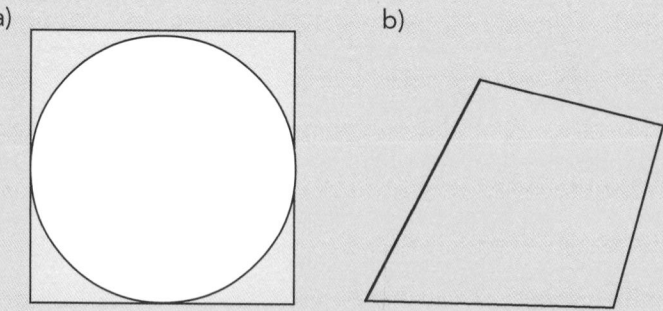

a)

b)

What fraction of the square is shaded?

Hint: if the radius is *r* what is the side of the square?

What is the area of the kite if the diagonals are 10 and 6 units long?

Hint: diagonals cross at right angles.

9. What is the surface area of these cuboids?

a)

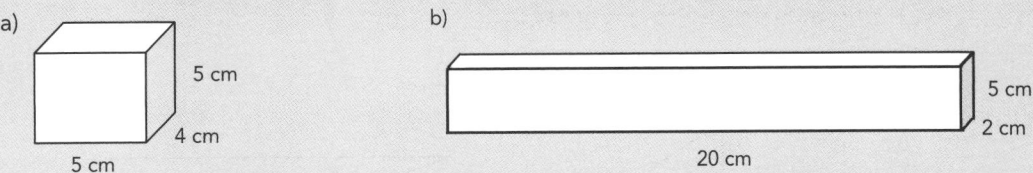

5 cm

4 cm

5 cm

b)

20 cm

5 cm

2 cm

c) What is the surface area of the prism? Work out the area of each face (both triangular ends and three rectangular faces) and total the amounts to give the surface area.

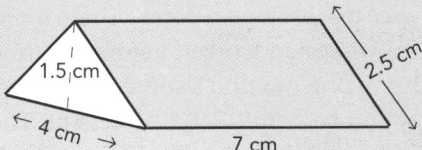

1.5 cm

4 cm

7 cm

2.5 cm

10. Try these:

a) If you drive at 30 mph how long will it take you to drive 150 miles?

b) If you drive 210 miles in two and a half hours on the motorway are you driving within the speed limit?

c) What would be better value – milk at 45p for a pint or £1.20 for a litre?

5 Problem solving, reasoning and proof

Human beings have always been involved in problem solving and mathematics has played its part in our search for answers. The Egyptians made use of their mathematical knowledge for practical purposes relying heavily on previous experience to 'get the job done'. Their approach when faced with a problem was to return to what had worked before and to explore how that could be adapted or extended in order to find a solution to the new problem. Approaching problems in this way can be helpful and successful. The weakness, however, in this inductive reasoning, in relying [on a] limited number of examples, is that success cannot be gu[aranteed.] [mathemati]cians rejected this practical approach on both cultural and [intellectual grounds.] [It w]as the role of others to carry out the everyday, menial ta[sks] [We] [kno]w that Plato believed that the trade of a shopkeeper was a de[gradation] [and] that Aristotle saw a perfect state as one in which no citi[zen] [practised a me]chanical art! Measuring fields was the business of farme[rs,] [not] [of] mathematicians and philosophers. These were matters, [which the] Greek mathematicians viewed as short-lived, imperfec[t] [whereas in] the abstractions that they saw the permanent, the ideal [Because of this], the Greeks were not likely to give themselves to solving [everyday problems and] they would not rely on inductive reasoning. Instead, th[ey sought to unders]tand the nature of what they were considering. What wa[s it that] [rem]ained true if it were divorced from its context, its concrete [form? In other] words, in their search for knowledge and understanding of t[he world, the Greek]s sought generality. Their knowledge would then be of what[ever they studie]s; in our example, they sought what could be said of *every* square irrespective of its context, size or orientation. Not content with this they then set out to prove that what they postulated was true. They did this by a process known as deductive reasoning. Briefly, in Kline's words, this '. . . consists of those ways of deriving new statements from accepted facts that compel the acceptance of the derived statements'. For example, if we have proof that the interior angle of any equilateral triangle measures 60° (the accepted fact) and we then make six of those triangles fit together to form a regular hexagon then the interior angle of the new shape must measure 120° (the derived statement). It *must* be so because the new angle is formed by bringing together one angle from each of two of the original triangles. We 'know', therefore, the size of the required angle whenever we bring equilateral triangles together in this way. The power lies in being able to predict, even to guarantee, the outcome. This is clearly an invaluable tool in problem solving. The Greeks provided us with a powerful means of solving mathematical problems. They may have had no interest in addressing the practical but their search for generality and proof and their development of deductive reasoning has allowed *us* to do just that.

The exploration of mathematics is conducted in the search for greater knowledge and deeper understanding. The 'problem' to be solved is within the mathematics itself. The research could arise out of intellectual curiosity or noticing the beauty of the way in which curves come together or mirror each other. Setting out on the adventure of exploring these phenomena is not prompted merely with an eye to practical application. Some people just get interested! Further, it is not always possible to identify, at the time, what the 'spin-offs' from such abstract and esoteric research might be, what might turn out to be 'useful'. Most of the time we count in 'tens' but we need not do so. Hundreds of years ago mathematicians demonstrated that the integers 1, 2, 3, 4, . . . could be recorded using a base of 2. This gives us 1, 10, 11, 100 and so on. In short the 'binary' system has been known about for centuries. Those who first recognised this surely never thought that the idea would be the basis of a machine that could perform calculations millions of times faster than the human mind! The application of the idea had to wait for the massive development in our knowledge in other fields for the system to form the basis of the machine on which this book was written; what has been described as the mathematical instrument *par excellence* – the digital computer. Combine this with the more specialised analogue version and we have the instrument that predicts the behaviour of weather systems; that can 'model' the solution to the problem of how to predict the trajectory of a rocket in its attempts to escape the earth's gravity and then follow a path to Mars; that attempts to identify the most likely time for future volcanic eruptions and in so doing could protect the lives of millions of people.

Davis & Hersh (1986) wrote of the 'mathematisation' of our world. They identified the contribution of mathematics to the natural sciences: physics, astrophysics and chemistry; to the 'life' sciences of biology and medicine; to the mechanisms controlling physiological processes; to genetics, morphology, population dynamics, epidemiology, ecology and economics. The list is by no means exhaustive. The development of our understanding of mathematics can, and does, contribute to our attempts to explain, modify, manipulate and control our world on a practical level. In other words, mathematics has a major role in problem solving today.

Further reading

Davis, P.J. & Hersh, R. 1986 *Descartes' Dream* San Diego: Harcourt Brace Jovanovich

Katz, V.J. 1998 *A History of Mathematics: an introduction* Harlow: Addison-Wesley

Kline, M. 1972 *Mathematics in Western Culture* Harmondsworth: Penguin

5.2 PROBLEM SOLVING, REASONING AND PROOF

CHAINS OF REASONING

A group of children is given three boxes wrapped in white, black and striped paper.

Using a balance the children find that:

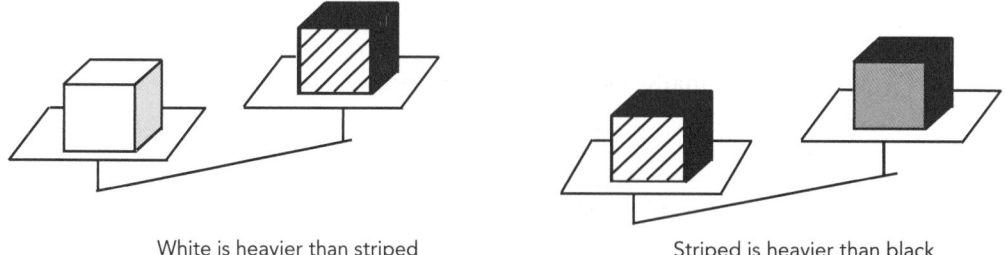

White is heavier than striped   Striped is heavier than black

Is the white or the black heavier? Do you need to use the balance again to find out?

The children might realise that as the white is heavier than the striped and the striped is heavier than the black they can predict that the white must be heavier than the black.

Constructing chains of reasoning like this to solve a problem is at the heart of mathematics and children start this process of reasoning from a very young age. Sometimes the problem solving is intrinsically satisfying and sometimes the methods devised will become well-established mathematical skills. For the child who insists that the white must be heavier than the black it is satisfying to use the balance to demonstrate that they are right. The chain of reasoning involved is an important step in logical thinking.

At a later stage a child might tackle the problem of deciding which is larger $\frac{3}{4}$ or $\frac{2}{3}$ by reasoning that:

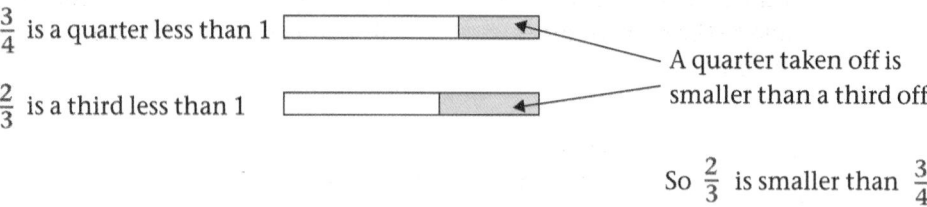

$\frac{3}{4}$ is a quarter less than 1

$\frac{2}{3}$ is a third less than 1

A quarter taken off is smaller than a third off

So $\frac{2}{3}$ is smaller than $\frac{3}{4}$

PROBLEM SOLVING

Well-chosen problems can help the child develop their ability to reason.

PROBLEM

Draw three lines which cross at a point and write any numbers you like in alternate segments.

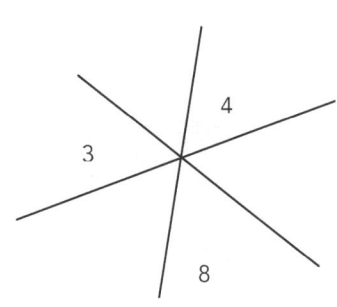

Add the numbers and write the total in the space between them

e.g. $3 + 8 = 11$

Continue until all the spaces are filled.

Finally add opposite numbers.

$7 + 8 = 15$
$4 + 11 = 15$
$3 + 12 = 15$

All the answers are the same!

Can you explain why this happens?

Will it happen if you choose different starting numbers?

With starting numbers 3, 8 and 2 the opposite numbers all add to 13.

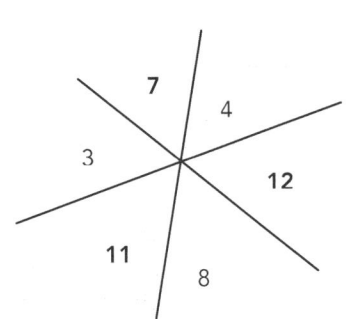

After a few attempts you will have convinced yourself that the final numbers are always the same.

Testing one more set of numbers will make you even more convinced – this must be true.

Misconception

Being sure something is true is **not** a mathematical proof. However many starting numbers you try you cannot be sure that some awkward number couldn't be found that wouldn't work. At this stage all that you can do is make an hypothesis.

Hypothesis

I think that whatever three numbers you start with opposite numbers will always add to the same number and that this number will be the sum of the numbers you started with.

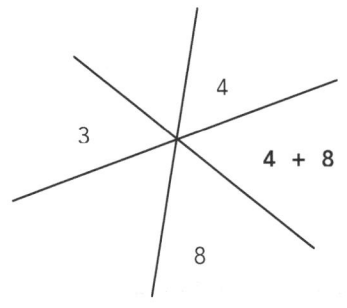

Proof

Working towards a proof

In between 4 and 8 goes $4 + 8$.
Then the opposite number 3 is added giving $3 + 4 + 8$.
This is 15, the sum of all the numbers.

Exactly the same would work for the numbers opposite 4.
Opposite 4 would be $3 + 8$ so the total would be $4 + 3 + 8$.

Finally opposite the 8 would be $3 + 4$ giving $8 + 3 + 4$.

So you would get the same answer each time and the answer would be the sum of the three starting numbers.

Although this chain of reasoning is just about one set of starting numbers, it is clear that the same reasoning would apply for any three starting numbers. So this is a proof.

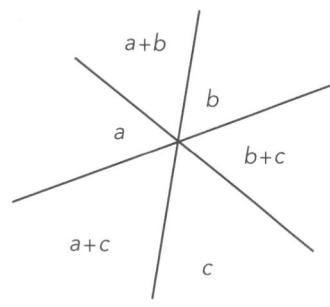

By the secondary school stage children would be able to present the proof more formally using algebra.

If the starting numbers are a, b and c

- The number opposite a is $b + c$ giving a total of $a + (b + c)$
- The number opposite b is $a + c$ giving a total of $b + (a + c)$
- The number opposite c is $a + b$ giving a total of $c + (a + b)$

Since $a + (b + c) = b + (a + c) = c + (a + b)$ the three final totals will all be the same and they will equal the sum of the starting numbers.

PROOF THAT THE ANGLES OF A TRIANGLE ADD UP TO 180°

Stage 1 Measuring

If you draw several triangles and measure the internal angles as accurately as you can and add them the results obtained will tend to be around 180°.

178°, 181°, 180°, 179°, 179°, . . .

So is it reasonable to assume that the angles of a triangle add up to 180°?

Measuring triangles suggests that the angles add to 180° but at this stage you can't be sure.

Stage 2 A visual demonstration

Before you start you need to know that a whole turn is 360°, and so half a turn is 180°.

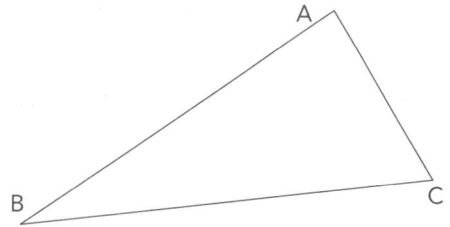
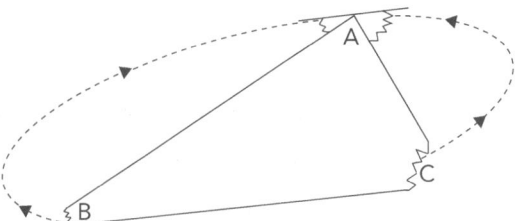

Start with a triangle ABC.

Tear off the corner at B. Turn it around and fit it on at the point A.

Tear off the corner at C. Turn it around and fit it on at the point A.

Visually it looks as if the three angles at A form a straight line.

The angles on a straight line form half a turn and so add up to 180°.

So if the angles really fit onto a straight line they must add up to 180°.

Stage 3 Proof

The formal proof is very close to the demonstration by tearing off corners but uses knowledge about the angles on parallel lines to show, for certain, that the angles add up to 180°.

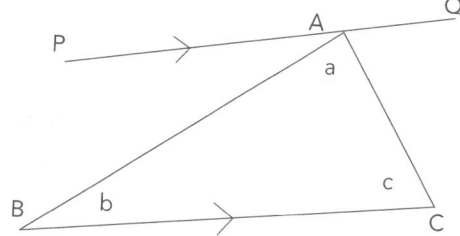

Given a triangle ABC,

draw a line PAQ through A parallel to BC.

$\angle PAB = \angle ABC = b$ (alternate angles)

$\angle QAC = \angle ACB = c$ (alternate angles)

The angles on the straight line at the point add up to 180°.

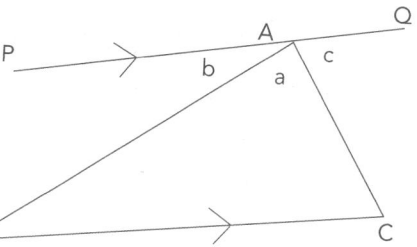

So $a + b + c = 180°$.

But a, b and c are the angles of the triangle.

So the angles of a triangle add up to 180°.

WHY IS PROOF NECESSARY?

If the answer appears obvious proof can appear unnecessary and rather pedantic. An example of a situation where something seems obvious but is quite wrong can show how important proof is.

One dot is placed on the circumference of a circle. The circle has just one region inside.

A second dot is placed on the circle and joined to the other dot to make two regions.

A third dot is added, all the dots are joined up to give four regions.

A fourth dot is added giving eight regions.

(*Note:* as many regions as possible are wanted so don't line the dot up so that three lines cross at a point.)

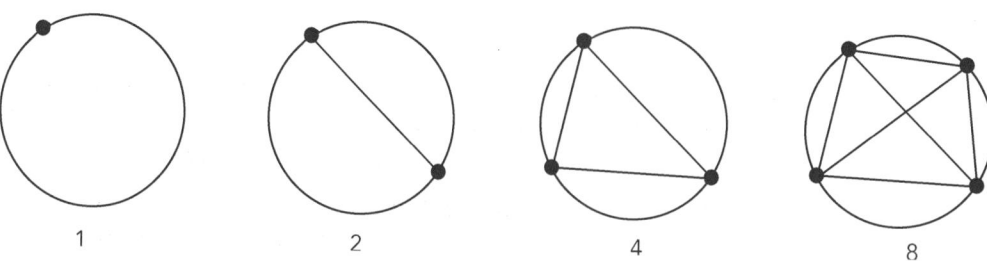

1   2   4   8

Most people would be very sure that the number of regions next time would be 16, and they would be right.

So the sequence goes 1, 2, 4, 8, 16, . . . What do you think the next number will be? 32 of course.

But it is **not** 32. The obvious number is not correct. Try it and see.

In this case of dots on a circle there is no reason in what we are doing why the doubling would go on at each stage.

Compare the situation of taking a piece of paper, folding it as shown and tearing down the fold.

You start with one piece of paper and now you have two pieces of paper.

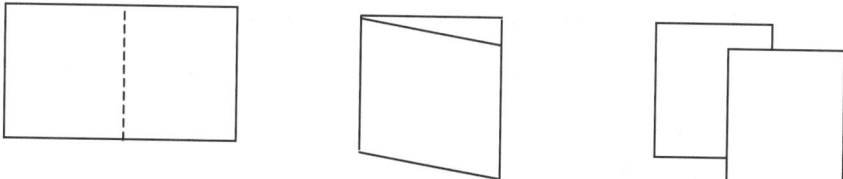

Put the two pieces of paper on top of each other, fold and tear again.

This will give you four pieces.

Continuing the process, you will have 1, 2, 4, 8, 16 pieces of paper. Just as in the points on the circle problem.

Just as before you will expect 32 to be the next number.

This time however you will be right and you have good reasons for knowing that you will be right.

At each stage the process of folding and tearing doubles the number of pieces of paper.

You start with one piece of paper and so the sequence will continue, doubling each time:

1, 2, 4, 8, 16, 32, 64, . . .

PARADOX

A faulty chain of reasoning can lead to a conclusion which clearly cannot be true. Mathematicians have been interested in paradoxes since the time of the Ancient Greeks because they make us look very carefully at our reasoning.

On squared paper draw an 8 × 8 grid and divide it up as shown on the left to give two right-angled triangles with sides 3 units and 8 units and two trapeziums with sides of 5, 5, 3 units and a sloping side.

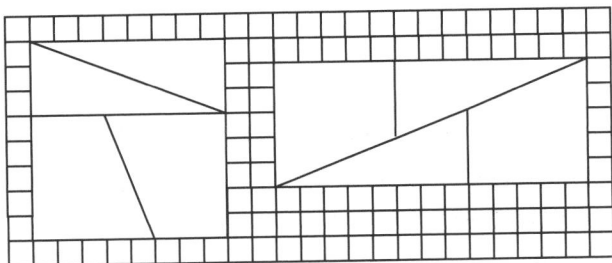

Cut out the pieces and draw a rectangle 5 units by 13 units.

You will find that the pieces fit into the frame on the right as shown.

The area of the square is 8 × 8 = 64 square units.

The area of the rectangle is 5 × 13 = 65 square units. This shows that:

64 = 65

But this is impossible!

There must be a fault in the chain of reasoning.

It is true that the 3 unit side of the triangle fits the 3 unit side of the trapezium, but they don't fit to make a straight line. It looks as if the pieces fit together but really there is a long thin gap in the middle.

This gap is the missing one unit

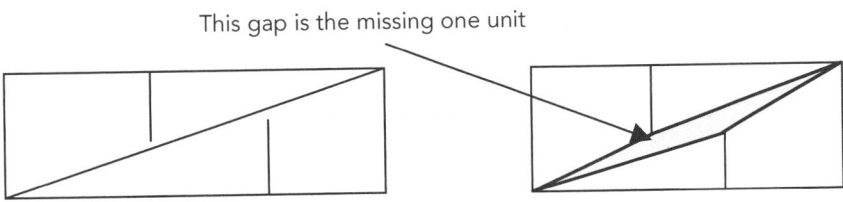

Cutting out shapes can be a useful demonstration of an idea but it needs to be backed up by logical reasoning to become a proof.

SITUATIONS TO ENCOURAGE REASONING

PEEK-A-BOO

A teacher holds a shape partly hidden behind a screen and asks the children to guess the shape.

Children's responses:
  It could be a triangle
  It could be a square.

More of the shape is revealed:
  It's not a triangle
  It could be a rectangle.

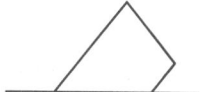

There is not enough evidence to be sure what is behind the screen. Any of the following shapes would be possible and many more . . .

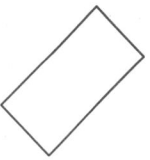 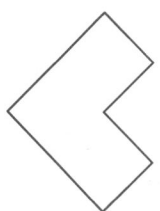 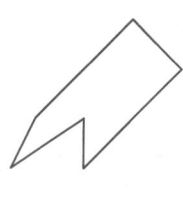 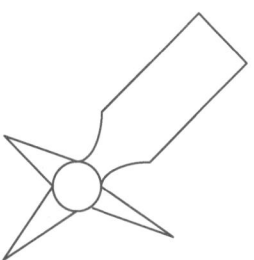

Putting on the constraint that the shape must be a quadrilateral makes chains of reasoning possible.

If that is a right angle it could be a square
  . . . or a rectangle
  . . . or a kite.

It's not a square or a kite.

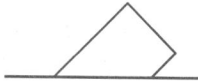

It's a trapezium.

A trapezium is a four-sided shape with a pair of opposite sides parallel.

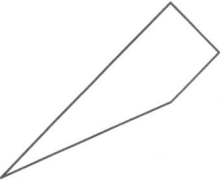

This type of reasoning is a simple form of 'proof by contradiction'.

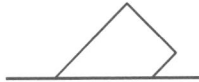 This shape cannot be a square because all the sides of a square are the same and in this shape two sides are **not** the same.

INFINITY

The idea of infinity is both fascinating and confusing. Many of the conclusions which mathematicians have come to about infinity are counter intuitive and yet they have led to the development of powerful areas of mathematics such as calculus.

The idea of infinity can crop up with very basic mathematical problems, such as:

$$What\ is\ 2 \div 0?$$

Not being able to give an immediate answer it can be useful to look at 2 divided by very small numbers.

What is $\quad 2 \div 0.1 \quad$ No problem, it is 20.
$$2 \div 0.01 \ = 200$$
$$2 \div 0.001 = 2000$$

As the number you are dividing by gets smaller and smaller the answer gets larger and larger.
You can go on and on dividing by smaller and smaller numbers without ever getting to zero.

The answer gets larger and larger without limit.

We describe this situation by saying that $2 \div 0$ is infinity. The symbol ∞ is used for infinity but it is not a number just a description of this process that goes on and on.

THE HARE AND THE TORTOISE

A paradox about the hare and the tortoise shows some of the confusions which can arise in thinking about infinity. Paradoxes of this kind were argued about by the Ancient Greeks as they tried to make clear the differences between the finite and the infinite.

The story goes like this: A hare and a tortoise agreed to run a race. The hare was so confident, because she knew that she could run ten times as fast as the tortoise, that she settled down for a snooze as the tortoise plodded off at a steady pace. When the hare woke up she saw that tortoise had already reached a tree 100 paces away. She set off after the tortoise and easily reached the tree where the tortoise had been when she woke up.

The tortoise however was plodding steadily on and had now moved 10 paces on to a bush. The hare raced on but when she got to the bush the tortoise had moved on. The hare got closer and closer to the tortoise but there was always a tiny further distance to go. The hare could never win the race.

Although each statement seems true, surely the hare will rapidly overtake the tortoise? What is wrong with the reasoning here?

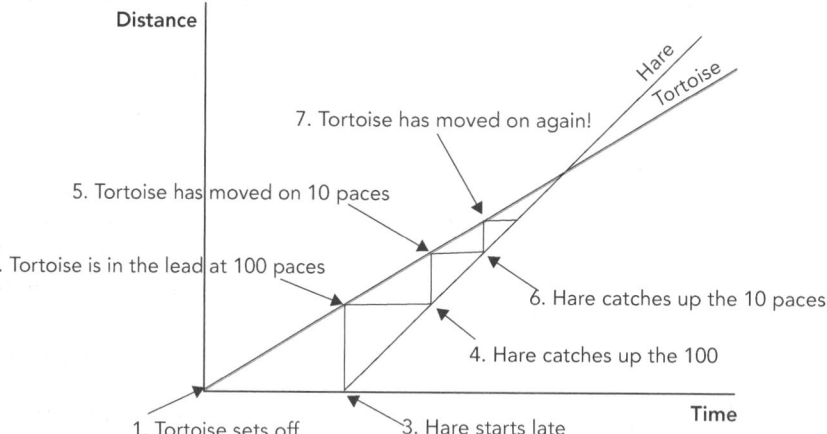

The heart of the confusion is that:

There are an infinite number of stages at which the hare is catching up the tortoise.

The length of these stages gets smaller and smaller each time.

If all these stages are added up they approach a finite distance in which the hare catches up the tortoise.

Try adding up the number of paces the hare must run: $100 + 10 + 1 + 0.1 + 0.01 + 0.001 + 0.0001 + \ldots$

The number of paces is 111.11111111111111111111111111111111 . . .

There is an infinite number of 1s but still the number of paces is certainly less than 112 paces.

The series may be *infinite* but its sum is *finite*. This is the source of the confusion.

The hare will catch the tortoise!

5.3 IMPLICATIONS FOR TEACHING

By deepening your level of mathematical knowledge you can teach for understanding and respond confidently to children's questions. Some issues considered in this section which could be helpful when you are planning your teaching are reasoning, observing and interpreting patterns, asking 'why?', considering alternatives.

The processes of problem solving and reasoning are important to learning. If a teacher can incorporate these into everyday teaching, then learning will be more effective, because they encourage children to make connections and to understand. For instance, children can learn multiplication facts or 'times tables' through recitation. However, if children say 'seven eights are fifty-six' and you ask them 'Why?' this encourages them to relate this fact to others. They might answer, 'Because . . . ':

> Seven eights is double seven fours, which are 28 (and that is double seven twos, which are 14.)
>
> It's one more lot of eight than six eights, which is 48.
>
> It's the same as eight sevens, which is one more seven than seven sevens (49).
>
> It's eight less than 64 (eight eights).

Recitation of multiplication facts, which works for some, is not effective learning for others, because in order to be stored and retrieved in long term memory, facts need to be connected in a network. Asking 'why?' prompts children to make connections and gives them a way to check their answer, should memory fail. Helping children to construct this network of understanding is what teaching is about.

Encouraging children to spot patterns and connections is also a more motivating way to teach. To discover that the digits of the multiples of nine always add up to nine is exciting and intriguing. Other patterns which are equally intriguing can be spotted in the multiplication tables, such as repeating digits in the multiples of three and six, or the way successive bending of fingers can represent the nine times table. It is much more interesting to discover and work out why three consecutive numbers always total three times the middle number, than to be told it. Using problem solving and investigation in this way can turn mathematics into a detective game. At a simpler level, children who have found there are eleven pairs of numbers which total 10 (0 and 10, 1 and 9, 2 and 8, 3 and 7, 4 and 6, 5 and 5, 6 and 4, 7 and 3, 8 and 2, 9 and 1, 10 and 0) can be asked how many pairs they predict with a total of 11. It is not a great leap from discovering there are twelve pairs for 11 to conjecturing a rule for any total and going on to test this out. This kind of activity engages children in some motivating and memorable learning about number bonds at a higher level of generality than just rehearsing 'sums'.

Asking questions like, 'Why?' and 'How do you know?' prompts this sort of enquiry.

With problem solving, questions like, 'Does this remind you of anything you have done before?' and 'Is there another way?' not only prompt connections, but encourage children to consider alternative methods and select the most efficient. Having alternatives also offers a way of checking. In problem solving there are many opportunities for discussion and articulation, which help to clarify thinking. Problem solving does not have to involve contextualised word problems; it is essentially about giving children choices. These could be about methods or resources, and also interpretations and assumptions, information to collect or ignore, resolutions and extensions. Asking children to justify their choices encourages explanation and reasoning. If children are asked to record in their own way, as well as obliging them to organise their thoughts, this provides teachers with valuable opportunities for assessment including children's understanding of symbols.

Presenting opportunities for problem solving and pattern spotting, giving choices and asking higher order questions like 'Why?' and 'How do you know?' are therefore key strategies for effective mathematics teaching. They help children to consider alternatives and make connections, to check, to communicate, to explain and reason. They also produce more motivating learning, which is both more memorable and produces greater understanding. Therefore not only are problem solving and proof at the heart of mathematics, but incorporating the 'Using and Applying' strands of 'Problem solving, Communicating and Reasoning' into any mathematics teaching will make learning more effective.

5.4 SELF-ASSESSMENT QUESTIONS   Problem solving, reasoning and proof

1.   To work out 4 nines using your fingers:

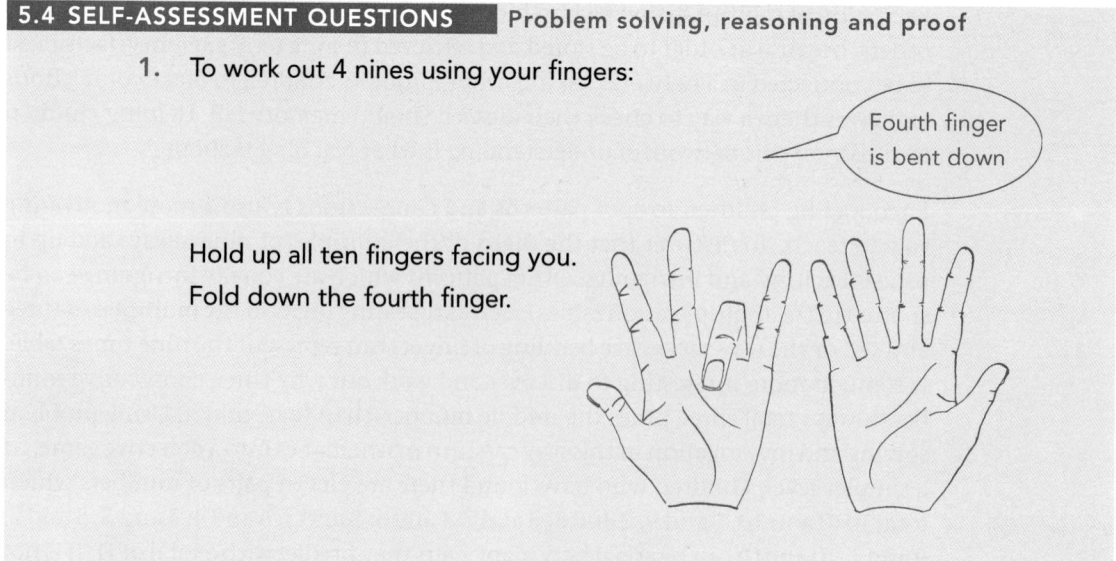

Fourth finger is bent down

Hold up all ten fingers facing you.
Fold down the fourth finger.

See that you have 3 fingers to the left of the folded finger and 6 fingers to the right.

So 4 nines are 36.

Use the fact that $4 \times 9 = 4 \times (10 - 1)$

$\qquad = 40 - 4$

$\qquad = 30 + 10 - 4$ to explain why this works.

Explain to a friend how it works for 7 nines.

2. Think of a number. Add 4. Double it. Multiply by 3. Divide by 6.

    Now take away the number you first thought of.

    Whatever number you start with you should always get the answer 4.

    Let x stand for the number you start with and by writing out each stage as an algebraic expression, e.g. $x + 4$, then $2(x + 4)$, try to explain why you always end up with 4 whatever the starting number.

    Invent a similar problem which always gives the same answer and try it with some children.

3. What is the last digit of 2^{112}?

    Well, I'll just do some superfast mental arithmetic – this really is a very large number – and the last digit is 6.

    Look at the pattern in the final digits of 2^1, 2^2, 2^3, 2^4, 2^5, . . . to see how this can be done at lightning speed.

Answers to self-assessment questions

A1. c) Work out 534 – 147

$$\begin{array}{r} 500 + 30 + 4 \\ 100 + 40 + 7 \\ \hline \end{array}$$

Considering the units: to take away 7 will need to adjust 30 + 4 to 20 + 14

$$\begin{array}{r} 500 + 20 + 14 \\ 100 + 40 + 7 \\ \hline \end{array}$$

Units are now OK but to take away 40 will need to adjust 500 + 20 to 400 + 120

$$\begin{array}{r} 400 + 120 + 14 \\ 100 + 40 + 7 \\ \hline 300 + 80 + 7 \end{array}$$

Subtraction is now straightforward and the answer is 387.

d) 489 ÷ 17

$$\begin{array}{r} 489 \\ -170 \\ \hline 319 \\ -170 \\ \hline 149 \\ -136 \\ \hline 13 \end{array}$$

10×17

10×17

8×17

$$\begin{array}{r} 28 \\ 17\overline{)489} \\ -34 \\ \hline 149 \\ -136 \\ \hline 13 \end{array}$$

489 ÷ 17 = 28 remainder 13

A2. a) As four-fifths is close to 1 the total will be about $1\frac{1}{2}$.

3 and 5 have no common factors so 3 × 5 = 15 is the lowest common denominator. Find equivalent fractions and then add.

$$\frac{2}{3} + \frac{4}{5} = \frac{10}{15} + \frac{12}{15} = \frac{22}{15} = 1\frac{7}{15}$$

b) $\frac{2}{3}$ of $\frac{4}{5}$ will be less than $\frac{4}{5}$ but more than $\frac{2}{5}$, say $\frac{3}{5}$.

$$\frac{2}{3} \times \frac{4}{5} = \frac{8}{15}$$

A3. a) $\frac{2}{3}$ of $\frac{3}{4}$ is just part of $\frac{3}{4}$ so the answer will be smaller than $\frac{3}{4}$.

$$\frac{2}{3} \times \frac{3}{4} = \frac{6}{12} = \frac{1}{2}$$ which is smaller than $\frac{3}{4}$.

b) $\frac{3}{4} \div \frac{2}{3}$ means how many $\frac{2}{3}$s fit into $\frac{3}{4}$. More than one will fit so the answer is bigger than 1.

$$\frac{3}{4} \div \frac{2}{3} = \frac{3}{4} \times \frac{3}{2} = \frac{9}{8} = 1\frac{1}{8}$$

c) How many thirds are there in 4?

Each whole one has three thirds so there are $3 \times 4 = 12$ thirds in 4. So answer is 12.

When dividing by $\frac{2}{3}$, the chunks are twice as big so fewer will fit . The answer is $12 \div 2$ which is 6.

A4. a)   0.07   0.17   0.625   0.65   0.71

b) These are just some of the possibilities:

	$5 \times 6 = 30$		
Divide by 10	$0.5 \times 6 = 3$	or	$5 \times 0.6 = 3$
Divide by 100	$0.5 \times 0.6 = 0.3$	or	$5 \times 0.06 = 0.3$
Multiply by 10	$5 \times 60 = 300$		
Multiply by 100	$50 \times 60 = 3000$	or	$500 \times 6 = 3000$

c)   For grid method partition 2.4 to $2 + 0.4$ and 5.3 to $5 + 0.3$

	2	0.4	
5	10	2	12
0.3	0.6	0.12	0.72
			12.72

```
      2 4
  ×   5 3
  -------
      7 2
  1 2 0 0
  -------
  1 2 7 2
```

For formal method calculate 24×53 and then divide by 100 to give 12.72.

d) $7 \div 1.25$

$1.25 \quad \times \quad 2 = 2.5$

$1.25 \quad \times \quad 4 = 5$

$1.25 \quad \times \quad 5 = 6.25$

$\dfrac{7}{1.25} = \dfrac{700}{125}$

```
           5. 6
   125 | 7 0 0.0
       - 6 2 5
       -------
         7 5 0
       - 7 5 0
       -------
```

So $7 \div 1.25$ is 5 remainder 0.75

Equivalent calculation is $700 \div 125$ which is 5.6.

A5. a) Give numbers to 2 sig. fig as 24 000 and 17 000.

b) Give length of pieces to 1 decimal place as you could not measure more accurately, so lengths are 6.3 cm to 1 decimal place.

c) Give answer to 1 decimal place, 201.0.

A6. a) 10% is 32, 50% is 160, 25% is 80 etc.

b) 10% is 32, 5% is 16, 2.5% is 8. Adding these gives 17.5% is 56.

A7. a) Percentages are just an alternative notation for fractions with a denominator of 100, so $40\% = \frac{40}{100} = 0.04$

Fractions to decimals and decimals to fractions – see 1.4 Links between fractions and decimals.

b)   0.42   0.425   0.6   0.625   0.65

A10.   1000 and 10^3 $\frac{1}{100}$ and 10^{-2} and 0.01   0.25 and 2^{-2}

A11. Numbers in standard form have a first number greater than or equal to 1 and less than 10 multiplied by a power of 10.

a) 5.26×10^0 and 9.26×10^{-3} are in standard index form

b) $358 = 3.58 \times 10^2$

$9.26^2 = 85.748 = 8.5748 \times 10^1$

$20.1 \times 10^4 = 2.01 \times 10^5$

In order of size, smallest first: 9.26×10^{-3} 5.26×10^0 8.5748×10^1 3.58×10^2 2.01×10^5

c) Height of a child 8.5748×10^1 cm, Length of a pencil 5.26×10^0 cm, Height of a room 3.58×10^2 cm, Thickness of a finger nail 9.26×10^{-3} cm, Cross-country run 2.01×10^5 cm.

A12. a) Roughly 3.1, $\sqrt{10} = 3.16$ to 2 d.p.   b) $\sqrt{16} = 4$

A13.

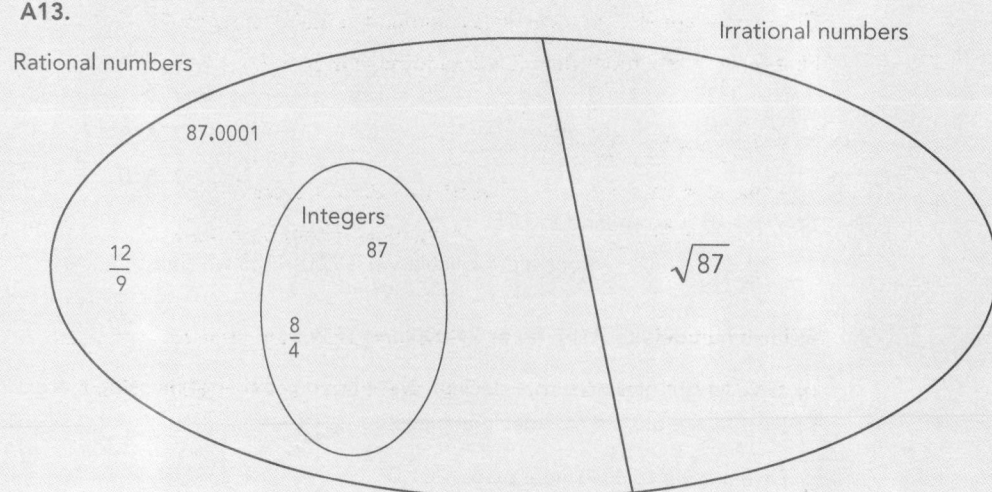

2.7 PROPERTIES OF NUMBERS, NUMBER SEQUENCES, ALGEBRA

A1. $3(x + 2)$ is the odd one out as $3(x + 4) = 3x + 12$.

$3(3x - 4) = 9x - 12$, $7x + 2(x - 6) = 9x - 12$ so the odd one out is $9x - 6$.

A3. An even multiple of 5 is a multiple of 10, so need a square number ending in 9 such as 9 or 49.

So $3 \times 3 + 1 = 10$ is one answer and $7 \times 7 + 1 = 50$ is another

Try other numbers ending in 3 or 7: $13 \times 13 = 169$ so 170 is an answer

$17 \times 17 = 289$ so 290 is another etc.

A4. $2 \times$ (3rd triangle number) $= 3 \times 4 = 12$

$2 \times$ (100th triangle number) $= 100 \times 101 = 10\ 100$

$2 \times$ (nth triangle number) $= n(n + 1)$

So nth triangle number $= \dfrac{n(n + 1)}{2}$

A7. a) 358   b) 799   c) 0.85 to 2 decimal places   d) 0.27 to 2 decimal places

A9.

Differences are all 2 so formula is linear and contains the term $2n$.

First term, 9, is 7 more than 2×1 so formula is $2n + 7$.

A10. $6x - 4 = 2x + 13$

$\begin{aligned}
6x\ &= 2x + 17 &&\text{Adding 4 to both sides}\\
4x\ &= 17 &&\text{Subtracting } 2x \text{ from both sides}\\
x\ &= 4\tfrac{1}{4}
\end{aligned}$

To invent equations with the same solution just do the same to both sides.

So starting from $4x = 17$ add 90 to both sides to give $4x + 90 = 107$ etc.

3.5 HANDLING DATA

A1. It would be appropriate to calculate a mean for the following:

a) Daily maximum temperatures for a month

c) Heights of children in a class

e) Examination marks for a school

g) Times for 30 children to swim 10 lengths of a pool

It would not be appropriate to calculate a mean for the following:

b) Examination grades for a school

d) National curriculum levels for a school at the end of a key stage

f) Colours of cars passing the school gate in a 30-minute interval

The mode would be the only appropriate average in each of these situations.

A2. a) A line graph is only appropriate for showing trends, for example over time. It does not make sense to use a line graph for frequencies. A bar chart or a bar line graph would be appropriate.

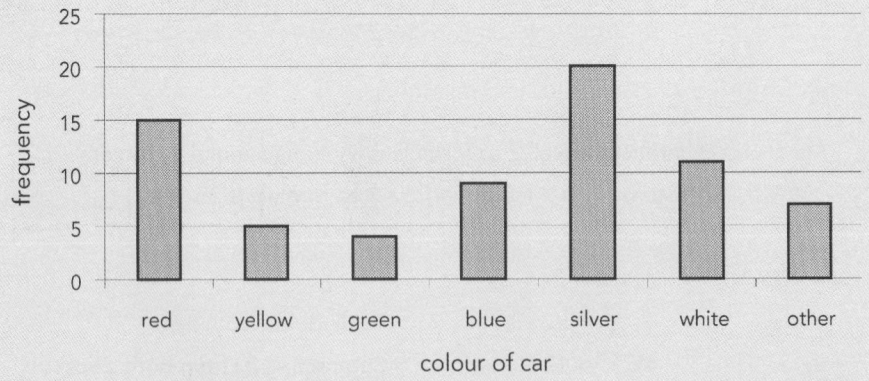

Colours of cars passing the school gate

b) Whilst a bar chart for discrete grouped data may be appropriate at Key Stage 2, a histogram is, strictly speaking, the most appropriate representation for this data. Having grouped together all the marks between 0–9 and 10–19, it doesn't make sense to have a gap between 9 and 10.

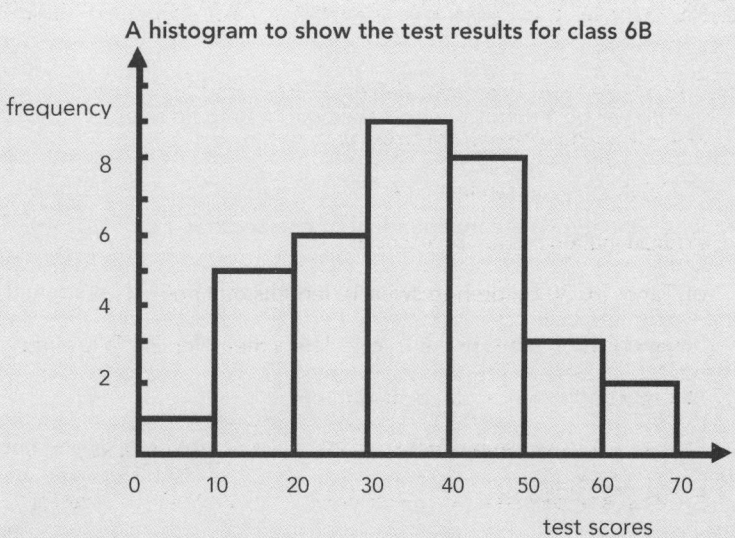

A histogram to show the test results for class 6B

c) The question 'What does the whole pie chart represent?' doesn't have a sensible answer. It is just the price of several cans of baked beans added together. Pie charts are for comparing proportions! A bar chart would be more suitable where the vertical axis represents the price (in pence) for the same sized tin in each supermarket.

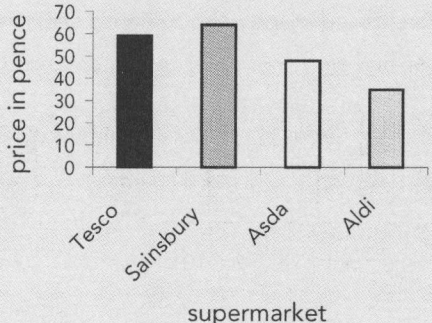

The price of baked beans

A3. a) The events landing buttered side down and landing buttered side up are mutually exclusive, so the probability is 1 – 0.6 = 0.4.

b)

i) $\frac{1}{6} \times \frac{1}{6} \times \frac{1}{6} = \frac{1}{216}$

ii) This will be 1 minus the probability of getting no sixes:

$1 - (\frac{5}{6} \times \frac{5}{6} \times \frac{5}{6}) = 1 - \frac{125}{216} = \frac{91}{216}$.

iii) $\frac{1}{6}$, the throws are independent of one another.

c)

	Straight sides only	Not straight sides only
Some right angles	4	0
No right angles	4	5

There are 13 shapes and 5 shapes that have no right angles and not straight sides only, so the probability is $\frac{5}{13}$.

4.6 SHAPE, SPACE AND MEASURES

A1. For a regular polygon all the angles must be equal too.

Example 1:

A rhombus is a quadrilateral with all 4 sides equal; this is only a regular polygon when all the angles are the same.

Example 2:

A triangle with equal sides will have equal angles too and so is regular.

A2. Polygons are closed shapes with straight sides only:

Polygons a) and c)   not polygons b), d), e) and f)

A3.

Shape	Order of rotational symmetry	Lines of symmetry
a)	3	0
b)	4	4
c)	10	10
d)	6	0
e)	2	2
f)	4	4

A4. 4.4.8: two squares and an octagon will not tessellate: $2 \times 90° + 135° \neq 360°$

3.3.6.6: two triangles and two hexagons will tessellate: $2 \times 60° + 2 \times 120° = 360°$

3.3.3.4.4: three triangles and two squares will tessellate: $3 \times 60° + 2 \times 90° = 360°$

4.6.12: square, hexagon and dodecagon will tessellate: $90° + 120° + 150° = 360°$

3.3.12 : two triangles and a dodecagon will not tessellate: $2 × 60° + 150° ≠ 360°$

A5. There are at least two possibilities: 4 cm × 3 cm × 2 cm and 6 cm × 2 cm × 2 cm.

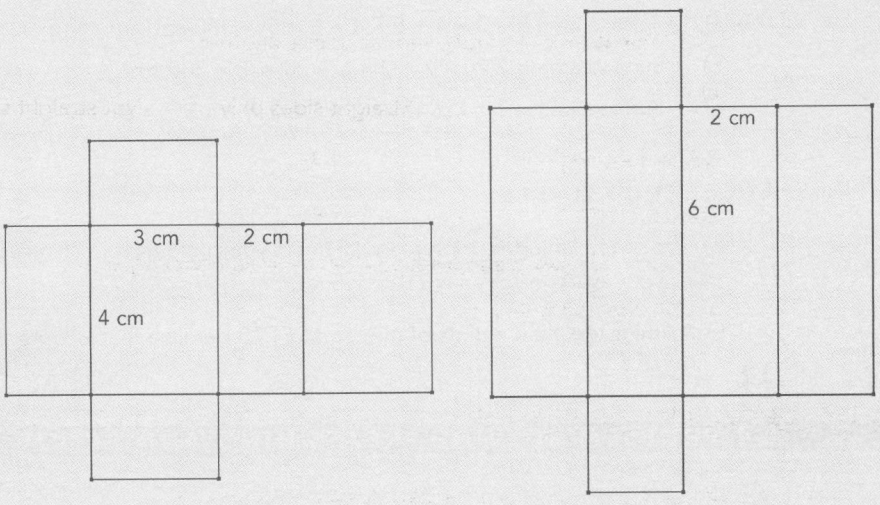

A6. a)   Perimeter = 6 + 8 + 10 = 24 cm

Area = $\frac{1}{2}$ × 6 × 8 = 24 cm²

b)   Perimeter = 5 + 12 + 13 = 30 cm

Area = $\frac{1}{2}$ × 5 × 12 = 30 cm²

It is unusual to have the area and perimeter numerically equal. For a 3, 4, 5 triangle the perimeter is 12 cm and the area is 6 cm².

A7. a)   volume = π × 2² × 10 = 125.7 cm³

surface area = 2 × π × 2² + 2 × π × 2 × 10 = 150.8 cm²
(both to 1 d.p.)

b)   volume = 4 × 5 × 6 = 120 cm³
surface area = 2(4 × 5 + 4 × 6 + 5 × 6) = 148 cm²

c)   volume = $\frac{1}{2}$ × 3 × 4 × 10 = 60 cm³

surface area = 2 × $\frac{1}{2}$ × 3 × 4 + 3 × 10 + 4 × 10 + 5 × 10 = 132 cm²

The cylinder has the greatest volume, followed by the cuboid and then the triangular prism.

The cylinder has the greatest surface area, followed by the cuboid and then the triangular prism.

A8. a) Area of square is $4r^2$, area of circle πr^2 so fraction that is grey is

$$\frac{4r^2 - \pi r^2}{4r^2} = \frac{4 - \pi}{4} = 1 - \frac{\pi}{4}$$

b) Area of kite is $\frac{1}{2} \times 10 \times 6 = 30$ sq. units

A9. a) Surface area $= 2(5 \times 4 + 5 \times 4 + 5 \times 5) = 130$ cm^2

b) Surface area $= 2(20 \times 2 + 2 \times 5 + 20 \times 5) = 300$ cm^2

c) Surface area $= 2 \times 2 \times 1.5 + 2 \times 7 \times 2.5 + 4 \times 7 = 69$ cm^2

A10. a) $150 \div 30 = 5$ hours

b) The speed limit is 70 mph so in 2.5 hours you could travel 175 miles. If you travel 210 miles your average speed is $210 \div 2.5 = 84$ mph.

c) A litre is less than 2 pints of milk so at £1.20 per litre that is more than 60p per pint.

5.4 PROBLEM SOLVING, REASONING AND PROOF

A1. For seven nines $7 \times 9 = 7 \times (10 - 1)$

$$= 70 - 7$$

$$= 60 + 10 - 7$$

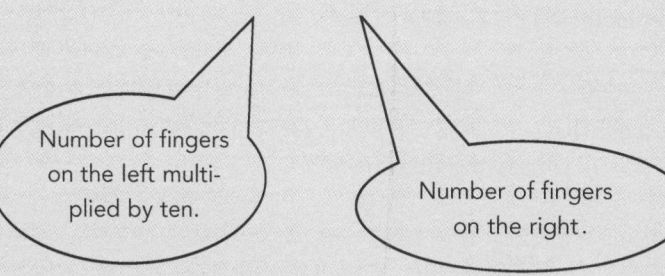

Number of fingers on the left multiplied by ten.

Number of fingers on the right.

A2. Think of a number x

Add 4 $x + 4$

Double it $2x + 8$

Multiply by 3 $6x + 24$

Divide by 6 $x + 4$

Dividing by 6 undoes the effect of multiplying by 2 and then by 3.

Take away number first thought of   4

To invent your own problem: Start with x, add or multiply and then undo the effect of each of the operations. Finally subtract the number you started with.

A3. The powers of 2 are 2, 4, 8, 16, 32, 64, 128, 256, 512, 1024, 2048, 4096, . . .

The pattern in the final digit is and must continue to be 2, 4, 8, 6, 2, 4, 8, 6, 2, 4, 8, 6

112 is a multiple of four so following the pattern 2^{112} must end in 6.

Index